The Grateful Dead
and Philosophy

Popular Culture and Philosophy®
Series Editor: George A. Reisch

Popular Culture and Philosophy®

The Grateful Dead and Philosophy

Getting High Minded about Love and Haight

Edited by
STEVEN GIMBEL

OPEN COURT
Chicago and La Salle, Illinois

Volume 28 in the inimitable Open Court series, Popular Culture and Philosophy®, edited by George A. Reisch

To order books from Open Court, call 1-800-815-2280, or visit our website at www.opencourtbooks.com.

Open Court Publishing Company is a division of Carus Publishing Company.

Printed and bound in the United States of America.

Library of Congress Cataloging-in-Publication Data

The Grateful Dead and philosophy : getting high minded about love and Haight / edited by Steven Gimbel.
     p. cm. — (Popular culture and philosophy ; v. 28)
    Includes bibliographical references and index.
    ISBN-13: 978-0-8126-9623-3 (trade paper : alk. paper)
    ISBN-10: 0-8126-9623-9 (trade paper : alk. paper)
    1. Grateful Dead (Musical group) 2. Music and philosophy.
  3. Deadheads
    (Music fans) I. Gimbel, Steven, 1968-
    ML421.G72G67 2007
    782.42166092'2—dc22

                                             2007010256

Contents

Set One—Who's to Guide You?
Ethical Questions in the Lyrics of the Grateful Dead 95

Set Two—What Shall We Say? Shall We Call It by a Name?
The Nature of Nature and Knowledge 161

Encore—Mysteries Dark and Vast
Metaphysical Quandaries 211

Half Baseball Game, Half Church

One of the standard jokes about Deadheads is that they're determined to find cosmic significance in every aspect of the band they love so much. Every lyric, song choice, onstage utterance, and even random glance—*Jerry looked right at me!*—was mined for arcane meanings by scruffy fans determined to believe that the universe is a conspiracy working in their favor.

It's not hard to imagine why several generations of kids raised in American suburbia would be eager to join a subculture that held out the promise of Eternal Secrets Revealed during a night of serious partying and adventurous rock 'n' roll. What's harder to understand for non-Deadheads is how often these secrets actually *were* revealed in the course of a show. I'm not talking about the stoned flights of fancy that evaporate in the harsh light of morning. I'm talking about the kinds of durable insights that are the foundation of any meaningful, creative, and responsible human life. For decades, Dead shows provided me and thousands of others with an opportunity to check in, take stock, set aside the distractions of daily life, and tune up the internal navigation system for the long and unpredictable journey ahead.

These insights were not given by the band to its audience, as esoteric teachings might be passed on by a guru to an earnest student. The band members had no special claim on enlightenment, and were put off by the notion that they were anything other than reasonably capable and occasionally hardworking musicians who had lucked into a good gig. But somehow, the totality of the experience—the music, the people, and, on those special nights, the psychedelics—provided a setting where it became easier to sift the wheat from the chaff and remember what's truly important.

That's not to say that the band didn't make an effort to provide guideposts for its audience along the road. The Dead's primary lyricist, Robert Hunter, is a wily craftsman of phrases that
yield a salty brand of wisdom while eluding facile exegesis. (It
didn't hurt that he came to his role in the band after immersing
himself in the writings of James Joyce and T.S. Eliot.) Of all the
musical gifts of the late Jerry Garcia, perhaps the most remarkable was his knack for spinning out improvised melody lines
that conveyed a sense of narrative development, as if each song,
each jam, each set, and each show was itself a story—stories
folded within stories.

And it's not as if the band didn't enjoy simply *fucking* with
notions of transcendence, particularly if those notions got too
staid, systematized, or pious. To uncover profound philosophical import in the Grateful Dead, you don't have to dig any
deeper than the name of the band. Dead . . . *and grateful?* And
there you are, standing in the middle of what Zen teachers call
the Great Matter, life and death, with a grinning skeleton as your
guide. (The fact that the band's name was the product of a
chance operation—one day in 1965, the band smoked DMT
while thumbing through a Funk and Wagnall's dictionary, and
the pages fell open to the fateful phrase, which none of them
liked at first—only makes it more Grateful Dead-ish. Garcia
once said that the moniker turned out to be "tremendously
lucky. It's just repellent enough to filter curious onlookers and
just quirky enough that parents don't like it.")

I once described the *Gestalt* of Dead shows as half baseball
game and half church. I can't think of another social setting that
conveyed such a pervasive sense of *permission*—to be however
you wanted to be, however you felt just at that moment. If you
felt inspired to move to the music, you could flail or flow grace-
fully anyway you wished, as long as you didn't step on too
many toes. If you felt like partaking in the sort of alchemical
molecules that have been employed for spiritual inquiry for
thousands of years, you could do so without being dragged
away by the cops. If you were suddenly moved to tears by a
juxtaposition of lyric, music, and personal circumstance, you
could even weep. It was all okay. (And then there were the big
sweaty guys who insisted on ripping off all their clothes during
the second set.) In this environment of collective liberty, people
were freed up to do what they naturally do—to play, to ponder

the mysteries at the heart of everyday existence, and to build community with kindred spirits.

In *The Dharma Bums*, a book much beloved by Deadheads, Jack Kerouac wrote, "Ho! What we need is a floating zendo, where an old Bodhisattva can wander from place to place and always be sure to find a spot to sleep in among friends and cook up mush." For thirty years, that's what the Dead and their fans offered one another—a familiar refuge that could be anywhere, in any town on any night of the week, for as long as the party lasted. This marvelous book records flashes of understanding experienced in that floating zendo, which remains open to any Bodhisattva, old or young, lucky enough to fall in love with this music.

STEVE SILBERMAN

Saying Thank You for a Real Good Time

Little did I realize then that all those years, all those miles, and all those boxes of blank cassette tapes were really just research. At the end of this long, strange trip, there are many people to thank for this volume. First and foremost are the authors of these wonderful chapters. They have approached these discussions in the same playful spirit that we celebrate in the Dead's music, taking themes we've heard many, many times before and making them seem fresh, alive, and packed with new insights. One always has to worry about putting Deadheads on a deadline, but their care, craft, and thoughtfulness is appreciated beyond words.

This project could never have become what it is without David Ramsay Steele and George Reisch at Open Court Publishing Company, our Bill Graham and Owsley. Their support, patience, and suggestions have allowed this volume to blossom into what it is.

Special thanks must be extended to Barbara McDonald, Linda Pniak, and everyone connected with the Grateful Dead whom we've had the joy and privilege of working with. Bob Weir and Dennis McNally truly went beyond generous with their time, memories, and insight. Their genuine kindness and grace in entertaining our odd, convoluted, and perhaps uncomfortable questions is an embodiment of the spirit that this volume tries to capture. We would like to thank Phil Lesh for reading the manuscript while it was in production. We are especially grateful to Alan Trist from Ice Nine Publishing and his kind help securing the permission to quote from the lyrics throughout the chapters and Sean McGraw of Spirit Two music for his helpfulness with John Phillips's "Me and My Uncle."

Thanks also to Sony/ATV for permission to use part of Merle Haggard's "Mama Tried" and Alfred Publishing for permission to quote from Dickie Betts's "Ramblin' Man."

Finally, I would like to thank the Grateful Dead for decades of bringing together those of us who felt apart from the society we were born into and thought a more free, caring, and funky world was possible. Of those folks, a special heart-felt thanks to Lar and Dave, Amy and Jack, C. Dan, Tim, Paul, Doug, and Andrea, and everyone else who I've seen a show with, taped a boot from, sold a tie dyed t-shirt to, or kicked a hack with.

Some Folks Trust
to Reason

It was a beautiful summer's evening on the lawn at Merriweather Post Pavilion. The Jerry Band was in true form. From the top corner of the hill, I could look out over the dancing colors down in the valley by the concession stand. On the next blanket over, my eye was caught by the guy next to me when he suddenly stopped dancing. His mouth was agape. His eyes were almost as wide as his pupils. He was in mid-revelation. He aggressively staggered for words that would allow him to explain his epiphany to his buddy, terms that would pull back the veil covering the consciousness of one who had not yet been touched. Finally, he pointed heavenward and blurted out, "Dude, don't you get it?! We're all *cats* under the *STARS!*" It is a very rare event when one receives authentic insight into the true nature of reality. I'm not sure whether that guy has found any yet, but it must have been one hell of a trip that night.

When you put the words "philosophy" and "Grateful Dead" in the same sentence, you run the risk of invoking precisely that sort of image—vapid, silly statements that collapse into the triviality of something you'd find in a fortune cookie when you take the time to think about it with a sober mind. And while we've all had those moments of artificial clarity, the fact is that some of those 2:00 a.m. dorm-room conversations sparked by a newly acquired bootleg really did focus on deep and interesting questions. Some of those folks sitting around cross-legged on the floor, looking through your couch for enough loose change to order a pizza went on to be come honest-to-goodness philosophy professors. And they are still having those conversations. To prove it, this book is a collection of them.

Perhaps more so than any other band, the Grateful Dead challenged norms. From their roots as the house band for the acid tests, they probed the nature of mind, testing to see if it was possible to tap into the creativity of the collective consciousness. Musically they attacked the cookie cutter three-and-a-half-minute template for rock songs and the walls between record store genres pulling influences from blues, folk, jazz, bossa nova, bluegrass, and the twentieth-century avant-garde movement. As an organization they championed unconventional business practices, making their crew part of the family, not only allowing, but helping, fans to tape their shows, and selling their own tickets.

This spirit gave rise to a culture all its own. The traveling carnival that landed in fields, parking lots, and campgrounds across the country several times a year was filled with folks eager to dance over all the conventions that were socially enforced in the white-bread world they sought to leave. Each tour was a living laboratory, an experiment that was one part social engineering and one part chaos theory. There was an ethos to the parking lot, a social code, an economy, and customs all its own. It was a nomadic culture within a culture that attracted those who felt that there must be a different way.

Whenever norms are being challenged, there is philosophy to be done. Philosophy is the art of questioning the foundations of our beliefs. The long history of thought about thought has evolved in many different directions, a number of which are represented in the chapters here. We have essays that look at eastern modes of thought and how Buddhist and Taoist traditions are elucidated in the lyrics of Dead tunes. Analytic philosophy tries to apply logic to clarify our thinking in problems like that posed by the story-teller in "Lady with a Fan" and understand how scientific results should inform our thinking about issues like whether the narrator in "Half-Step Mississippi Uptown Toodle-oo" was fated to a life of misdeed. Contemporary continental thought looks at the social and political influences on our lives and lets us think about the nature of Deadhead community and whether we should in fact be grateful for death. Classical philosophy presents us with many of the traditional moral questions, such as the nature of justice which we may see illustrated in considering whether the Uncle of "Me and My Uncle" was getting his just deserts when he was gunned down by the nephew he had trained. American philosophy has a decidedly worldly, practical bent and we see not only one brand of that tradition reflected in the lyrics of "Eyes of the World," but we can see the Grateful Dead itself, arising from the beat movement of the generation before it, as an instantiation of the great American intellectual narrative.

This volume in no way purports to answer these questions. The point of philosophy is not to conclusively end discussion, but to provide insights that advance it in ways not previously expected. Robert Hunter was precisely correct: Some of the time you *do* see the light in the strangest of places if you look at it right. The aim of these chapters is to allow you to look at life in a slightly different way when viewed through a pair of glasses with one lens focused on philosophy and the other crafted from aspects of the Grateful Dead's music and deadhead culture.

Well, "you know it's gonna get stranger, so let's get on with the show."

In the Parking Lot—
Fireworks, Calliopes, and Clowns

The Culture of the Dead

1

Keep Your Day Job: Tie Dyes, Veggie Burritos, and Adam Smith in the Parking Lot

STEVEN GIMBEL and
BRENDAN CUSHING-DANIELS

There was nothing like selling tie-dyed t-shirts in the parking lot. Weaving between cars and tents, watching the drum and hacky-sack circles, smelling the veggie burritos and chicken kabobs cooking, dueling bootlegs, each as good as the last, occasionally pausing to let an interested eye browse my wares. They were quality shirts: bright colors from the Procion fiber reactive dyes and tight patterns—off-centered diamonds, double spirals—they were solid ten-dollar shirts.

But they *were* ten-dollar shirts, not twelve-dollar shirts and certainly not fifteen-dollar shirts. A ten-dollar shirt was a well-made tie-dye or a plain shirt with a silk-screen design. A twelve-dollar shirt was either a silk screen with a nice complementary dye job or a design that was particularly beautiful and intricate or had a slogan that was novel and clever. The fifteen-dollar shirts were the new injection dyed shirts that were suddenly the rage. The old school tie dyers would bitch amongst ourselves that they didn't fold, they sewed the shirts to get the designs so perfect; they cheated by using syringes to perfectly place the dye instead of mastering the spray bottles and rubber bands; and most of all the guys selling them weren't the ones who made them anyway, they just bought them in bulk. But no one denied they were stunning. Whether it was a mushroom, a globe with actual continents, or Jerry's face, the designs and the colors were incredible. They *were* fifteen-dollar shirts.

It was a rebel life; escaping the boredom of a straight job to make cool shirts, sell them at shows, and then fall asleep in a tent reading Karl Marx's economic critiques. Campgrounds instead of corporate offices, tie-dyes instead of neckties, it was an end run around The Man and his materialistic ball and chain. But, of course, the irony is that the attempt to opt out of the capitalist system led directly to the free and open marketplace of capitalism. Was it naiveté? Was it hypocrisy? Was it what Ben Cohen and Jerry Greenfield would later term caring capitalism if none of the profits went to charity, but rather for tickets, gas, and food?

It turns out that it was actually right along the lines of the picture of capitalism that Adam Smith had in his head in the 1770s, an economic system that would change mightily with technological advances and the concentration of wealth. While Marx's critiques may have been right on the money for the corporate capitalist life I was avoiding, they missed the mark with the eye-to-eye, hand-to-hand, homemade marketplace that was the Dead parking lot scene. It was a kinder, gentler brand of capitalism.

Take a Silver Dollar, Take a Silver Dime

Capitalism began as a far out left-wing notion, as an economics of liberation. In European societies which were agriculture-based with long-standing monarchies, where the property was owned and controlled by a few nobles, but worked by serfs and generation after generation there was not even the possibility of economic, social, or political mobility, the idea that just anyone could make money, and lots of it, was quite radical. The idea that any Joe Schmoe could just have a better idea, work harder, build a factory, and suddenly have wealth and power was part of the movement that championed democracy with everyone voting and trials by juries instead of politically appointed judges. It was a movement that distrusted authority and tried to put the power in the hands of the people, all the people. No one had special rights, all humans were created equal—equal in terms of being rational and therefore equally entitled to opportunity.

The theory of economics that came out of this movement, the Enlightenment, is classical capitalism and is largely associated with the name Adam Smith. Smith's masterwork, *The Wealth of Nations*, is an owner's manual for a mercantile economy, for a marketplace based on trade.

The theory begins by redefining the basic notion of wealth from assets—gold silver, national currency, land holdings, . . . to consumable goods. Wealth resides in having something that you can trade for something else. When you have more than you need of a tradable commodity, you can use it to get other things you want or need, especially when one is able to take the surplus and through labor, turn it into something more valuable in the marketplace. You can buy t-shirts and dye and through your labor, create t-shirts worth more than what you paid for the parts.

Indeed, if you have sufficient excess, you could pay someone else to help you turn your materials into manufactured goods and have even more to sell that is even more desired. (Dude, help me sell these shirts and I'll pay for the gas and campground.) This is not only good for you, but also good for the worker who had no surplus, except time and the ability to labor. And it is good for the person who chooses to buy your manufactured good, as she now has something she desired, but did not possess. T-shirts and money change hands and everyone becomes more and more satisfied.

Smith sought to find the rules that governed the movement of wealth. Surely a price in the marketplace that was too high was like a dam on a stream that was too high; it stopped the flow that would otherwise take place. There was a natural order to the economy, just as there was a natural order to the physical universe. If there was an "invisible hand" that guided a cannonball in the same perfectly smooth arc every time it was fired from the same cannon, then the conditions of the marketplace ought to have the same sort of "invisible hand" guiding the flow of wealth. If you know the amount of powder, the angle of the cannon, and the weight of the ball, you can perfectly predict, using Isaac Newton's laws of motion, how high the cannonball will fly and exactly where it will land. In the same way, Smith thought, there are economic properties that govern what happens in the marketplace. Lots of veggie burrito stands, lower prices; lots of hungry folks after the show, some with serious munchies, higher prices.

Too high, though, and people may want it, but they won't buy it because those people are rational consumers. They have surplus cash to blow, but not so much that they'll waste it. Similarly, those selling the shirts are rational. They need cash for gas, tickets, food, and campgrounds. They would like to make as much as possible and that means both maximizing how much they make off each shirt and how many shirts they sell. This means they will sell as many shirts as they can at the market price as long as they are covering their costs. How do they figure this price out? For the most part, they don't have to—the marketplace figures it out for them. Multiple buyers and multiple sellers in repeated interactions at every Dead concert drive the market to its equilibrium price. Just like a box of ping pong balls behaves according to Newton's laws, so self-interested humans in a marketplace act like rational ping pong balls. Self-interest, like gravity, is a basic force of the world determining the course of the system.

But humans are not just ping pong balls and Smith knew this. We are ping pong balls with feelings, and that is where ethics comes in. Smith argued that ethics comes from our ability to be sympathetic, to understand the feelings of others. When we see something wonderful or tragic happen to someone else, we know how they feel, or at least, how we would feel in their shoes. Because of this, we can always evaluate our potential actions in terms of the way they will affect others. When we are children being taught a moral lesson, we are asked, "How do you think that made Suzy feel?"

Ethics guides us in how we ought to act, even in the marketplace. The economy runs best when everyone is self-interested, but that self-interest needs to be tempered with sympathy. In this way, we all reap the benefits of trade and have a world where we treat each other with the respect we deserve . . . or, at least, so thought Adam Smith.

Self-Centered to the Extreme

But if Newton's theory was the model for Smith's picture of capitalism, a new scientific theory a few generations later would reshape that view in the minds of many prominent thinkers—Darwin's theory of evolution. The idea that there was an invisible hand in biology favoring the fittest members of a species was a radical notion. Those who prospered did so because they were stronger and their strength makes the species stronger and the suffering of the weak makes it less likely that they will leave weak offspring. The less fortunate were not to be pitied, they were a menace to the overall health of the herd. If they had to be sacrificed, it was for the natural order of things and it had to be so. Having them culled may strike the more sentimental among us as sad, but in the end it is for the best.

There is, of course, an easy analogy for the slogan "survival of the fittest" in terms of wealth distribution. Natural selection turned to economic selection. The poor, like the weak and sickly runt of the litter, were poor because they were inferior and should be weeded out for the greater good. Since it was the invisible hand that was keeping them down, any outside interference like governmental welfare programs or church-based aid to give them a "hand up" would upset the natural balance.

The advance of capitalism with rapid industrialization created a radical division in Europe between those with wealth and those without that was the economic descendant of the noble-peasant distinction. Those who had accumulated great wealth under the new system saw the state of the poor and were keen to justify the disparity in standard of living. So by combining Darwin's and Smith's ideas "Social Darwinism" was born. To be altruistic and care about the downtrodden became immoral because it would upset the structure that brought about the best overall state. Given the choice between some people suffering and more people suffering, the proper choice was obvious. If you really cared about human suffering, you needed to become a self-centered SOB who didn't care about human suffering. We began to see human nature "red in tooth and claw."

It's Brother to Brother and Man to Man

Writing in London during this period, Karl Marx observed the effects of this industrialized social Darwinism firsthand. Marx's attempt to predict and advocate for the economic order that would follow capitalism has gotten the most press merely because the implementation and opposition of some forms of it happened to be the single most important geo-political factor in the twentieth century. But there's another part to his work. We can set aside his notion of communism and just look at his analysis of the effects of capitalism on people. He argued that there were four ways in which people experienced alienation in a society governed by its marketplace.

The first sense of alienation is from your labor. Your time is yours. You have free will and may do what you please. But when you sell your labor, you trade for money your ability to make decisions about what to do. You may want a little drink of water, but the big boss man decides whether to let you stop.

The second sense is from the product of your labor. When you sell your labor, the thing you make is not yours. Contrast this with a work of art. I may buy one of Picasso's paintings, but it is still Picasso's painting not mine. But a line-worker who makes an SUV he can't afford is estranged from the product of his work. The baker's family should never be in need of bread. By creating something, you put yourself into that thing; but when you sell your labor, the thing that should be part of you is removed from you.

Alienation also occurs with respect to other people. When I am treated as a tool, I begin to see others as tools. I see fellow laborers not sympathetically, but as competitors. I don't identify with them or try to find joy in our common humanity, but try to sabotage them for my own interests. The process of becoming a dehumanized worker leads me to dehumanize others.

The final sense is alienation from what Marx terms our "species being." Humans are creative by nature, he argues. That is just a fact about who we are. But when people work for a living, they are forced to treat their ability to do things as if it were a thing itself. You are what you do and if you do what you love, then you are what you love, you are who you would want to be. But when you are forced to sell your labor in order to get what you need to survive (food, clothes, and shelter), then you are no longer you, you become an object instead of yourself. You have been stripped of that which forms your very nature.

In these four ways, Marx argues that capitalism causes us to relinquish our humanity and remove it from one another. It sets us up as mutual enemies instead of bringing us together as a human family.

Wave the Flag, Pop the Bag

The general framework that Marx created failed to predict the future of economic progress. Planned economies have generally failed to live up to hopes and the underlying assumption that economic progress is always based on two competing, and ultimately clashing, classes proved far too simplistic to describe the real world. But as the economy transformed, the notions of alienation that he pointed out only deepened.

After World War II several factors altered the American economy in major ways. The biggest, of course, was the baby boom. Suddenly there was a huge new demographic to market to. A hit with the kids could mean huge profits, so the focus turned to entertainment and other products that would appeal to them.

Second, those who served in the armed forces during the war were given the opportunity to attend college under the GI Bill. Previously, higher education was limited to the well off. But once college graduates were no longer in short supply, the employment opportunities of those without a diploma changed significantly. This was exacerbated by the 2-S draft deferment that could keep you out of Vietnam as long as you were pursuing higher education. As such, anyone who could go to college did. This meant that there was suddenly a glut of white-collar workers looking for white-collar positions.

You also had the rise of the military-industrial complex and the beginning of the service economy. While corporations had played a major role in the American economy before the war, afterwards, their influence and size increased markedly. This created a whole new set of positions for mid-level managers, jobs just perfect for those newly minted college grads.

When all of these factors combined with the suburbanization of the middle class, a new way of life with new expectations became entrenched. The TV dinner button-down life gave the children of those who suffered through the depression and the world wars a sure path to white bread security and stability. But it was not a path embraced by all . . .

The work-a-day office world created a new wave of alienation. Now you were not only alienated from the product of your labor, it was more often than not unclear exactly what the ultimate product was. The suburban life was safe, but sanitized. Individuality, creativity, those parts of our species being that Marx argued were essential parts of us were being suppressed. And there was a backlash.

The hippie movement in San Francisco that gave rise to the Grateful Dead was a reaction to this new order. Laws and mores were challenged. Freedom from the old social, political, ethical, and economic strictures was championed. It was not a move to subtly tweak the social order, it was dropping out, turning on, and tuning in to a new and completely different way of life.

Some projects, like the Hog Farm, worked to build alternative, self-contained spaces for this new approach to life, but most remained embedded within the larger capitalist society. This presented logistical problems. A house full of people living together, stretching their consciousnesses, and enjoying free love still had to eat. Groups like the Diggers provided free food and other goods in an attempt to sustain the movement, but ultimately hippiedom in its late-1960s formulation proved unsustainable and not capable of being universalized. The Diggers required donated or stolen food and this led to hippies becoming what economists call "free riders." If the counterculture movement around the Dead was to survive and expand beyond San Francisco and Berkeley, it would need to find some sort of economic model that could shield it from many of the influences and mores of the larger society and yet still be sustainable over the long run.

Need that Cash to Feed that Jones

And so we return to the parking lot. Deadheads who toured were generally faced with two options, either take a temporary job where you could save up the financial resources needed to sustain yourself on the road or find a way to make cash while on tour. The first is to be a part-time member of the standard capitalist structure, but the second was to become a member of an alternative capitalist structure, one that in certain ways is reminiscent of the picture that Adam Smith had two centuries before. Back were the marketplaces where the chasm between producer and consumer were bridged and back came sympathy as an economic virtue.

When you would catch a Dead show or two close to home and you bought a shirt, burrito, or new window or bumper sticker, you knew you were not just acquiring more stuff—you were also doing something to keep the scene alive. You may not be able to tour for whatever reason, but you could help keep the community going. That shirt would not only be a beautiful addition to the wardrobe, but also represent your contribution to making sure that there was a place to hang out for hours before and after the show, and a scene that would be there if and when you were ready to tour with the band. You could put yourself in the place of the person selling their wares and you could feel what they were feeling—that mix of joy and passion living on the road and the vague nagging that they had to make sure they sold enough shirts to fill the tank and the stomach. You could sympathize with those touring even when you weren't and that sympathy tempered self-interest. It was simply uncool to screw over a fellow deadhead.

But self-interest did not disappear altogether. The market forces were still there in all their glory. Anyone who tried to sell a ten-dollar shirt for fifteen dollars didn't sell many shirts—even to those who might have been willing and able to pay fifteen dollars. Those selling fifteen-dollar shirts they bought in bulk, were selling fifteen-dollar shirts and even if they hadn't made them, they were providing a valuable good—even according to those of us who bitched about them. No one begrudged them their place selling their goods when it came right down to it. It was capitalism, pure and simple—literally pure, simple, uncomplicated, non-corporate capitalism.

And the interesting thing about it was that while we were capitalists, we weren't alienated. I loved making shirts. It was an expression of creativity. Working over a basin, rinsing the loose dye out of yesterday's shirts, seeing if that new pattern came out the way I expected; it was always exciting. Watching people, for no apparent reason, instantly connect with a shirt and have to have it was amazing—especially since I could sympathize. I would have the same feeling, knowing the very instant I unfolded it beneath cold running water, that this one was destined for my shirt drawer as soon as it dried.

Robert Hunter wrote that "Day Job" was taken off the playlist because Deadheads disliked it so much. The embrace of the corporate capitalist lifestyle perhaps struck too close to home to be taken as ironic. But where the unease with the social and economic expectations imposed on them by the larger society was just as much there as it was with the hippies that started it all, the negotiated solution was ultimately not a full-fledged dropping out of capitalism, but something closer to what Ben and Jerry would later call "caring capitalism," a model that would try to meet needs, foster respect, and lead to a sustainable alternative way of being in the world.

2

Community at the Edge of Chaos: The Dead's Cultural Revolution

HORACE L. FAIRLAMB

> For me, the lame part of the Sixties was the political part, the social part. The real part was the spiritual part.
>
> —Jerry Garcia (*Rolling Stone* interview, #566, 11/30/1989, p. 73)
>
> We would all like to able to live an uncluttered life, a simple life, a good life . . . and think about moving the whole human race ahead a step . . . or a few steps.
>
> —Jerry Garcia (interview, *Anthem to Beauty,* Rhino VHS, 1997)

Everyone knows that the 1960s was a decade of idealism, activism, and social upheaval. What it all meant, however, has never been clear. Where the liberals took credit for its political successes, and where conservatives renounced each and every excess, the counterculture radicals have been dismissed, misunderstood, or marketed for nostalgia. According to one standard view, the counterculture was a utopian illusion born at Woodstock and buried at Atlamont. More charitably, some say that the counterculture was a political failure but a cultural success: Marx and Mao are out, but alternative identities and diverse subcultures are in. The culture-politics dichotomy was codified early on by the contrast between Hippies and Yippies—the drop-outs versus the radicals, the stoners versus the bomb-throwers. But it oversimplifies the counterculture to enforce the separation of politics and culture. For many in the counterculture, what was most radical about their vision was

that a change in consciousness (including its appropriate culture) would be the vehicle for—whether or not it qualifies as
politics or ideology—a new way of living.

The counterculture's ambivalence toward politics is captured
by Jerry Garcia's remarks quoted above; he seems at some times
to reject politics while at other times to promote utopian hope.
This political ambiguity is typical of the Dead, the doyens of San
Francisco counterculture, who not only survived the Sixties, but
went on to become the most successful touring band in concert
history (Introduction, Adams and Sardiello, eds., *Deadhead
Social Science: You Ain't Gonna Learn What You Don't Wanna
Know* [Walnut Creek: AltaMira, 2000], p. 28).

On the one hand, the Dead—like many in the counterculture—repudiated the militant politics of the time. On the other
hand, their "dropping out" of mainstream society meant *dropping in* to a new form of society not based on the struggle for
power. Their success story shows that theirs was a utopian
vision that worked. But what sort of utopia was it? And how was
it supposed to come about? To understand the ideology of the
Dead, one must abandon the traditional notion that politics
frames culture in favor of the view that politics follows culture
and the consciousness that animates it.

Before the Counterculture: The Promise and
Betrayal of Liberal Freedoms

Where did the notorious counterculture of the Sixties come
from? Conservative critics typically characterize it as the *reduc-
tio ad absurdum* of liberal permissiveness. But whether the
counterculture was the degeneration of Liberalism or the Good
News fulfilling the Old Law depends on one's priorities. One
could say that the counterculture was (1) the logical extension
of Jefferson's right to pursue happiness, and (2) a radical
embodiment of John Stuart Mill's liberal classic, *On Liberty*. Mill
argued that the state could not legitimately intervene in private
affairs except to prevent *involuntary* harms. Moreover, Mill's
argument praised the social benefits of eccentric experiments
in living. Whether or not "be-ins" were what Mill had in mind,
the Sixties counterculture was nothing if not an experiment in

living.[1] In these ways the counterculture was truly the logical extension of liberal permissiveness.

On the other hand, if the counterculture had been merely permissive, it would have been indistinguishable from economic libertarianism. While the counterculture did radicalize the eighteenth century's legacy of *political* liberalism (limiting the power of the state), it also challenged the *economic* liberalism that arose alongside it.

Economic liberalism began with Adam Smith's defense of the free market (1776) although liberalism gradually evolved to counteract the damage of unregulated capitalism. As nineteenth-century markets played havoc with the working class under industrial capitalism, American liberalism tried to mitigate its worst effects, at first with Progressivism at the turn of the twentieth century, and then with the New Deal programs of the Depression. Liberalism came to mean the welfare state. With the decade of prosperity after World War II, the Liberal Establishment became firmly entrenched in the mainstream of American politics, claiming to have found a workable balance between the dictatorial state-run economics of the Soviets and the market radicalism of the anti-communist American right. Where anti-socialists typically followed Friedrich Hayek's argument in *The Road to Serfdom* that ("creeping") socialism led inexorably to totalitarianism, Liberal defenders of "mixed economies" (markets limited by regulatory agencies and Keynesian deficits) attributed postwar prosperity to co-operation among the elites of government, business, and labor (whom C. Wright Mills called the "power elite"). This Liberal Establishment claimed to have found the right mix of freedom and management, meritocracy and public service, inequality and social safety net. The apparent success of this liberal pragmatism prompted Daniel Bell to proclaim "the end of ideology."

The Sixties proved Mills's critique of the Liberal Establishment more prescient than Bell's prediction of a final status quo. At first the Kennedy-Camelot aura distracted political observers from the signs of impending trouble. America's Cold Warriors were already spreading disinformation about Soviet arms and

---

[1] The experimenters have been far more candid than their critics regarding the sometimes hard lessons and its mixed results, see the interviews with former activists in Mark Kitchell's documentary *Berkeley in the Sixties* (1990).

East Asian dominos. In the landmark year of 1962, Michael Harrington's *The Other America* showed how many Americans were still off the gravy train, Rachel Carson's *Silent Spring* showed how the market was not disciplining the corporation pollution of the environment, and the leftist Students for a Democratic Society issued its Port Huron Statement, shifting the Left away from the totalitarian model of the Soviets and toward a more democratically co-operative politics.

Unfortunately the New Left mistook the signs of the times. Militants interpreted deteriorating race relations, increasing disapproval of involvement in Vietnam, disruptions on college campuses, and Lyndon Johnson's hastily cobbled together War on Poverty for a potentially radical moment. But the forces were not in line for deep changes. In the face of social protest and official violence, the Liberal Establishment stagnated rather than collapsed: it was too hidebound to cure the deeper causes of militarism and inequality, but strong enough to fend off challenges from the left and the right. As a project in political transformation, the New Left failed by its own populist standard. With the help of the mainstream media's thirst for drama and exaggeration, the Left lost its populist base when its militancy outstripped that of its target constituency: the mass of Americans outside the establishment.

Nor surprisingly, the failure of the New Left has distorted the collective memory of the counterculture as mainstream commentators pronounced the New Left too radical. Yet it is more illuminating to see how the New Left was *insufficiently radical* regarding the politics of the future. The New Left allowed the traditional politics of force and confrontation to overwhelm its more progressive impulse, which was to find social alternatives to force and greed. By contrast, the forerunners of identity politics realized that radical political changes must begin with changes in *political consciousness*. But this insight was already afoot in the more visionary elements of the counterculture. In that spirit, the musical phenomenon known as the Grateful Dead proved a more successful experiment in utopian possibilities than the New Left, not by imposing their agenda onto society at large, but by creating their own alternative culture out of which a remarkably successful mini-society grew of its own accord. Theirs is the success story of the revolutionary Sixties.

Art and Life at the Edge of Chaos

Despite the conformism of mainstream America in the Fifties, the seeds of a more adventurous culture were already being planted by the Beats, by experimental music, by folk music, by rock'n'roll, and by the residues of Leftist politics. Perhaps even more than the Civil Rights movement, the cultural avant-garde of the early 1960s was the *radical* edge of change. High brow and academic composers pushed the compositional envelope by throwing away old rules, integrating randomness into composition, and enlisting electronic computers for musical production. Out in the streets, mainstream radio cobbled together folk, rock, pop, and country, which were then synthesized by Dylan, the Beatles, and their successors into the self-consciousness of a generation. In San Francisco, social protest merged with folk lyricism and the poetic independence of the Beats to fuse high and low culture, poetry and politics.

For the Dead, these influences were synthesized and turbo-charged by the Acid Tests that began in 1966 when Ken Kesey, Neal Cassady, and others sponsored experimental "happenings" with psychedelics, music, and widespread cavorting. As house band for the Tests the Dead found a venue for unlimited creative interaction.

> The audience didn't come to *see us*; they came to experience something altogether different. So we could play or *not* . . . we had the luxury of being able to experiment freely in a situation that didn't require anything of us. It didn't require that we be good, it didn't require that we repeat a song; it didn't require that we be intelligible on *any* level. (Garcia, *Anthem to Beauty*)

That freedom liberated the band in two ways. On the one hand, those experiments allowed the band to abandon predetermined musical structures altogether. "What the Acid Test really was," Garcia notes, "was formlessness. It's like the study of chaos. It may be that you have to destroy forms or ignore them in order to see other levels of organization" (*Rolling Stone*, 1989, p.73). What they found on the other side of prefab structure was not meaningless noise, but subtler levels of meaning, "the form that follows chaos." They found that they when they "throw everything out and lose all rules, and stop trying to make anything happen on any level, other stuff starts to happen" (Garcia,

Anthem to Beauty). The Acid Tests showed the Dead that art could be lived, as complexity theorist Stuart Kaufmann describes life itself, "at the edge of chaos." From then on, the Dead's music remained dedicated to growth, innovation, and adaptation.

On the other hand, the Tests also changed their interaction as a band, their "own interior politics" (Garcia, *Anthem to Beauty*). Improvisation came to characterize not only performance, but song formation as well. Instead of fixing arrangements in advance, the Dead combined song elements by allowing each player to explore his own approach: "The arrangements are almost nil. The intraband collaboration is almost total . . . [Apart from] melody, lyrics, and chord changes . . . it's what everybody finds to say" (Garcia interview, *Conversations with the Dead* [New York: Da Capo, 2002], p. 36). The Acid Tests, Garcia concluded, was "one of the truly democratic art-forms to appear in [the twentieth] century" (*Anthem to Beauty*).

Anarchy, or Zen and the Politics of No-Politics

No one would be surprised that the secret of the Dead's famed improvisational jams is knowing how to get from structure to openness, spontaneity, creativity, and novelty. What might be more surprising is the Dead's commitment to turning this aesthetic ideal of free formation into a way of life on a large scale, a social vision of minimal supervision lived at the edge of chaos. For Garcia, for instance, New York City exhibits functional anarchy: "a place that's basically not being governed, and it runs pretty well. . . . When you're there, you have this feeling of out-of-controlness which is unreal, but it somehow works." New Yorkers are not ego-less robots, and yet "all those people are able to exist as governments of one, and do business, play their games, whatever, on their own terms" (*Conversations*, p. 83)

As every social philosopher knows, unity in diversity is the essence of the social problem. From the start, the strong personalities of the band posed that challenge. As David Gans surmised, and Phil Lesh confirmed, they were "more or less an anti-social bunch of guys individually who found more comfort together" than apart (*Conversations*, p. 201). The internal rapport of the band and its method of collaboration was not the spontaneous product of selfless yea-sayers, but more like the opposite. It was the product of strong personalities who shared a vision with enough commitment to make it work.

The principle of inclusive diversity was equally true of the wider Dead community. Deadheads are not the passive, homogeneous hippie stereotype sometimes portrayed for laughs: "there are people who in any other place but the GD scene couldn't talk to each other." Perhaps surprisingly, there was "very little unanimity on any subject in the band, the organization, or the Deadhead community" (Gans, *Conversations*, p. 6). "You look at the range of human types . . . they all can hang together and find something to talk about . . . It's a microcosm" (Gans, *Conversations*, p. 204).

The social ideal that Garcia speaks of —a spontaneous order —has sometimes been called *anarchy*. But that word is ambiguous. Literally it could either mean "no principles" or "no dictators." When we look at the politics of the Dead world, we do find principles but we find no dictators. No doubt, many have imagined Garcia in the role of leader. But the Dead have repeatedly denied having a leader. "Nine times out of ten if someone tried to *take* charge," said Lesh, "it would just dissolve in their hands" (*Conversations*, p. 205). As Bob Weir observed of their collaborative non-arranging approach: "I don't know anyone who has the energy to tell six other strong-willed musicians, 'Play this, you play that' —you get a lot of: 'Hey, eat my shorts. I'll play what I feel man' . . . it's pointless to try to do that with the GD" (*Conversations*, pp. 10–11). The Dead don't tolerate control trips over themselves or their audiences: "We want for the GD to be something that isn't the result of tricks," Lesh noted. Wary of power, Lesh notes, "we don't trust ourselves with it. We certainly don't trust anyone else with it" (*Conversations*, p. 54). This lack of fixed subordination to person or idea explains the band's ability to evolve: if anyone had imposed "any one particular direction, [the band's music] would eventually narrow down." Always free to explore, the group spirit could blow where it listed, which is to say, go "its own way, as long as it's running, performing as a unit" (Lesh, *Conversations*, p. 110).

On the other hand, ethical principles need not be formalized and notarized in order to bind people together: "Community is not about agreement, it's about acceptance and diversity" (Gans, *Conversations*, p. 6); "you have to be able to allow the entire range of human possibility. Here. Right here and now on this earth, in this life" (Garcia, *Conversations*, p. 210). The key to functional anarchy is finding the subtler unity among extraordinary diversity. The music was able to achieve it in performance, the band was able to achieve it in working together, and the Grateful Dead community was able to achieve it in living together, at home and on the road. For the Dead, this was not merely a practical possibility, but a spiritual ideal: "It just seems to me that consciousness wants that to happen—that's where we're trying to get to, something along those lines" (Garcia, *Conversations*, p.83).

Many have wondered, however, how could a subculture of that size even *be* an organization? When the time comes to put pen to paper, hand to the wheel, how is it done?

The Rules of the House

To emphasize its evolving character, Garcia once described the Dead as "a process rather than an event" (*Rolling Stone* 1989, p.73). But processes too have structure. Insider David Gans even remarked of the Grateful Dead: "I've gone past being embarrassed about having seen that it is a machine, not a miracle. Now I can see that miraculous nature of the machine itself" (*Conversations*, p. 199). So how did the machine work? The Dead household may have had no paterfamilias, but every household has some kind of rules, some kind of organization. Since the Greek word for "rules of the house" is *economics*, the commercial side of the Dead world should further illuminate the group's domestic coherence.

From the start the Dead did not fit the mold of the music industry. Radio and records were geared to 3.5-minute hits. Recording standards emphasized precision and predictability. In time the Dead learned not only to accommodate the recording studio but to take advantage of it. Yet even as the Dead's organization and fan-base grew, it never succumbed to the normal business dictatorship of efficiency and profit. As Gans observed, "You could run an analysis of this business and drive an ordinary consultant berserk with the contradictions and waste in it. And yet . . . everybody works hard when they have to, and they have the leisure to work leisurely" (*Conversations*, p. 204). The Dead business resisted the typical corporate subordination of people to profits.

Indeed, the Dead were in the business of tolerating as much insubordination as possible. Their flattening of the business hierarchy was possible due to their organization's extraordinary *esprit de corps,* as shown by the corporate status of their road crew. According to the standard capitalist division of labor, managers hold the top of the pyramid of power and pay while manual labor sinks to the bottom as skill requirements decline. This division of work and pay has been the source of the labor-management class warfare of the last two centuries. In the Dead organization, by contrast, all staff members are partners and some of the road crew hold top management positions:

- Lawrence "Ramrod" Shurtliff: caretaker of drums; president of the GD corporation
- Bill "Kidd" Candelario: caretaker of bass and keyboards; head of GD merchandizing
- Steve Parish: caretaker of guitars; manager of Jerry Garcia Band.

Where the old business paradigm was impersonal rationality and efficiency, the Dead never wanted success at the expense of personality. "I don't want a mindless automaton who's just a fuckin' technical expert . . . I want somebody who's a real person" (Garcia, *Conversations,* p. 228). Conversely, the crew aspired to the dignity of skilled collaborators on whom the performers depend from moment to moment. Steve Parish's account of the crew's discipline sounds remarkably like the performers': "when you start getting [into] habit, you always make mistakes . . . When we just start doing stuff because it's there, and we stop feeling what we're doing . . . you start getting into a routine . . . The brain, when it gets into one little pattern, it stops branching out and seeing . . . But it doesn't happen to us because we don't let it" (*Conversations,* p. 219).

The result of this shared philosophy and praxis was a business that did what businesses are supposed to do—grow—but in an entirely unconventional, people-centered way. "We're like the exception to every rule. We're in some kind of nonformula, nonlinear developmental path which is definitely growing" musically, financially, and as a community: "it's not like we're just dragging along the same audience, we're actually getting new people" (Garcia, *Conversations,* p. 51). Gans calls this success the *real* American Dream. Not the "bogus sort of consumer version," but the dream of having self-determination, an original culture and a business that respects every individual in the band and everyone around them" (*Anthem to Beauty*).

In this account of the GD organization, every member would recognize a communal ethos that is an essential element of its unique *modus operandi*. But any deadhead would also know that we have not yet discovered the key to the GD community, the element that elevates the community experience to a sacrament.

Corpse Mysticum

There is a good reason why deadhead vehicles often bore the bumper sticker: "There is nothing like a Grateful Dead concert." Unfortunately, when something is not like anything else, it is very hard to describe. Like psychedelics, you just had to be there. No wonder that commentators have turned to the language of religious experience. But could it really be *that* serious?

The *seriousness* of the Dead experience began with their initial dedication to music. Individually the members began paying their dues before the Dead had formed, but once formed, they worked long hours to develop their own particular combination of expertise and innovation. The festive atmosphere of Haight-Ashbury was the environment in which their musical innovation was born, but hedonism was never the point. As Lesh observed: "nobody in the GD was interested in a perpetual party. We were all interested in being musicians—if not together, separately, although it never came to that" (*Conversations*, p. 207).

Yet that seriousness soon went beyond the music: "When we get onstage, what we really want to happen is, we want to be transformed from ordinary players to extraordinary ones, like forces of a larger consciousness" (Garcia, *Rolling Stone* interview; #616, 1991; p. 37). This special quality overshadowed the superficial trappings of success: "After this many years, man [1981], there's nothing awesome about it all, except the moments. Those moments, when you're not even human anymore—you're not a musician, you're not even a person—you're just there" (Lesh, *Conversations*, p. 110).

The Dead recognized early on that this extraordinarily intense communal experience was their goal. Phil Lesh explained it this way:

"The word 'blesh' is used in Theodore Sturgeon's novel, *More Than Human,* which is essentially the story of how certain human beings communicate with each other telepathically and form a greater organism. And when we first started playing together at the Acid Tests and in the bars it slowly became apparent that that's what was happening to us on the musical level in the sense that we were manifesting this togetherness or this unity or this single organism and it just grew and grew in that direction" (*Anthem to Beauty*).

The band members discovered that this group consciousness had a life of its own. "*It* is informing all of us," Lesh noted. Or as Garcia observed: "from the point of view of being a player it's this thing that you can't make happen, but when it's happening, you can't stop it from happening" (*Conversations*, pp. 52–53). Not only did the spirit of the GD not care if most of America didn't like it, Lesh noted, it "doesn't even care whether *we* like it or not" (*Conversations*, p. 196). As it turned out they liked it a lot, along with thousands of others.

The comparisons with religious experience are inevitable. Percussionist Bill Kreutzmann speculated that "there is some great power, be it God or whatever, that enters the GD on certain nights, and it has to do with us being open and getting together with the audience."[2] More cautiously, Garcia calls the experience "some kind of intuitive thing," though he doesn't "know what it is or how it works" (*Conversations*, pp. 52–53). Shan Sutton and Amanda Hirsch have analyzed Dead concerts into the three stages of Victor Turner's model of ritual: separation, liminality (living on the margins), and reincorporation (Turner, 1977, pp. 94–95). Fans trek to concerts at the margins of society. The power of the music lifts consciousness out of its normal channels. The various rhythmic cycles of concerts—sets, songs, and solos—allow for alternations between release and reincorporation, an easy passage of individuals between their sense of self and sense of group while never entirely leaving the

---

[2] Jerilyn Lee Brandelius, *The Grateful Dead Family Album* (1989), p. 193; quoted by Shan Sutton in *Deadhead Social Science*, p. 122. Garcia's suspicion of institutions prevents him from being entirely comfortable with that category. "It's a religion to me, too, on a certain level," he allows while insisting: "I don't like the word *religion*. It's a bad word" (*Conversations*, p. 214). Taking a more Zen attitude toward the Spirit, Garcia would prefer not to have that concept. "I don't want to assign a word to it. Why limit it?" (*Conversations*, p. 214).

other behind. As Shan C. Sutton sums it up: "This achievement of communitas and the mystical transformation from individual to group consciousness formed the heart of the Deadhead ritual process" (Shan Sutton, "The Deadhead Community," in *Deadhead Social Science*, p. 115). This rhythmic process explains the legendary intimacy of the Dead experience. "At this point [1989] it's gone beyond even blood," Garcia remarked. "The GD have been the most intimate kind of relationship I've ever experienced . . . that's what we're after—a kind of community. And we have it" (*Rolling Stone*, 1989, p. 73). The loyalty and diversity of the deadhead community confirm the extraordinary breadth of that intimacy.

Here too the deadhead stereotype may mislead. The Dead experience was not simply a mass hallucination or a mob psychological obliteration of the self. Both band members and deadheads find that the group experience arises through a heightened awareness that allows for diverse experiences ("everybody experiences it on their own terms," Garcia; *Conversations*, pp. 52–53) despite an absorption into the group experience: "It's like we're all orbiting around the sun. By the very nature of that situation, we each look at it in a different way" (Lesh, *Conversations*, p. 214). No doubt the music's provocation heightened consciousness was supported by some of the most thoughtful and sophisticated lyrics in popular music.

If the Dead's politics are unorthodox for their spiritual overtones, their spirituality is unorthodox for its ironic overtones. True, the Dead aesthetic—especially in the hands of visionaries like Rick Griffin—rose to the level of true iconography. But the Dead eschewed the temptation to sanctimonious leadership. Their attitude—like Schiller's concept of aesthetic play—has always been *both* ironic *and* serious: "our best attitude to [our community spirit] is . . . stewardship, in which we are custodians of this thing" (Garcia, *Conversations*, pp. 52–53).

The Gathering of the Tribe:
Ironic Sacramentalism

So what sort of society is the Dead society? From the point of view of modern social contract theory, the Dead are ahead of their time. Hobbes's social contract theory was based on the need to tyrannize the masses to keep them in line. Locke's version was based on the need to protect private property. Rawls's more recent version was based on a self-interested optimizing of the worst case scenario. The Dead seemed to have found an imaginative space in which the attraction of a maximally inclusive world—a world at once individual and collective, tragic and comic, serious and ironic, folksy and sophisticated, ancient and modern, absurd and divine, ordinary and magical—is powerful enough to transcend significant differences while leaving them in place. This is not politics as usual. But neither is it miraculous. The Dead's powers of transubstantiation do not depend on miraculous ingredients, but rather on cleansing the doors of perception so that the universe appears in a grain of sand: "I don't believe we're doing anything extraordinary," Garcia confided, a truth that has mystified other, more technically proficient musicians. "We're just doing what can be done" (*Conversations*, p. 59). That it can be done shows the political power of consciousness.

Does the GD "process" have a future? Toward the end, even some band members wondered if the Dead were too large a community to sustain their legendary cohesion. Kreutzmann complained: "In the very beginning we were a real tight family but now it's different. You know, toward the end, we had separate limos, stuff like that. It's hard to get six giant egos in the same place" (Sarah Bruner, "Just a Guy Who Plays Drums: An Interview with Bill Kreutzmann," *Jambands*, March 1999). Since 1995 the band's immortality has devolved to the question of life-after-Jerry. Of course, any loved and talented person will be missed. But lyricist Robert Hunter once speculated that even when there is no more Grateful Dead there may still be "a community formed that needn't wither simply because they don't have their band anymore . . . And if there can be a strong liberty-loving community at that point, which has evolved its own ethics, I think that community can hold together" (*Conversations*, p. 285). As of Year Eleven A.J., the community still lives and is paid the tribute of numerous jam bands who, while not yet reaching the achievement of the Dead, keep the process evolving.

3

The Everyday Miracle of the Occasional Community

JOHN DRABINSKI

Only a god can save us.

—Martin Heidegger

We must love one another or die.

—W.H. Auden

When someone wants to make fun of the Grateful Dead, the barbs inevitably take aim at Deadheads. You know the parade of stereotypes, many (if not most) of which are often true: stoner, dropout, smells bad (or good, if you like patchouli and sandalwood), druggie, free-love anarchist, aimless, and so on. One can surely debate whether all or any of these are actually vices. Most are usually quite fun and generally life-enriching which is a good distance toward becoming a virtue in my book. But my concerns here are not with the ethics of the Deadhead scene and its accoutrements; rather, I want to pose something quite opposed to the mocking stereotypes: that the Deadhead scene is actually an enormously important space of hope, especially when posed against the worst excesses of modernity. By "modernity," I mean that peculiar form of life most of us currently inhabit, a form of life dominated by crushing uniformity, familiarity, and repetition, all of which impair our ability to think about community. What would it mean to think about the freak show that was the Grateful Dead parking lot as an occasional redemption of modern life? How might this occasional character of redemption be an example of how, in the increasingly sterile, inhuman space of daily life, we can carve out meaningful human space? If modernity intervenes to fracture our sense of community, then what sense are we to make of the occasional communities found in daily life? What relation might those occasional communities have to the Dead parking lot? In other words, what lessons can we draw from the Deadhead scene?

It's All on the Same Street

I used to be a commuter. I spent over two and a half hours per day commuting from Amherst, Massachusetts (my home) to Worcester, Massachusetts (my former workplace, Assumption College). I drove these hours four days per week—often all five, and from time-to-time a day over the weekend. This is Western-to-Central Massachusetts, so the drive was quite beautiful, especially in the fall and spring. Leaves changing, pretty snow, typical New England stuff. Nevertheless, in its life form it was always the same departure and arrival: I leave early in the morning and return at suppertime.

By "form of life," I am loosely drawing on Ludwig Wittgenstein's notion in *Philosophical Investigations*, where forms of life are those meaningful spaces within which we live with one another, within which our speaking and being have public, rather than merely private, significance. In that context, we can say that commuting is as much a language and meaning as it is bare departure and arrival. Commuters have a language, a set of gestures and jokes that make sense in the sub-cultural context of commuting life. Only a commuter can roll their eyes in that peculiar way that says "I know, I know . . . that part of the day is such a drag."

Commuting put me in contact with a very particular *world* in which life unfolded in a distinctive way, with its own rhythms and harmonies. Whatever the reputation and stereotype—often well-earned—of professorial life as genuine leisure, my commute set my daily habits squarely within the rhythm of 9-to-5ers. Awakened before daylight, returned after sunset. The sheer repetition could be deadening, for it was always a repetition without excitement or difference. Different day, same shit. All those clichés.

Yet, we (and the first person plural is important here) were human, so that repetition always opened up alternatives: occasions of community. As I was still a philosopher, I found a bundle of philosophical insights in this repetition and its alternatives that led me back to, of all places, the fabled parking lot of Grateful Dead shows.

If commuting means repetition, then driving from Amherst to Worcester meant a whole lot of ritual: usual routes, familiar sites, and daily stops. This of course means one's personal habits, from showering to eating to paying bills, take on a routine structured around the commute; over two hours per day of driving puts a real squeeze on free time. But the ritual is also on the road. One stops at the same mini-marts in the same small towns, gassing up on petrol, coffee, and snacks. Visiting the same fast-food establishments for something to eat on the drive. And so on. In each of these places—and this is crucial— *one sees the same people*. Humans populate this repeated space as co-constituters and co-conspirators, which means that, to return to Wittgenstein, commuting becomes a form of life rather than a private language. This is social space in the cracks and breaks of front seat solitude. That said, I wouldn't go so far as to call this space friendship or community. Unlike other social spaces, we rarely (if ever) exchanged names or personal information. I knew the cars and the faces, as well as, if pressed, what she or he typically purchased: diet cola, peanuts, or whatever. We almost never spoke, but regularly gave greeting in eye-contact and nods. Smiles, in fact. We were a *community* in our commuting, no matter how strange the term sounds in this context. But the qualifier *occasional* is key for making sense of this community that happens in the cracks and breaks of solitude.

Why this community? Why call it occasional? Our common associations with the word 'community' are of deep and abiding connections. Family roots, common social vision, love and dedication—that sort of stuff. Whatever the importance of this occasional community in my daily life, I would never say we held much in common other than the fact that, for a few minutes for a few days per week, we occupied the same space. And that, perhaps surprisingly, this fellow occupation *mattered*. When I was on break and not commuting to Worcester, my return to this shared space would elicit a whole series of comments about my return, though rarely inquiries into the personal reasons why I'd been absent. Just a greet and some form of "missed ya!" Physical gesture or spoken, there was recognition that this community was real, revealing its reality at the moment it was absent, then present again. Missed ya!

What could this have to do with the parking lot of a Grateful Dead show? On first glance, there is very little—especially if we keep things at the level of aesthetic appearances. The commuters were mostly well-groomed, nicely dressed, low-level white-collar workers on their way to offices small and moderate sized (so I imagined). The Dead-show hosts a decidedly different crowd, to put it politely. This is a very different aesthetic. Deadheads smell of patchouli, dress in worn t-shirts/skirts/jeans, and drop out of daily life while living out of a classic VW van. This miracle, however: to walk into the mini-marts on Rte. 9 in central Massachusetts and to stroll through the stadium lot at University of Oregon are remarkably similar human events. Indeed, those walks stand out as some of the finest human moments outside my circle of intimates. No exaggeration. The human recognition in both spaces rejected what is most common about recognition in most spaces; we didn't need to know anything about one another, except that we occupied this space, at this time, and that this was sufficient for connection, even community. Entering the occasional community of the commuter *or* the occasional community of the Deadhead parking lot is akin to exiting much of what defines modern life. What do I mean by this?

The Other One

We live in a peculiar age. Whether one calls it modern or postmodern, our age is one of mutual alienation and mediated connection to others. Modern life is "bureaucratized" and "technologized," which is to say that life is managed either by others for us (to the extent that we follow orders) or by us against others (to the extent that we strategize for self-benefit). We see this in the routine that is typical of working life, some of which I sketched out above as the commuter's form of life. But working life is only one part of the management of life. Friendship, love, family are all subject to scheduling and meeting "set goals" offered to us in too many self-help books. Even death, as Zygmunt Bauman argues in his *Mortality, Immortality, and Other Life Strategies*, is managed by medical technology; death has become something we postpone with good medicines, managing its inevitable presence until the last moment like Enron accountants. The management of life most fundamentally changes our relation to others. The other person ceases to be a singular individual with demands, needs, or even just generous, human exchange. Rather, the other person's relation to me is mediated by a whole set of social demands, values, and structures, all of which alienate us from one another. We needn't look to high theory for glimpses into this alienation. Indeed, this alienation is reflected by too many pop-culture sayings. The one that always comes to mind for me is from my own college days: "He who dies with the most toys wins." And we can find variants of this same sentiment from any period of the past handful of decades. Whether it's "a dog-eat-dog world" or "a war out there," the prevailing sentiment seems the same: other people are our enemies at worst, zero-sum competitors at best. I take these cliché's and sayings seriously. They are genuine windows into our lives together. Are our lives pitted against one another? Is life really a competition? Or, more directly, is community dead in American life? It is always worth asking these questions, for, if modernity is a form of life, then we are justified in asking whether or not the speaking and being through which that form of life is composed is legitimate.

In his *One-Dimensional Man*, Herbert Marcuse makes the case that, through the constant presence of technology and other forms of managing life, Western culture has become "one-dimensional." Life is reduced to one dimension, which means for Marcuse that our lives are modeled on work-a-day efficiency and little more. The management of this life is total, prompting Marcuse to describe one-dimensional life as laboring under a *totalitarian regime*. For sure, this sounds like an exaggeration , but Marcuse's rhetoric has its purpose. What we consider "normal," this management of life, is actually an exercise in deadening our participation *in* life. This totalitarian "regime" operates at the level of micro-management by lodging itself in private and public life, ranging from the inflexibility of social rules of work and family to the repetition of one and the same vision of life throughout our media sources. No one would describe one-dimensionality as particularly optimistic; a bleak vision, for sure, but not without a lot of merit. Societies operate according to pivot-points of identity, and in a society such as the United States, those pivot-points have very little shared history from which to draw. So, we find that our identity in the United States is often formed in a vision of being an efficient worker and diligent consumer—a vision that is inclusive, surely, yet utterly one-dimensional. Perhaps Coke does add life in this one-dimensional world? Now *that's* pessimism.

Pessimism, however, cannot rule the day. Not entirely. Whatever the leveling effect on us by the regime of one-dimensionality, the human person *as a human,* with voluminous desires and needs beyond what the one-dimension offers, contests such a reduction of life in the breaks and cracks of life's one-dimensional flow. Bits and pieces of the other two (or more) dimensions show themselves dramatically in rebellious social movements (the sexual revolution is Marcuse's chief example) *and,* albeit with less drama, in quirky, daily routines that re-inscribe human contact within a world insistent on eliminating such community. Sadly, those glimpses of a bigger, more passionate life quickly recede as we return to duties of work and sleep. Glimpses are fleeting, for sure, but they are also where a sense of hope takes root.

What hope is there in a one-dimensional world? How might our multi-dimensional desires help form relations with other people *against* the threat of one-dimensionality? The stakes of this question could not be higher. Indeed, our thriving and flourishing as humans is put in question by one-dimensionality, so re-forming these relations is tantamount to overcoming what is most stifling about modernity. Let me be blunt: we need a new "ethic" to revive a sense of community, to reconnect across competitive alienation, and so to reopen the dimensionality of life.

What do I mean by "ethic" here? We need to be precise, for common associations do not quite capture what I have in mind. The word "ethic" suggests rules for right and wrong, good and evil, and in that way seems just *the opposite* of what we need in a world reduced to one-dimension by routine and repetition; rules manage life, threatening our relations with others with the specter of a kind of moral one-dimensionality. Instead, to get at this quirky term "ethic," I want to turn to Martin Heidegger's sense of the term, which derives from the Greek word *ethos.* *Ethos* meant something very different for the Greeks, something to be distinguished from rules and principles. According to Heidegger, *ethos* "means abode, dwelling place. The word names the open region in which man dwells. The open region of his abode allows what pertains to the essence of the human and what in thus arriving resides in nearness to him, to appear (Martin Heidegger, "Letter on Humanism," in *Basic Writing* [New York: Harper and Row, 1988], p. 233). *Ethos* names the place—the home, even—in which we abide. The crisis of one-dimensionality is therefore obvious: our very home constricts us. Opposed to the openness that Heidegger describes as a dwelling place, the one-dimensional life is closed to the point of near-suffocation.

Yet, Heidegger connects the openness of our abode, our home, to the essence of the human. To be human is to abide in this openness; without it, we are lost and yearn. Yearning transforms one-dimensionality, I would argue, because it is that part of us that rebels, however quietly, against the forces that might limit our sense of life. Occasional communities open this one-dimensional space with the human voice, embodied in the hello, the acknowledging smile, or the simple head-toss greeting. The problem with thinking about hope for an open abode or alternative *ethos* in terms of the occasional community represented by the commuter's stopping points is simple that it is too occasional. Too brief. Too constricted, even as the constriction is opened up by human contact. We need an alternative *ethos*, the movement into which is more dramatic, even jarringly so.

For Werner Marx, one of Heidegger's more creative students, the movement into an alternative *ethos* is provoked by a shocking experience, one completely foreign to the normal and normalizing flow of life, and so by an experience that is *transformative*.

> In the one who has been taken out of his everyday attunement of indifference, the capacity for compassion thus acts as the all-pervading force that is alive in his overall relation to the world, fellowman, and community. It is the measure that exists here on earth, determining him through and through in all his contexts of meaning. (Werner Marx, *Toward a Phenomenological Ethics* [Albany: SUNY Press, 1992], p. 140).

Forgetting the Love We Bring

Does the commuter's occasional community really transform, or does it allow for hints and suggestions of an alternative without disrupting the flow of one-dimensional life? I fear the latter.

What sort of occasional community might take us out of our everyday attunement of indifference with the possibility of crippling—rather than setting aside—that indifference?

Again, let us return to the parking lot. The sheer volume of smells, dope, people, colors, and sounds is enough to alter one's attunement. It is utterly overwhelming and impossible to take in, except insofar as we take in the fact that it is so overwhelming. And lovely in its overwhelmingness. But a stroll through the parking lot is not a spectator sport; it is a human event. Without put on or pretension, the human event of the stroll through the parking lot is *personal* and *familiar*. It is as if you already know everyone. At first, this might sound like false intimacy or just a matter of using the right words and phrases to *feel as if* it were an intimate space.

The stroll itself is something altogether different. The parking lot is a marketplace of two very different things: commodities and friendship. Everything you need for the show and after is for sale. If you're hungry, there's plenty of cheap food: sandwiches, beans and rice, fruit. You can certainly get high. The Grateful Dead's famous libertarianism about taping shows appears as well, as tapes of famous and unknown shows are available for cheap. All of this is available from folks who love The Dead, folks who by virtue of being *in this lot, at this very moment*, are your friend. The lot itself is a community, not just a space in which community may or may not form.

The parking lot is not a *possibility* of overcoming the kind of alienation from one another inherent in one-dimensionality. The parking lot is the given and uncontested community within which hostility and indifference are tantamount violent acts against the meaning of the shared space. This is what is meant by the *vibe* of the Grateful Dead parking lot. For all of those people, high as shit, anxious to see the show, and packed in close, I never saw a hint of aggression. It just didn't seem possible.

A legitimate hesitation, though. *Commodities and friendship*— this seems completely contradictory, for we are justified in asking if the very idea of a marketplace, of exchange and profit, is not yet another repetition of the very sort of alienation from one another against which I am claiming the Dead parking lot works. What kind of marketplace is this? Certainly things are sold: food, dope, t-shirts, bootlegs, and so on. What distinguishes this mode of exchange from profit-driven, alienation-laden marketplaces?

Simply put, it is the saturation of that space with friendship. The exchange that characterized the parking lot was communal, yet communal in a very peculiar sense. To be sure, for those Deadheads who followed the band around for months, a year, or years, we can begin to talk about community in a conventional sense: a collection of humans that share something essential and decisive in common. In the case of the Deadheads, it is the ritual of packing and unpacking with the band. But the parking lot is a community of hardcore Deadheads *and* the occasional concert attendee. Those attendees have an affection for the Grateful Dead in common, sure, but that is hardly grounds for calling the gathering a community. The concert-goers ranged from frat guys to hippies, teenagers to old farts. *I went to two shows with my own hippie-cum-yuppie father, with whom (at the time) I had in common little more than a last name, a ticket, and mutual distrust.* Yet, there was community.

On the one hand, it may be enough to say that this communal sense is explainable by what I call the occasional community. Dead concert-goers share an occasional, temporary form of life; there is a whole way of speaking and being specific to the scene. The crowd's response to certain lyrics or to that sound only Jerry Garcia can make with a bent note are as much a form of life as random pleasure. The grammar, to evoke Wittgenstein again, of the show makes a total being possible in that space.

Dope is not incidental here, as it is one (important on the scene) way in which forms of life were enhanced and shared on the concert floor (and previous to the music, in the parking lot). The fact that such a random assembly of people could be held together in this space is testimony to the power of occasional communities. But that randomness is also the moment in which the occasional character of the parking lot and concert transcend mere occasionality. There is, rather, an authentic transformation of who you were before you walked into the parking lot into who you would be for the show. Not a put on. A genuine transformation. And always for the better. Unlike the commuters who share form of life and meet within that form in occasional community, the Grateful Dead parking lot is a site of conversion.

What does this have to do with an *ethos* of compassion? If we take the term compassion, as does Werner Marx, in its root sense, the undergoing (passion) of the scene together (com) is the moment where we overcome not just our alienation from one another, but also take that leap across a sense of connection to an undergoing together. *Com-passion.* This means the good trip and the bad trip. This means the smile exchanged between the frat guy and the long term Deadhead as a favorite lyric is uttered. This means the comforting of the old fart who smoked a joint too strong for his "experience" by the college kid who knows better. *Undergoing together* is in fact the very essence of the freak show that was the Grateful Dead parking lot. It is easy to remember the freak show as a collection of dropouts in some sort of glorious performance art piece. But the real freak show of the parking lot was the freakish collection of authentic freaks, part-time freaks, and just plain normal dudes there for a good show and mix tape. That's to say, the real freak show was the idea that such an assembly could be, against so many forces to the contrary, a genuine alternative *ethos.* That an occasional community transcended its occasional character through its sheer endurance across decades, generations of Deadheads, and more than a couple of keyboard players. In your town and mine, there was this everyday miracle of the parking lot. We need it now more than ever. We need that kind of hope.

4

Performance and Property: Archive.org, Authorship, and Authenticity

PETER BRADLEY

Tapers—Grateful Dead fans who make and then share recordings of live shows—subscribe to one of the most comprehensive, grass-roots enforced, black-and-white moral systems around. Studio recordings designated 'off-limits' by the band are not shared while recordings made of live performances, sometimes even off the official soundboard, are shared widely. Those who break this code are ostracized. Taking (or even asking for) money for the taped recordings is an even greater moral violation than pirating studio versions. The taping ethos suggests a new attitude towards the rights entailed by intellectual property and authorship in general.

Consider how Deadheads distinguish between performances that are band property—which it would be a moral violation to share—and performances they consider public property. The music of a studio performance is distinguished from its live performance counterpart only with respect to engineering: acoustics, post-production mixing, and interference from the audience. Artistically, studio recordings are often free from errors but the bootlegged live performances more authentic. But neither of these distinctions seem morally relevant.

Could the distinction be grounded on mutual trust and respect between a band and its fans? But is the desire of an artist enough to impose such a moral duty on me? If so, which artist? Jerry? John Perry Barlow? Or Bob Weir? For that matter, on what basis can someone *own* their performance?

All of these issues came to a head on November 22nd 2005 when Archive.org, without warning, blocked users from downloading all taped performances (although non-soundboard recordings could be streamed from the site). Users of the site found this message when they logged on: "Based on discussions with many involved, the Internet Archive has been asked to change how the Grateful Dead concert recordings are being distributed on the Archive site for the time being . . ." Chaos ensued. Petitions were started. Fingers were pointed. The nascent blog-o-sphere erupted with rumors. Bob Weir, who by all accounts has been implicated in making the request to Archive.org, defended his actions thus:

> We had to cover our asses. What they're doing is illegal, unless there are arrangements made . . . particularly in the case of covers—other people's material. If we're perceived to be distributing their songs without their agreement, they have every right, and really every obligation, to sue us . . . We had to take it down. We had no choice . . . the "information wants to be free, man"—those folks . . . this is not information, this is music. It's kind of value-added information. Some people prefer to call it art. . . . We had to go ahead and do the right thing, and it upset some folks. I'm really sorry about that.

Bob is right. At least, he's right about the covers. The legal and moral obligation to respect the property rights of an artist do not end when another artist performs their work. On the other hand, if the bands covered by the Dead subscribed to the same ethos of sharing as the Dead, Bob's argument would hold no water.

The legal protections offered by copyright extend the rights beyond what authors are morally entitled to. These special rights are based on a fiction of individual creativity perpetuated, in part, by authors themselves. The truth of the matter is that authors are no different from other artists and creative performers—and they should all be entitled to protect the integrity of the products of their creativity. And as the free duplication and exchange of artistic products over the internet has made perfectly clear, the protections to which artists are morally entitled are slightly different than those currently protected by the legal standard of copyright.

Conventional versus Natural morality

Every society has conventions. We follow these conventions not because it is *right* to do so, but because they make the society run more smoothly. Suppose everyone decided one day to drive on the left side of the road, as they do in England. We wouldn't be committing a moral violation to do so. At the same time, it would be foolish for me to suddenly start driving on the left without a change in the society's driving behavior just because there is no moral obligation to drive on the right.

It would be wrong of me, however, to kill everyone who wore purple. Even if I lived in England. Even if I lived in a country where the Government allowed it. And even—and perhaps most especially—if I lived in a country where the Government required it.

This is the core distinction in moral thinking, and it is one that most children grasp at an early age. If you ask a child of four or five, "Suppose the teacher said it was okay to hit Jenny on the playground. Would it be okay to hit Jenny?' they will respond "No." But if you ask, "Suppose the teacher said it is okay to put your elbows on the table when you eat. Would it be okay to do so?," they will respond "Yes." This distinction, incidentally, is one that psychopaths are never able to make. Ted Bundy famously considered murder and jaywalking to be on equal moral footing.

Making the distinction between protected canonical recordings and public taped recordings on the basis of the band's wishes assigns the taper's ethic to conventional morality. Suppose that the band said it wasn't okay to share taped recordings. Would it be okay to continue to do so? But the legal argument —insisting on the property rights of covered artists that are ensured by copyright—does exactly the same thing. Neither argument offers any truly (that is, natural) *moral* reason not to share studio recordings.

And that's the rub. If it is wrong to share studio recordings contrary to the wishes of the band, there must be a reason. And that reason has to be more than the reason we don't jaywalk. Or drive on the right. If it is wrong, it's wrong in a society that lacks copyright. If it's wrong, it's wrong even when the artist doesn't care.

Author Intent and Respect

After the Archive.org decision, a petition addressed to Grateful Dead Merchandizing and signed by numerous fans made its way around the Internet, which contained this paragraph:

So here is our resolution. You want to change the rules as you go along, so will we. We don't care anymore; we've lost all respect for this organization. Between the utter disgust of your decisions with Jerry's guitars, and now taking away our access to the music we care about most, we refuse to support any aspect of GDM until we see change. No more CD's, no more tickets, no more merchandise. We ask all deadheads to join us in this protest.

More often than not, the taper ethos is defended in these terms: mutual respect between the fans and the band. But what does that mean? One cannot just 'respect'. One must respect someone or something. And one must exhibit some quality of property worthy of respect (even those who demand to be respected simply as a matter of birth, like monarchs, usually justify that respect in terms of being chosen by god).

Respect differs slightly from emulation. We emulate those who are like us, but who have achieved something that we wish we could achieve. Respect is a broader term. We respect those who have achieved something great —something that we sense it might be good to achieve, but we don't necessarily want to achieve it ourselves. I respect the hell out of Lance Armstrong for having survived testicular cancer. But I don't emulate that — because I don't want to get testicular cancer. If I do get testicular cancer, then I'll almost certainly emulate him. But for now, I'm happy with respect.

The Dead did something that is worthy of respect. They performed music in a way no one else could. Each performance is irreducibly unique. And I respect that. I don't want to play in exactly that way—I can't, but that's irrelevant—I respect them because they can. It may not be as stunning and life-affirming as Lance's recovery from testicular cancer, but nonetheless, I respect the Dead for their artistic creativity and integrity.

Notice that respect based on artistic qualities does not privilege songwriters over the other performers. Compare this kind of respect based solely on an author's intent, which underlies Bob Weir's argument quoted above. Respect for an author's intentions for how his or her work can be used cannot be extended to cover other artistic expressions. Respect for the irreducibly unique nature of each and every performance can be. Hence, respect for authorship cannot provide the justification for intellectual property protection we are seeking, but respect for creativity of expression can.

Special Status of Authors

Lawrence Olivier—considered by many to be the greatest actor of his generation—first broke through when he played Hamlet. In the early part of the play, Hamlet meets his father's ghost who relates the details of his murder to the young prince. This is the pivotal moment in the play: without this information, none of Hamlet's actions are comprehensible.

Traditionally, this scene is played by two actors, one portraying Hamlet and the other his father's ghost. Olivier played both roles—*à la* Gollum in the "Lord of the Rings" movies. In his film version (1948), the ghost is Olivier's voice, recorded and distorted for effect. Olivier's creative, artistic choices suggest a very different interpretation of Hamlet's state of mind and force us to reconsider the entire play.

Olivier was given due credit for his insight—but he cannot copyright it. If I were to play Hamlet today, I could use the same technique without paying Olivier's estate. Copyright is reserved for authors. Consider Bob Weir's comments about the Archive.org controversy. His primary concern was not for his own performance, but for the authors of songs that they had covered live. According to Weir, it was the author's right—or even obligation—to sue Archive.org or the Dead to stop distribution of their property without their permission.

But why this special status for authorship? Woody Guthrie 'copyrighted' "This land is our land" with the following:

> This song is Copyrighted in U.S., under Seal of Copyright # 154085, for a period of 28 years, and anybody caught singin it without our permission, will be mighty good friends of ours, 'cause we don't give a dern. Publish it. Write it. Sing it. Swing to it. Yodel it. We wrote it, that's all we wanted to do.

Producing a work of art as complicated as a play—or, for that matter, a Dead show—is a collaborative effort. Every person who works on such a show makes creative, artistic decisions that contribute to the overall artistic experience. Yes, Olivier's Hamlet would not have appeared in the West End had Shakespeare not written it, but it also wouldn't have appeared if the lighting designer hadn't been able to light the stage effectively.

We tend to prize authorship because we imagine that authorship is an individual effort. We extend copyright to authors in part because it is easy to pay one person. It is extraordinarily hard to split income with lighting designers.

But artistic individualism is a myth. Authors do not work in a vacuum. Without Marlow, Shakespeare would not have been such a great author. Without Woody Guthrie, neither Jerry nor Barlow would have been such a great lyricists. Without the right people to perform their words, play writers and songwriters would never be heard.

This is not to argue against copyright. The tradition of copyright law is well aware of influence of author on author. Indeed some of the very first lawsuits about copyright under English Common Law challenged the distinction between an original *idea* and an original *means of expression*. Many people wrote books about whaling in the late nineteenth century—some even about albino whales. But only Melville wrote *Moby-Dick*. The distinction is one of the *manner of expression*, not the idea. That is what copyright was designed to protect.

Recall that tapers routinely make a hard and fast ethical distinction between studio recordings and live recordings made by amateurs, for which the manner of expression is unique to each performance. So there is little there to support the special moral status claimed for studio recordings over live performances.

Moreover, given that some of the later recordings are made directly off the soundboard (and hence, mixed by a professional) the only significant difference is post-production mixing. Post-production mixing is not considered one of the 'high arts' or 'individual arts' or even 'acts of genius' that would entail special protection like authorship. Again, there is little reason to think that post-production mixing, alone, commands the special moral responsibilities allotted to studio recordings.

In order to distinguish between studio recordings and live taped recordings, we must delve further into the notion of 'property'—in particular, that odd beast 'Intellectual Property'.

Intellectual Property: A Very Brief History

You know those room-makeover shows where they show a 'dream' room, and then create a knock-off for one-third the price? Why is that legal? After all, interior designers work hard to design those rooms. They have as much training as many musicians and authors. The same argument can be made for the faux-fragrances that are sold on college campus across the nation. Or all the mimicry that happens in the fashion industry. So why are performances of music and poetry protected by copyright and interior design not?

In 1853, Harriet Beecher Stowe sued a German company who had produced a German translation of *Uncle Tom's Cabin* without her consent. The circuit court of appeals ruled that the "creations of the genius and imagination of the author have become as much public property as those of Homer or Cervantes . . . A translation may, in loose phraseology, be called a transcript or copy of her thoughts or conceptions, but in no correct sense can it be called a copy of her book". The reasoning is this: if the products of one's labor are mere ideas, then those ideas are shared publicly, and hence cannot be owned. If the product of one's labor is a physical book, then it cannot be copied. Harriet Beecher Stowe's product was ideas: and they, once released, were in the public domain. So long as a person was not physically copying her book, they were allowed to replicate her ideas.

This reasoning has been revised in intervening century and a half: photographs were admitted to copyright in 1884. Recordings of musical performances were added in 1971 (by an act of Congress, not the ruling of a judge), computer software was included in the early 1980s; and, recently, architectural works. On the other hand, 'Intellectual Property' has been expanded beyond copyright to include trademarks, trade 'dress', and other intangibles. For example, in 1983 Johnny Carson successfully sued a proprietor of portable toilets who used his catch phrase 'Here's Johnny' as a slogan. In 1988, Bette Midler won a lawsuit against Ford for using a singer who sounded like her in a car commercial. And in 1992, Samsung was found to have violated Vanna White's intellectual property when it produced a commercial with a robot that wore a wig and used her 'distinctive stance'.

A recent landmark case occurred in 1992, when a taco chain named 'Taco Cabana' expanded from San Antonio to open their first restaurant in the Houston area. Taco Cabana had a distinctive interior design, including the use of pink and green as their primary paint colors, and garage doors as awnings. Unfortunately, there was another chain already operating in the Houston area called 'Two Pesos', who also used green and pink and garage doors. Taco Cabana sued Two Pesos on the grounds that their interior design violated Taco Cabana's 'trade dress': the distinctive features of their restaurants that allowed consumers to immediately recognize the brand. They won.

Suppose I start a pizza joint. Can I decorate it with red-and-white checkerboard tablecloths, candles stuck in old wine bottles, dim the lights, and put old wine casket logos on the walls? My interior design is certainly not original—but can it be protected under intellectual property law? No. In order to be protected, the products of one's intellectual labor must be sufficiently original. In Taco Cabana v. Two Pesos, the Supreme Court ruled (at least implicitly) that the use of garage doors in Interior design, and the combination of pink and green as the primary colors combined to make a sufficiently unique, distinctive style that deserved protection. When you apply for a patent, the patent office must determine if the invention would be 'nonobvious' to a person having ordinary skill in that area. The same is true here: if my interior design is obvious to a person with normal skill in the area of restaurant décor, it just isn't protected as intellectual property.

That's why authorship gets special privilege over the other performance arts: because we tend to believe (falsely) that John Perry Barlow and Jerry Garcia did something that was 'nonobvious' to the normal person, while everyone else (performers, sound engineers, lighting designers, etc) are doing something just anyone can do. Again, this is wrong. Sound engineers are highly talented people who make creative decisions all the time. So are drummers. And they deserve the same respect as authors.

What Kinds of Things Can Be Owned?

I own the products of my labor. If I produce something, I own it—simply because I'm the only one who produced it.

I own a car. Okay. But what does that mean? I didn't produce it. And the money I used to buy it was borrowed. Yes, I'm paying it back—but I'm doing so with money gained from talking to undergraduates and grading papers, not selling my labor on an open market. It's true that I have a piece of paper stamped by the state of Maryland stating my ownership—but that paper doesn't change anything about my relationship to the car. Suppose I lost the paper. Nothing would change. That is, unless someone asked me to legally *prove* my ownership. The title merely *demonstrates* ownership, it neither establishes nor constitutes ownership.

Ownership is constituted by the right to control. The first thing I control is my labor. I can extend this control through various technological advancements: I own my car because without me, it doesn't do anything (except rust, of course). Everything it does I 'tell' it to do. If it is stolen—a crime against property—the thief has blocked my ability to control my car. Our society has agreed that the right to control *is signified by* possession of a title. But it is not so constituted.

Consider the difference between iTunes and Napster. When you purchase a song on iTunes, you own that song. But when you purchase a song from Napster, you don't own the song, you are 'leasing' it. Your rights to choose when and where that song is played are curtailed, and the company could, at any time, without your consent, revoke your continued right to listen to that song. If iTunes goes out of business, you still have your song. If Napster does, you have bupkiss.

This reasoning works in the opposite way as well: if one cannot control a thing, one cannot be said to own it. But here is where it gets tricky. When we say that 'one cannot control something', we might be saying it in the moral sense: that it would be immoral to control that thing. And we might be saying it in the metaphysical sense: that this thing is impossible to control, just because it is the kind of thing that it is.

For example, try as I might, I can't control another person. Yes, people are often manipulated by propaganda, threats, behavioral conditioning, and whatnot. But they are not controlled in the same way my car is. Try as hard as you can. People will always resist. Even in the notorious Guantanamo Bay detention facility, prisoners committed suicide, staged huger strikes and engaged in resistance activities. My car never refuses gas. And it never threatens to drive itself into oncoming traffic. People can't be controlled—because they are people. Hence, it is metaphysically impossible to own a person, and therefore, immoral to try.

So what has this to do with the taping ethos? Copyright—which Bob Weir cited as the motivation for changing the Archive.org policies—is the equivalent of my car title. It is a socially agreed upon document that extends one's right to control that which one produces. Copyright—like my car title—signifies ownership and relying on it turns a matter of natural morality into a matter of conventional morality. Not owning people is a matter of natural morality because it is metaphysically impossible to control another person. To which morality category does taping belong?

Is a Performance the Kind of Thing that Can Be Controlled?

No. A performer can choose not to perform. A performer can choose to perform badly. But once the performance is completed, it's hard to say that the performer can control his or her performance. The same holds for ideas. Once Harriet Beecher Stowe gave the world the idea of Uncle Tom, the character was outside of her control. At least, that's what the judge ruled in 1853.

In his 'academic' (as opposed to 'musical') life, John Perry Barlow is best known for an article titled "The Economy of Ideas: Selling Wine Without Bottles on the Global Net." In it, Perry points out that all existing intellectual property law is based on the ability of a user to *physically* control the objects of his or her labor. He goes on to argue that this notion of property is simply inapplicable to the digital world. I control my car because I control a physical object (the key) that is physically required to start the car. Digital media, however, has no such physical limitations. Once a performance is digitized, it is infinitely replicable.

Consider my ownership of this chapter. By buying this book (or when you will buy this book) you buy something physical. I transferred my right to control where this chapter appears in print to the publisher of this volume *because they have access to networks of readers that I lack.* In short: they can produce a physical book and get it displayed in Barnes and Noble, while I can't. It is to my advantage to give up some control in exchange for access to that network. And it is in their interest to get me to write this chapter (or else, they'd have nothing to publish).

Digital information, according to Barlow, is different. You and I and Bob's crazy uncle from Montana all have that same access to the Internet as Barnes and Noble. Thus, you and I and Bob's crazy uncle from Montana gain no advantage by working with traditional publishers. Except, of course, avoiding the loss of control.

Bookstores routinely destroy unsold books and return them to publishers. Information placed on the Internet never, ever truly disappears. Recently, while browsing Archive.org to research this paper, I decided to look up some of my (very) old websites. When I first set up the original website of my alma mater, Antioch College, I started a 'Too Much Coffee Man' fan site on the side. In a moment of nostalgia for the good ole' days when the Internet was young and Netscape was in beta-testing stage, I decided to look it up on Archive.org. It came right up. And there—in all its poorly-designed glory —was a coding error I made over eleven years ago. The agony! The embarrassment! A minor error (which I'm sure I fixed eventually) was captured and preserved for all netizens to witness for all time. Oh, if only I could rip the cover off and return it to the publisher.

But maybe I'm just a perfectionist. Performers routinely make minor errors while performing. And they live with it. They know that people notice. That is exactly what makes performances authentic. A written work is subjected to constant revision *up until* the exact moment it is published. The published version is made rigid and considered canonical. Mistakes that slip through to the canonical version haunt you, personally, for the rest of your life.

Maybe what is wrong in my story is just my desire for perfection in published form. Maybe if I thought about authorship more like performance—constantly subjected to revision and improvization—I would be more comfortable seeing old versions of my work. And maybe, just maybe, this drive for perfection arose from the process of rigidifying works of creativity via publication: the technological ability to physically control information allowed by printing presses—and not the other way around.

As I argued earlier, authorship does not appear to be distinguished from other creative endeavors in terms of originality or individual genius. Why, then, should it be distinguished in terms of its rigidification? Musicians often complain that their audiences (not Deadheads, notably) demand the same old songs performed in the same old way again and again and again. Any deviation from the canonical version is met with skepticism if not outright hostility.

Douglas Adams, author of the *Hitchhiker's Guide to the Galaxy*, changed the text for each medium in which it appeared. The original radio show differs from the BBC TV show, which differs from the original movie, which differs from the book, which differs from the comic book, and so on. When the Disney movie version appeared in 2005, many fans complained that it was different from—what? Which of those versions is to be considered 'canonical'? Which was the 'real' version?

Rigidification is the death of artistic performance. The whole point of seeing a band live is to hear deviations from the canonical versions. Authors are no less artists than the other performers on stage. Their work should be treated in the same manner: as an ongoing improvisational artistic performance, not as a canonical physical product that can be controlled.

A Solution: Dissolving Special Status

Authorship is not sacred. The digital revolution has reduced or eliminated the author's ability to control the products of his or her creative output. But no more so than performers are unable to control what happens to their performances once the performance has finished.

At the same time, we can distinguish between recordings of live performances and studio recordings. Live performers are given respect. Olivier became famous because of his performance innovation. The Dead are respected by Deadheads more than any other band is respected by their fans, precisely because they perform in an irreducibly unique ever-changing manner. Perhaps this is the solution: if we begin to think of authorship as an artistic expression on par with performance, we will treat authors in the same manner we treat performers. Published instances of a written work should be treated like recordings of a performance, not as the canonical version from which all others deviate. Authors should be respected as innovators and collaborators, not isolated static geniuses.

The approach I am advocating entails changes not only in our understanding of intellectual property and copyright but also our aesthetic appreciation for authorship. Authors would lose their special privileged status in the art and legal world, but gain respect for and better appreciation of their work as an irreducibly unique manner of expression.

Soundcheck

Describing a Band Beyond
Description

5

The Electric Nietzsche Deadhead Test: *The Birth of Tragedy* and the Psychedelic Experience

DAVID MACGREGOR JOHNSTON

To use your head, you have to go out of your mind.
—Timothy Leary

"The music started and everybody was dancing. Nobody was dancing with each other; they were just all kind of dancing. Everybody's up and down. I looked at all these freaks and thought, 'What the hell is goin' on?' Then I looked down and all of a sudden I'm dancing. All these heads are going this way and that way, but pretty soon there's a groove going and all of a sudden everybody's dancing together. Everybody's like one, and the crowd gets excited. Then the band starts getting excited, and then the crowd gets more excited. Everyone just starts feeding on everything and then this magical thing just happens. It's just so beautiful. You see, when you listen to music, it comes in, but when you listen to Dead music, it comes out."

That's the way one tour veteran in the 1995 documentary *Tie-Died* described his first show. Whether he was tripping on LSD or some other hallucinogen we can only guess, but it was clear that he was caught in the magical moment that was the Dead show.

About ninety-five years before the Dead first played together, Friedrich Nietzsche addressed just these sorts of magical moments in his first book, *The Birth of Tragedy out of the Spirit of Music,* but he was interested in a different sort of ritual: the drunken revelry honoring Dionysus, the ancient Greek god of wine and ecstasy. An ambivalent source of decency and depravity, Dionysus's myths and fables tell of drunkenness, madness, and wild ritual, all recapitulated in the festivities known as the Dionysia or the Bacchanalia. It was this unruly Dionysian aspect that later brought a musical element in to Greek drama, and that raised the more constrained ideal found in Apollonian sculpture to what Nietzsche considered the most developed form of art: tragic theater.

Although he claimed that both Greek tragedy and German culture had lost this mystical musical element, Friedrich Nietzsche believed that we would some day recover the Dionysian aspect of our lives and our art:

In the end I lack all reason to renounce the hope for a Dionysian future of music. Let us look ahead a century; let us suppose that my attempt to assassinate two millennia of antinature and desecration of man were to succeed. That new party of life which would tackle the greatest of all tasks, the attempt to raise humanity higher . . . would again make possible that excess of life on earth from which the Dionysian state, too, would have to awaken. (Friedrich Nietzsche, *Ecce Homo* [New York: Vintage, 1969], p. 271).

Move ahead that century and we find that the psychedelic experience of the Dead show offered a fortunate group of modern revelers the chance to immerse themselves in a contemporary synthesis of Apollonian structure and Dionysian impulse that Nietzsche explores in *The Birth of Tragedy*.

A Bus Came By and I Got On

When Ken Kesey and his Merry Pranksters finished that bus trip with the cowboy at the wheel, it's hard to believe that their minds remained completely "unbended." In any case they knew they still had "furthur" to go and other minds to bend. So Ken Kesey invited his friends, then known as the Warlocks, to provide some musical weirdness at a series of house parties that came to be known as the Acid Tests. As we know, the band had to change its name with the discovery that on the other side of the country another band (that would become the Velvet Underground) was already recording as the Warlocks. By their second appearance at the Acid Tests, in December of 1965, the Grateful Dead had been born, and the music that developed was weaned on the LSD-laced Kool-Aid that was a staple of those parties.

It's no surprise that Owsley "Bear" Stanley, creator of the Wall of Sound—the largest "portable" sound system ever constructed (seventy-five tons and 26,400 watts) and co-creator of the *Steal Your Face* lightning bolt, met the Dead soon after the Acid Tests began. Owsley was widely regarded at the time as the world's finest manufacturer of high quality LSD, and had become Ken Kesey's primary supplier before the Acid Tests officially began. Kesey took his first dose of acid around 1960, when he and Robert Hunter were exposed to a wide variety of powerful psychedelics as part of the CIA's experiments at the Menlo Park Veterans Hospital and the Stanford Research Institute. Ironically, as Hunter recalls, the United Sates government was in a way responsible for creating the Acid Tests and the Grateful Dead, and thereby the whole psychedelic counterculture.

The CIA was particularly interested in the use of hallucinogens as part of a mind control program, but LSD's discoverer, Albert Hofman, was more interested in its mind-expanding opportunities. At a recent conference honoring his one-hundredth birthday, Albert Hoffman told the gathering, "LSD wanted to tell me something. It gave me an inner joy, an open mindedness, a gratefulness, open eyes and an internal sensitivity for the miracles of creation" (Quoted in Ann Harrison's "LSD: The Geek's Wonder Drug" in *Wired*, January 16th, 2006, p. 1).

It was just that sort of miracle of creation that the Acid Tests were designed to produce. With advertising posters asking, "Can you pass the acid test?" the Merry Pranksters invited hipsters and squares to turn on with LSD and helped start "a revival of the most ancient human values," a psychedelic return to the Greek Dionysia, complete with a sound track provided by the Grateful Dead. The infamous renditions of "Drumz" and "Space" find their origins in the primordial improvisations at the Acid Tests, and "like everything else here, it grows out of—*the experience*, with LSD. The whole *other world* that LSD opened your mind to existed only in the moment itself—*Now*—and any attempt to plan, compose, orchestrate, write a script, only locked you out of the moment . . ." (Tom Wolfe, *The Electric Kool-Aid Acid Test* [New York: Bantam, 1999], p. 59. Wolfe's emphasis). Connecting with the moment on a sacred level was the point of it all, and the psychedelic ritual space that was the Acid Tests provided at least one of the two main aspects that all of the Sixties' acid gurus agreed were the keys to a good trip: set and setting. In other words, if you came with the right mind-set, the Merry Pranksters and the Grateful Dead would provide the right environment.

"They weren't just playing what was on the music sheets. They were playing what was in the air. When the Dead are at their best, the vibrations that are stirred up by the audience is the music that they play," recalled Ken Kesey in an interview appended to the *Tie-Died* DVD release. So, once LSD was criminalized in October of 1966 and the Acid Test held its graduation, it's no surprise that the people "on the bus," as Kesey called the ones who passed the test, climbed into all manner of vehicles to follow the Dead on their continuing journey and to keep the spirit of the acid parties alive, whether in the Dead shows themselves or in the drum circles that populated countless parking lots and campgrounds. "'Now you're either on the bus or off the bus. If you're on the bus, and you get left behind, then you'll find it again. If you're off the bus in the first place— then it won't make a damn.' And nobody had to have it spelled out for them. Everything was becoming allegorical, understood by the group mind, and especially this: 'You're either on the bus...or off the bus.'" (*Electric Kool-Aid Acid Test*, p. 83) Deadheads were on the bus.

Out of the Spirit of Music

The followers of Dionysus were on the bus, too. In ancient Greece, the Dionysian festivals signified a break from the routine of everyday existence that foreshadowed the weirdness at the Acid Tests. Friedrich Nietzsche warned that when the Dionysian "fever" was allowed to run rampant, ". . . precisely the most savage beasts of nature were unleashed, including even that disgusting mixture of voluptuousness and cruelty which always seemed to me the real 'witches' brew'" (Friedrich Nietzsche, *The Birth of Tragedy*, (New York: Random House, 1967), p. 39). So the Dionysian drive had to be kept in check by the Apollonian force. The wild musical impulse of the revelers comes together only within the "principle of individuation" provided by the form-giving force of Apollo, and the static genius of the Apollonian power is fully understood only with the ultimate abandon of the Dionysian chaos. True beauty is the result of Apollo's triumph over Dionysus, where Dionysus represents the destructive yet necessary dynamic element without which the creation of the highest aesthetic expression and experience would not be possible. Thus, the Dionysian and Apollonian energies remain in a dynamic contest of opposites, each representing an interpretive stance on the entirety of existence and each operating in classical Greek tragedy.

Each stance was a response to what Friedrich Nietzsche called "the question mark concerning the value of existence." The Apollonian attitude came out of that god's association with epic poetry and the plastic arts, such as sculpture and painting, which best exemplified the notions of limits and balance as essential to the exactingly executed work of art. Apollo represented the individuality of creation, the strength to mold one's own character and works of art into precise forms out of the chaotic raw materials of nature. Dionysus, on the other hand, was associated with lyric and dithyrambic poetry, music, and drama that were performed at public spectacles, and represented the instinctual elements that seemed to defy all limitations: intense emotional drives, intoxication, and lunacy. "Unlike Apollo, Dionysus was thought to inspire collective outbursts of ecstatic celebration, wherein the individual insensibly lost possession of himself and became part of a larger whole through chants, recitation, music, and song" (David B. Allison, *Reading the New Nietzsche* [New York: Roman and Littlefield, 2001], p. 19).

The Grateful Dead and the Merry Pranksters were obvious descendants of the Dionysian revelers. As part of a formal ritual, the early Dionysia were usually accompanied by tremendous quantities of wine, and sometimes included narcotic and hallucinogenic substances. The revelers re-enacted bizarre and horrific episodes from the tales of Dionysus and exhibited "those awesome, joyful, and occasionally fear inspiring expenditures of energy and eroticism that transgress the general rules, norms, and codes of individual and social existence" (*Reading the New Nietzsche*, p. 19). Although ancient writers recount that a wide variety of animals, including various humans, were torn to pieces and ingested as part of the Dionysian rites, Kesey and the Pranksters were never reported to have gone to that excess, even when the Hell's Angels were guests. All the same, the above description seems to characterize the Acid Tests reasonably well, and we know that Sixties squares viewed the freaks from the San Francisco scene as almost as much a threat to society as the ancient Greeks saw the early followers of Dionysus.

Still, Nietzsche's highest art must simultaneously contain the Apollonian element, which the Dead tie into through the structure of the concert format. Remember, it was the combination of the Apollonian form and the Dionysian exuberance that Friedrich Nietzsche viewed as holding the highest aesthetic value and as providing the resources for a healthy culture. "This would be a culture imbued with a generous understanding of and toleration for the whole of human experience, with a strength to survive in the face of personal and political adversity, a culture that would admit a wide latitude in the pursuit of individual creativity, coupled with a deep-seated feeling of social and political identity" (*Reading the New Nietzsche*, p. 25). Again, by jumping ahead that prophetic century, we find just such a culture on tour with the Dead. The Acid Tests and the hundreds of concerts that followed provided the communal ritual that gave concrete form to the psychedelic groove that permeated Deadheads and the Dead.

Friedrich Nietzsche addressed this same creative impulse as it arose in the competing forces of Apollo and Dionysus, as they worked themselves out in ancient Greek tragedy. The Apollonian element was found in the two or three actors on stage, who used masks to portray the various characters from classic myths and who strictly followed the playwright's script. The Dionysian element was found in the larger chorus positioned off stage, which sang and danced between the scenes, commenting on the previous action, and whose leader engaged in dialogue with the characters during the drama. "In the light of this insight we must understand Greek tragedy as the Dionysian chorus which ever anew discharges itself in an Apollonian world of images" (*Birth of Tragedy*, pp. 64–65) Through the synthesis of these elements, the dynamic tension and the specific resolution enacted in the play are vitally and immediately experienced, not as an Aristotelian catharsis, but as an "orgiastic delight," in which the audience is immersed in a mystical here and now. "But from orgies a people can take one path only, the path to Indian Buddhism . . . these rare ecstatic states with their elevation above space, time, and the individual" (*Birth of Tragedy*, p. 124).

The Book of the Dead

The true aim of the Dionysian impulse was the total identification with the world beyond the individual, what Friedrich Nietzsche called "dispossession," or the removal of one's own individuality. It was only through immersion in the Dionysian essence of the primordial unity of being that a person could find a way to escape the fate of all mortals, which is death, but it was only within the confines of the Apollonian structure that a person would not risk being totally swallowed up by the chaotic Dionysian instinct. Foreshadowing the acid gurus' warnings about set and setting, Nietzsche recognized that Greek tragedy satisfied those concerns and established the ritual confines of public performance that the Dead perfected in a mystical musical incarnation. In either case, the Dionysian immersion in the ecstatic, living moment must be harnessed and directed by the Apollonian configuration of the spectacle.

Just by chance, 1964 marked not only the start of the Merry Pranksters' bus tour; it also hailed the publication of Timothy Leary's seminal trip guide *The Psychedelic Experience*. Along with two colleagues from the scandalous Harvard LSD experiments that got him and co-writer Richard Alpert (later the Hindu-Buddhist teacher known as Ram Dass) fired, Leary compared the psychedelic trip to the cycle of life, death, and rebirth outlined in the *Tibetan Book of the Dead*. Claiming that the scripture is more accurately understood as a guide to assist the living rather than (or at least as much as) a ritual to assist the dead in their passage to the next life, Leary and the others argued that reciting appropriate passages at specific points during an acid trip would help the trippers find a sort of spiritual awakening. Echoing key features of the Dionysian impulse, their guidebook begins:

> A psychedelic experience is a journey to new realms of consciousness. The scope and content of the experience is limitless, but its characteristic features are the transcendence of verbal concepts, of space-time dimensions, and of the ego or identity. (Timothy Leary, Ralph Metzner, and Richard Alpert, *The Psychedelic Experience: A Manual Based on the Tibetan Book of the Dead* [Secaucus: Citadel, 1964], p. 11)

By providing a Buddhist structure to the frenzy of an acid trip, Leary and the others bring forth the stabilizing Apollonian attitude that informs the psychedelic experience.

One story of the Dead's naming draws a surprising parallel to Timothy Leary's trip manual. According to Phil Lesh, "Jerry picked up an old *Britannica World Language Dictionary* . . . In that silvery elf-voice he said to me, 'Hey, man, how about the "Grateful Dead"?'" The definition there read, "A song meant to show a lost soul to the other side." (Phil Lesh, *Searching for the Sound: My Life with the Grateful Dead* [New York: Little, Brown, 2005], p. 62) Since their inception, the Dead played the songs that guided blown minds to the other side of their trips. The communal space that was the Dead show mirrored, in many cases quite literally, the amphitheaters of ancient Greece, and many Deadheads agree that outdoor shows were the best. Indoors or out, the Apollonian-Dionysian tension was equally present, the structure coming from the instrumentation, amplification, and set-list of a performance and the chaos induced by a variety of mind-altering sights, sounds and substances.

Even today, the acid-fueled music guides all kinds of journeys. "It must be changing something about the internal communication in my brain. Whatever my inner process is that lets me solve problems, it works differently, or maybe different parts of my brain are used," said Kevin Herbert, an early employee of Cisco Systems, who admits to solving difficult computer programming problems and pondering major career moves by taking LSD and listening to the Dead. He continued, "When I'm on LSD and hearing something that's pure rhythm, it takes me to another world and into another brain state where I've stopped thinking and started knowing" ("LSD: The Geek's Wonder Drug," p. 2). A small number of well-known computer pioneers reported using LSD to enhance their creativity, ironically at about the same time that Timothy Leary left the promotion of psychedelic drugs as the path to enlightenment and turned to the mystical aspects of modern computing.

But it remains the show, with that awesome sound and the collective energy that brought so many Deadheads to the ecstatic heights of the psychedelic ritual. As one *Tie-Died* Deadhead put it, "There are very few places in the world that you can go and truly feel like yourself, truly be yourself, and that's OK because the people around you are truly being themselves. The Dead shows to me are one of the last vestiges of free zones . . . Now the ego has a chance to drop away and cleanse itself."

When the Doors of Perception Are Cleansed

The psychedelic trip and the Dead Show, with or without each other, are vehicles to access what Carlos Castaneda in *The Teachings of Don Juan* called "non-ordinary reality." As part of a sociological study, the shaman of the title instructs Castaneda in the ritual use of a variety of mind-expanding substances. In a remarkable parallel to the Apollonian-Dionysian opposition, Don Juan broadly categorized these hallucinogens as allies, whose powers could be controlled by the shaman, or protectors, whose forces remained untamed. In any case, allies and protectors acted as teachers on the way to becoming a "man of knowledge," the Yaqui name for a shaman, who could access a mystical way of being in the world that is beyond our ordinary perception. Starting in 1961 and continuing until just two months before the first official Acid Test, Don Juan led his apprentice on a path to spiritual awakening, insisting on a specific set and setting, not to mention involved preparation, for each psychedelic substance used.

It was precisely this search for spiritual enlightenment that guided many of the early LSD researchers, who most often considered the drugs merely a medical aid to achieve what mystics from a variety of cultures could accomplish through intense training and self-purification, if not also psychedelic experience. Carlos Castaneda writes that a man of knowledge no longer needed to take some substances in order to make use of their mind-altering powers. Of the two categories of psychedelic substances Don Juan used, only one of them actually required ingesting it to access its power. Eating peyote buttons was the only access to the protector called "mescalito," and the quality of the experience was entirely determined by the spirit that visited you. On the other hand, the inspiration of allies could be harnessed without actually using those hallucinogens. When discussing the mushroom based herbal mixture called "the little smoke," Don Juan says, "Because the smoke is my ally, I don't need to smoke anymore. I can call him anytime, anyplace" (Carlos Castaneda, *The Teachings of*

Don Juan: A Yaqui Way of Knowledge [New York: Washington Square, 1996] p. 98).

For the Ancient Greeks, the magical spirits were invoked during the communal rituals. As with other festivals, the later public Dionysia, held twice a year, were special occasions for bonding with a community of like-minded revelers. What mattered in these festivals, as opposed to the earlier clandestine rites of violence and mayhem, was the public spectacle. During a tragic drama, a sober viewer could be carried away by the Dionysian spirit of music to that world beyond the formal appearance of the Apollonian persona. By being part of the collective revelry and ecstatic bliss that the chorus called forth during the play, the spectator accessed the frenzied spiritual awakening to the infinite, invisible existence beyond our ordinary modes of perception. As Friedrich Nietzsche saw it, the ultimate access to that mystical other world arose just as much out of the magical musical element as the Sixties acid gurus saw spiritual enlightenment arising out of the mind-altering substance.

The same goes for Wharf Rats, as sober Deadheads are known. "It's magic without the dope; it's totally magic," said one *Tie-Died* Wharf Rat. On the one-year anniversary of his first sober show, another one claimed, "I get the same trippy experience that someone who is tripping on acid would get from the Dead, just because I can be there, and I can be free, and I can be dancing, and I'm around friends." Perhaps the acid has acted as an ally, allowing this particular Deadhead to conjure the specter of LSD as an aid for his sober trip. From Nietzsche's perspective, it is just as likely that the collective spirit of the spectacle that was the Dead show infiltrated him in the same manner that the Apollonian-Dionysian tension in theater opened ancient Greeks to the non-ordinary reality otherwise accessed through psychedelic drugs. "The Grateful Dead's music was the essential agent for the transformation of consciousness in the Deadheads' pursuit of mystical experience. The dancing and hallucinogenic drugs were supplementary means of achieving transformation" (Shan C. Hutton, "The Deadhead Community: Popular Religion in Contemporary American Culture" in Adams and Sardiello, *Deadhead Social Science: You Ain't Gonna Learn What You Don't want to Know* [New York: AltaMira, 2000], p. 117). Yes, it was the music that kept the Dead atmosphere alive with the mystical potential for enlightenment.

The Music Never Stopped

If the spirit of the primordial Acid Tests never left the Dead, perhaps it's best explained by the fact that for almost thirty years the public performance of the music that drove those magical moments never stopped, but it was precisely the loss of Dionysian music that Friedrich Nietzsche saw as the decline of Greek drama. He traced this decline to Euripides, who lessened the chorus's connection to the main action of the drama and focused on more realistic representations of the characters. By including a spoken prologue that accomplished the narrative function of the chorus, as well as songs that now often had nothing to do with the events on stage, Euripides destroyed the delicate balance of Apollo and Dionysus that Nietzsche saw as fundamental to a true work of art. Since each force depended on the other, reducing the influence of the Dionysian chorus simultaneously undercut the Apollonian power in favor of the Socratic belief that absolute knowledge should form the path to enlightenment. With Socrates as his guide, Euripides transformed Greek tragedy into what Friedrich Nietzsche considered merely a type of embellished story telling. Without the play of Apollonian and Dionysian forces, the theater had lost its ability to present the world in its greatest intensity.

Thus, we see that in a way Friedrich Nietzsche gave the musical element a privileged status. While Socratic rationality operates only at the level of words, Dionysian music transports us to a realm beyond language, and so allows us to rise beyond consciousness and to experience our immediate identification with the whole of existence. "Quite generally, only music, placed beside the world, can give us an idea of what is meant by the justification of the world as an aesthetic phenomenon. The joy aroused by the tragic myth has the same origin as the joyous sensation of dissonance in music" (*Birth of Tragedy*, p. 141). Nietzsche believed that music was the only form of artistic expression that could adequately represent the infinitely changeable nature of a vibrant world. The creative tonal resources that enliven every musical nuance provide an infinitely variable supply of creative elements. "It does this not by representing one single state, a static 'image' of the world as the language of concepts does, but by manifesting the very nature, essence, or idea of its general dynamic properties" (*Reading the*

New Nietzsche, p. 47). But these dynamic properties can only be accessed if the listener is moved or transformed by the music, if the listener actually experiences a state of relative dispossession. Through the entire life of the Dead, LSD fueled such lettings go of the self and explorations of what Friedrich Nietzsche alternately called the "primal reality," the "Dionysian ground," and the "heart of all things." The modern day revelers known as Deadheads hoped to gain a glimpse of that Dionysian world without order, rules, or restraint.

One century after *The Birth of Tragedy*, the Grateful Dead brought a musical element back to the mind-expanding public spectacle, and so reinitiated the dynamic tension between Apollo and Dionysus. Audiences could once again go beyond the formal appearances from the Apollonian attitude and revel in the primordial unity of existence accessed from the Dionysian impulse. As Ken Kesey commented, Deadheads are "looking for magic. When you see something like that, there's a crack in your mind and you know it's a trick, but you can't figure it out. That crack let's in all the light. It opens up all the possibilities. When that little split second thing happens, when the Dead are playing and everybody in the audience goes, 'Wow, did you see that?' that's the moment that puts them in touch with the invisible."

6

How Dead Beats Became Deadheads: From Emerson and James to Kerouac and Garcia

GARY CIOCCO

Dennis McNally recounts how, at one of his first meetings with Jerry Garcia after becoming the biographer of the Dead, Jerry's dressing room "was decorated with two pictures, one of his late friend and musical cohort, Pigpen, and one of Jack Kerouac" (*A Long Strange Trip: The Inside History of the Grateful Dead* [New York: Broadway, 2002], p. xiv). McNally had sensed a fundamental connection between these two phenomena, the Beats—Kerouac in particular—and the Dead (indeed, he became the biographer of both). It may seem a stretch to attempt to connect these two icons of post-World-War-II American bohemia with pragmatism, America's indigenous philosophical movement, but to understand Ralph Waldo Emerson and William James is to know that these American philosophers would heartily approve of being linked to the hipster poetry, prose, and music of the twentieth Century.

Their philosophies point to a transcendence of philosophy; not a complete transcendence, mind you, but a view from which philosophy can be seen as only one piece of a larger reality. The Beats and the Dead are able to do what Emerson and James could only talk about. One cannot philosophize while one is doing. But when the doing is timely, the result is timeless, just like philosophy can be. Plato said that to be is to do, Aristotle said to do is to be, and Jerry Garcia said only at a human be-in can a human being be free.

Emerson and James: Multiplying Nonconformists and Electrifying their Minds

In his book *The American Evasion of Philosophy*, Cornel West points out that Emerson sets the tone of the pragmatism to come with his evasion of the modern philosophical obsession with the technical concerns of what we can know and how we can know it. Emerson instead emphasizes the idea of expansiveness, summed up by his claim that "'the only sin is limitation', i.e., constraints on power" (Cornel West, *The American Evasion of Philosophy: A Genealogy of Pragmatism* [Madison: University of Wisconsin Press, 1989], p. 17). The movement begun by Emerson continues today and has created a philosophical climate more akin to "a continuous cultural commentary" that tries "to explain America to itself at a particular historical moment" (*Evasion*, p. 5), rather than one searching for solutions to perennial problems. The central concerns are power, provocation, and personality, and Emerson's prescription emphasizes self-reliance and nonconformity, which should keep us away from a "foolish consistency." Emerson himself claims as his own just "one doctrine, namely, the infinitude of man (*Evasion*, p. 28)." To be infinite is to have endless energy, constant action; a person with such uncontrolled energy would be inherently nonconformist. Both Kerouac and the Dead tapped into that energy. To truly link doing and being is to get beyond the joke of the seriousness. This was the goal of the bohemian counterculture, a goal that still resonates because of its philosophical and spiritual depth.

West points out that William James is both the most famous American philosopher and the most "exemplary Emersonian embodiment of intellectual power, provocation, and personality" (*Evasion*, p. 54). James is also unique in that he crosses disciplinary boundaries with ease, from psychology, to medicine, to philosophy. James is focused on the mystery and possibility inherent in life as experience. As West points out, James emphasizes the "heroic energies and reconciliatory strategies available to individuals" and he has a consistent moral goal—to make us "more fully alive, more attuned to the possibilities of mystery, mortality, and melioration" (*Evasion*, pp. 54–56)" This could serve to sum up the Dead's goal as well, with their best meliorating forces being those of music and mushrooms, meditation and marijuana. In the Preface to *The Varieties of Religious*

Experience, James explains how the psychological issue he confronts—what he calls "Man's Religious Appetites"—began to so overwhelm the metaphysical issue of their "satisfaction through philosophy" that the psychology filled all twenty lectures. Thus his philosophic conclusions in the book are by his own admission "suggested rather than stated" (*The Varieties of Religious Experience* [New York: Touchstone, 2004], p. 1).

James is an unabashed promoter of the power of experience, which reflects a unity in diversity, especially a diversity of feeling. He tells us that "resemblance among the parts of a continuum of feelings (especially bodily feelings), experienced along with things widely different in all other regards, thus constitutes the real and verifiable 'personal identity' which we feel" (William James, *Principles of Psychology* excerpted in Leonard A. Kennedy, ed., *Images of the Human*, [Chicago: Loyola University Press, 1995], p. 312). It can be as simple as feeling what is real, and going with the flow, even if it is troublesome, as in the final half of the refrain from "Casey Jones": "trouble ahead, trouble behind, and you know that notion just crossed my mind."

In good times or bad, we cannot stop the notions from crossing our minds; as James says, "the passing Thought then seems to be the Thinker" (*Principles*, p. 314). His idea of a "live option" furthers this development of personal identity, with an abiding concern for a special symbiosis between belief and action, between thinking and doing. A 'live option' makes an "electric connection with your nature," which means that it is a hypothesis upon which you are ready to act. A belief option also can be categorized in two other ways: as either "forced or avoidable", and as either "momentous or trivial". James' position is put best and most famously on the issue of religious faith: If belief in God (or not) is a live option for you (that is, if you understand and empathize with what is meant by "God"), then your choice of belief or not is both a forced and momentous one, as opposed to an avoidable and trivial one. James claims that it's better to risk chance of error than loss of truth, not *vice versa*. In such *momentous options,* it *is* your choice, but you must beware that a "maybe" answer is more like a "no" than it is like a true middle ground. Sitting on the fence in such circumstances is as good as falling off.

James's position involves a fundamental ethical shift, putting desire on an equal footing with reason as the motivator and the goal of our actions. James does not mince words: "In truths dependent on our personal action, then, faith based on desire is certainly a lawful and possibly an indispensable thing" (*Varieties*, p. 117). James treads on the borderline here, since he advocates constantly expanding the universe of possibilities. After all, philosophers are supposed to tell the *truth,* not just expand the *possibilities.* Artists on the other hand, perhaps especially *movements* of artists, are all about expanding the possibilities. James, like Emerson before him, is excited when disciplines interconnect, and the disparate ideas and realities of many options can come together. Something new will result; perhaps not just a new art form but a new mode of life itself.

Kerouac and Ginsberg: The Beat Begins

Jack Kerouac and Allen Ginsberg, the dual heart of the Beat Generation, were both born in the 1920s. Like Emerson, James, and the Dead, they all shared a desire to make life become art *and* art become life, and that *was* their philosophy. The lasting legacy of the Beats is that they began to bring to fruition the vision of Emerson and James, blurring and tiptoeing the line between thinking and doing.

For the Beats, the writer is not only defined as one who creates art, but rather the life of the writer itself can become the art. For them, it is not simply that the "truth is what works," but that the truth can also be *created* by heroic energy. If the "truth is what works," then it is clearly beneficial to expand *what works.* By an incredible concomitance of circumstances, the Beats succeeded in their time, searching for their own expanded version of the varieties of religious experience. In one of the most-quoted passages from *On the Road*, Kerouac explains his passion for life as a cross between madness and mysticism: "I shambled after as I've been doing all my life after people who interest me, because the only people for me are the mad ones, the ones who are mad to live, mad to talk, mad to be saved, desirous of everything at the same time, the ones who never yawn or say a commonplace thing, but burn, burn, burn like fabulous yellow roman candles exploding like spiders across the stars and in the middle you see the blue centerlight pop and everybody goes 'Awww!'" (*On the Road* [New York: Penguin, 1999], p. 5).

The fact that Ginsberg would begin his most famous poem, "Howl," with his own reference to the madness of the best minds of his generation shows the collective disaffection that the Beats had. Their disaffection tapped into a cultural moment, and permitted them, a collection of very different personalities, to become a movement, and to attempt to function as a single, many-headed organism. The Beats were a case of powerful opposites attracting one another and creating something larger than themselves due to the cultural moment. The atomism of this opposition was one of its greatest flaws. In 1968, this was the concluding paragraph of an article in the six-month-old magazine, *Rolling Stone*:

> The Beats . . . were a relative instant in history: Their art was personal, urgent, tense, and separate from life, possibly so much so that the Beats could not survive. Hippie art, by contrast, is functional, integrated entirely into the daily life of the subculture. It lacks the individuality of most of the old Beat art, but as an art movement, it will probably last much longer. (Parke Puterbaugh, "The Beats and the Birth of the Counterculture," in Holly George-Warren, ed., *The Rolling Stone Book of the Beats: The Beat Generation and American Culture* [New York: Hyperion, 1999], p. 356)

The Grateful Dead were about to show the world the prescience of this claim. They would become the answer to the answer man, man.

The Dead Bring the Beats New Life

The Beats represent the first sweeping example of the reign of power, provocation and personality in the twentieth-century American arts scene. Until—the Beats became the Beatniks, and the Grateful Dead became what Jung refers to as a "psychic epidemic" (Mary Goodenough, "Grateful Dead: Manifestations from the Collective Unconscious," in Robert G. Weiner, ed., *Perspectives on the Grateful Dead* [Westport: Greenwood, 1999], p. 175). Only Garcia's death could begin to put a dent in what was a nearly forty-year run of inspiration and innovation. Born in 1942, twenty years after Kerouac, Garcia had much in common with his fellow avatar. Both were born into strong ethnic families, both experienced the traumatic death of a male in the family, and each became entranced with the joys and sadnesses of the life of an artist and rambler. The idea of moving, drifting, and just "being" as a form of doing, was as central to Garcia as it had been to Kerouac, who was very much alive in the early Sixties, but was already on a downward spiral into alcoholism and anachronism. Kerouac was often incoherent in the 1960s, and manifested a conservatism and even anti-Semitism, both of which were perhaps latent within him.

As the King of the Beats was in his swoon, the Dead were rising and, as Jason Palm puts it, were developing "a fascinating and realistic critique of the American Dream" (Jason Palm, "The Grateful Dead Versus the American Dream," in *Perspectives*, p. 150), which fueled their longevity. The Grateful Dead's stance was anything but simple; their realistic and even harsh aesthetic was paving a "path into the American psyche" by ignoring the present and harkening to the past of the American West, says Palm. The no-name character of the song, "Loser," is a "noble marginal character who is doomed to failure in spite of his determination and good heart" ("Versus," p. 151). And August West, the blind alcoholic bum of "Wharf Rat," entertains the narrator with his story of pain and lost love. In the end, the narrator is left to move toward his own current love, and yet shakily, as he must reassure himself of her loyalty.

Such characters, says Palm, are typical of the Dead's mythic America: lovable losers who will never succeed. We can sympathize, empathize, and also mythologize—our dreams are not only "illusory and doomed" like theirs, but also as valid and filled with heroic struggles. The Dead, like Kerouac and Jack London before them, began to put before us their visions of the "glory and wreckage of the American Dream as it drifts west and crashes headlong into the rocky Pacific Coast" ("Versus," p. 152).

Palm is only half right here, for the untimely demise of Jack Kerouac is a good metaphor for the dissolution of the Beats into the Deadheads. It is also to oversimplify a bit to claim that the Dead's "best work" harkens to the American West. The harkenings of the Grateful Dead, befitting their tie-dyed image, explode in colors in all directions, including in the direction of Neal Cassady.

Cowboy Neal Was at the Wheel

Neal Cassady must get his due. As the bus driver for the Merry Pranksters, Cassady is the figure who literally connects the Beats and the Dead. But he was so much more than this. He was Kerouac's muse, the centerpiece of *On the Road*, and of all things Beat. To call him the "Socrates of the Beats" is no exaggeration—he wrote almost nothing (or at least not much publishable), yet his life was the inspiration for the methods of the Beats—talk fast, live faster, and ask questions later. The myth of the Western hero was alive in Neal Cassady, at least as far as Kerouac was concerned. Cassady is the cowboy of energy and experience to Kerouac's role of the great Chronicler. Cassady was an individualist's individualist, pure energy and feeling wrapped in sinew, bone and brains. As a result, he did not have the difficult transition into the Sixties that Kerouac had.

So what did he do for the Dead? He drove into and through their lives, literally and figuratively. For all of his own desire to go careening on a long, strange trip, it is no surprise that Jerry Garcia expressed admiration for Cassady; but it is more than a little ironic that he also expressed concern and fear! Even as he could call Cassady a "tool of the cosmos," Garcia also admitted that riding with him "was to be as afraid as you could be, to be in fear for your life" (Steven Watson, *The Birth of the Beat Generation: Visionaries, Rebels, and Hipsters, 1944–1960* [New York: Pantheon, 1995], pp. 289–290). Garcia must have noticed that Cassady was "driving that bus, getting high on us," and that Casey Jones was not the only maniac who had to watch his speed.

As the center of energy of the Beats, Cassady also embodied their attitude of sexual exploration and obsession. Manically sexualized, and ardently bisexual, he was the Adonis of the Beat's male-centric movement which served to explode the role which unrepressed sexuality can play in the culture of power, provocation and personality. In his book *Subterranean Kerouac*, Ellis Amburn makes a very strong case for the fact that the entire trajectory of Kerouac's life was somehow connected with his own troubled sexuality. Cassady's role in each movement, the Beats and the Deadheads, is a key clue to the differences between them. To the Beats, he was *the* Muse, the hard-driving, conflicted ball of energy who symbolized and united their rebellious, individualized energies. To the Dead, he was still the hard-driver, but he was part of a crew, and a sign that the inevitable lessening of energy with age could be overcome by meshing with the energy of others. The Dead opened up more possibilities precisely because they advocated a unity in diversity in the musical experience itself, instead of a highly personalized, ultimately atomizing unity with your own particular Muse. The Dead's rebellion is at a higher level, and represents as such an evolution.

As a result, the issues of male-centrism and hyper-sexuality were not at the forefront for the Grateful Dead. Each of the Beats had an individualized trajectory that was bound up with his being on the fringe until the end—outcast, sometimes jailed, oversexed, drugged, alcoholic, and so forth. It's not really that the Dead or Deadheads were wiser or more controlled than their Beat and hipster counterparts, but rather that they were, over time, more fulfilled and more fulfilling. I am thinking here of Aristotle's term *Eudaimonia,* which is normally translated as "happiness," but which makes much more sense as referring to the fulfillment one gets from living a good life. For as much craziness as the Beats and Dead shared, the Dead were poised to move our cultural icons from those of outcast, hipster rebels (think James Dean, and then view some photos of Kerouac and Cassady in their early days) to happy-go-lucky, trippy love-freaks. Where the Beats were, in a very real sense, rebels without a cause, rebels who simply lived off of their very rebellion, the Grateful Dead represented a unified community of experience-seekers that was able to roll and grow right up until the death of Garcia.

The Dead was able to avoid the atomistic splintering that ravaged the Beats because they were able to take the Jamesian goal which they shared with the Beats—to experience all of life in the heightened state or fever pitch of a "religious/spiritual" experience—and turn it into not just an *individual* goal, but *a common* goal. Hence, while Kerouac suffered the burden of being the religious center of the Beats (the appellation was applied by both himself and others), Jerry Garcia was able to orchestrate a "moveable feast" of consciousness-raising, with so many people coming together over him and his band, even as he often was personally falling apart. It could be argued that the sex and drug scene encircling the Dead from the beginnings until the end was, as compared to both the Beats and to many other developments in Rock as well, a "kindler, gentler" sex and drug scene. Shared experience was always the goal, as opposed to mainly atomistic epiphanies, variously exchanged. As tragic as Garcia's demise was, he was vital and true to himself up to the end, unlike Kerouac. He was *organic* through and through. It was always about the Band.

Tough *and* Tender, The Dead Keep Truckin'

The organism that the Dead became was evolutionarily much more advanced than the organism that was the Beats. A famous distinction of William James's can shed some light here. James discusses the differences between two temperaments—the "tender-minded" and the "tough-minded." The tender-minded are devoted to abstract and eternal principles, and also are intellectualistic, idealistic, optimistic, religious, free-willist, monistic, and dogmatical. The tough-minded emphasize empirical facts, and are sensationalistic, materialistic, pessimistic, irreligious, fatalistic, pluralistic, and skeptical. Although most people fall variously on both sides of the tough and tender line, James claims that the history of philosophy shows a lack of balance, as it is populated by extremists in one of these directions or the other. The dissolution of the Beats in general, and Jack Kerouac in particular, can be understood within this framework, as it appears that they and he made a nearly wholesale transition from tender-minded to tough-minded, a radical experiential transition that happened much too fast and disparately and was thus cataclysmic to the organism. The Dead, though, showed the ability to feed the hunger for the good things on both sides of the divide in a much more consistent manner.

In his article about being gay and a Deadhead, Edward Guthmann relates a conversation he had with Steve Silberman, in which Silberman praises the ecstatic happiness of a party for gay Deadheads: "[It] is profoundly healing: It generates community, and it's profoundly overlooked in the Christian tradition. The beating heart of Christianity is a guilty one. The central metaphor is one of obligation, whereas the central metaphor in the Grateful Dead world is one of fulfillment" (Edward Guthmann, "A Tale of Two Tribes," in David G. Dodd and Diana Spaulding, eds., *The Grateful Dead Reader* [New York: Oxford University Press, 2000], p. 224.

All can be fulfilled, all can be one—it is a very high aspiration. But the communal high that was the Grateful Dead allowed so many more to reach these heights than ever before, by expanding the possibilities for "live options" and fulfillment. One man, or a small group of men, cannot do it alone. The Dead scene was not primarily one of idol worship, because the band was able to blend in with the Deadheads. The ambiguity of reality can be "fully electric" and a "live option" in the sense in which James used these terms. This ambiguity was fully alive in the Deadhead scene. The tightrope that everyone must walk between the tender and tough-minded is widened in the Deadhead scene. What Silberman has described is the co-existence of opposites—free will and determinism, religion and irreligion, one-ness and many-ness—that cannot be fully explained or reasoned about, but must be *lived*. To experience this unity is an aesthetic experience and it *is* good for us. Robert Hunter's lyrics from "Terrapin Station" are both clear and sadly prophetic, "The storyteller makes no choice, soon you will not hear his voice, his job is to shed light and not to master." To experience this enlightenment at a Dead show was to do it in a way that the Beats or even The Rolling Stones could not provide. Perhaps we can call it *The Oneness of Dead Calm.*

The music is and was the medium of this lived experience, of course. As Garcia said, "Magic is what we do. Music is how we do it" (Blair Jackson, *Garcia: An American Life* [New York: Viking, 1999], p. xi). Jackson points out that Garcia's musical genius was always overshadowed by the force of his personality—he began as "Captain Trips" and ended as a bemused, ancient grandfatherly figure. But he was all along dedicated to the diversity of musical styles that inspired the Dead's music—bluegrass, folk, country, rock, jazz, blues. He was not afraid to grow and innovate until the end; he had an inexhaustible desire to move forward. If as Jackson says, "his musical legacy is larger than his life" (*Garcia*, p. xiii), his life may also be large enough for us to see the reign of power, provocation, and personality that began with the Beats take a powerful turn for the positive.

In his book The *Tipping Point*, Malcolm Gladwell talks about the power of certain people to cause changes which otherwise might seem mostly accidental. These powerful people effectively create "viruses," for good or ill, and thus many of our important changes can be considered as "epidemics." When these changes are for the good, the provocative people who enact them fall into three categories: Connectors, sociable personalities who unite people; Mavens, who accumulate and transmit knowledge; and Salesmen, who are skilled at persuasion. This twenty-first century idea is simply an update of Emerson's and James's ideas on power, provocation, and personality. Such people, argues Gladwell, span the range of possibilities of roles in society. The Beats and the Dead represent two of the most forceful twentieth-century artistic and social movements, and can be judged by their excellent abilities to fulfill the roles of Connectors, Mavens, and Salesmen. Jack Kerouac and Jerry Garcia, the respective centers of each movement, undoubtedly fit the bill in all three categories as well; especially as Connectors, they shared a love of people and an undeniable ability to also attract others to them like magnets. As mavens and salesmen, however, the Dead and Garcia, were much more successful than the Beats and Kerouac, in the sense that they were able to take a certain level of achievement and raise it several notches.

If it's true that both groups brought to fruition what Emerson and James could only talk about, then we can perhaps take that train of thought one small step forward: the Dead were able to revive an organically dying beast, the Beat counterculture, by tapping into the power of music over words. As much as Kerouac succeeded in creating a "be-bop", jazz-inspired prose or poetic style, he was still limited by the fact that it *was* prose or poetry. Writers themselves, especially poets, are often commenting on their status as failed musicians, either literally or figuratively. The heightened, jazzed and bluesy religious experience that the Beats had tried to evoke with the necessarily limiting medium of the written and spoken word, the Dead had exploded into its more natural and meliorating medium, the experience, at once personal and communal, of listening to music. The movement from Jack Kerouac to Jerry Garcia is the movement from The Great Chronicler to The Great Enabler. There *is* calm at the center of Deadhead culture. Indeed, Jerry Garcia and the Grateful Dead evoke and invoke a calm craziness where, in the spirit of bringing opposites together, and expanding the "live and electric" possibilities, the madness became, and continues to be, properly mundane. Through the Dead's vision and action, new and larger doors of perception opened even wider, to a "new" cultural moment, which has lasted forty years. It *is* possible to purely expand the possibilities *and* retain a communal conscience—this is what kept, and will continue to keep, the Dead's heart beating.

7

Tolstoy's Favorite Choir

MICHAEL GETTINGS

> They're a band beyond description, like Jehovah's favorite choir
> People joining hand in hand while the music played the band,
>   Lord
> They're setting us on fire.
> —"The Music Never Stopped"

Besides shaggy beards, what do Leo Tolstoy and Jerry Garcia have in common? One devised an influential theory of art and the other played lead guitar in a band that brought that theory to life. In his 1898 essay "What is Art?" Tolstoy says that real art communicates feelings of the artist to the audience, uniting all who take part into a community of fellow feeling (*Tolstoy on Art* [New York: Haskell House, 1973]). Jerry Garcia, and the Grateful Dead as a group, communicated feeling, uniting audience members into an incredibly close-knit community. Tolstoy thought real art was usually the product of ordinary people. From folk music and dances to clothing, dolls and decorations, the works of common people in nineteenth century Europe tended to convey more feeling to Tolstoy than the works of the most esteemed artists of his day. This makes Tolstoy a populist when it comes to art—he has little tolerance for the elitism of high art, preferring the mundane but powerful works of ordinary people.

A Band Beyond Description

In 1965 a group of otherwise ordinary people formed a band that evolved into the Grateful Dead. This band, more than any other musical group in history, came to be known for their live performances and the throngs of Deadheads who followed them from venue to venue on tour. The Grateful Dead played to packed stadiums, concert halls and outdoor arenas for nearly three decades, a vast subculture following in their wake. If Tolstoy is right about the definition and function of art, the music of the Grateful Dead ranks among the greatest works of art produced in the last century. If Tolstoy had been born one hundred years later, he might even have been a Deadhead.

Words and Art, Thoughts and Feelings

Early in his essay, Tolstoy compares words to art, saying "by words a man transmits his thoughts to another, by means of art he transmits his feelings" ("What is Art?," p. 171). This comparison is telling. Tolstoy believed that art was as important to human society as language. At one point he says that without the capacity to receive the thoughts of others through words people "would be like wild beasts," and without the capacity to receive feelings through art "people might be almost more savage still, and, above all, more separated from, and more hostile to, one another" ("What Is Art?," p. 174) To credit art with the maintenance of civilization might be hyperbole on Tolstoy's part, but he is idealistic about the power of art. This idealism of Tolstoy's matches the idealism surrounding the music of the Grateful Dead during the 1960s in Haight-Ashbury. And for the subculture of Deadheads, or as Jerry Garcia called them this "little society out there," a unified community formed around the music.

Would You Hear My Voice Come Through the Music?

What unifies the community is feeling. Tolstoy defines art in this way: "Art is a human activity consisting in this, that one man consciously, by means of certain external signs, hands on to others feelings he has lived through, and that others are infected by these feelings and also experience them" ("What Is Art?," p. 173). A friendly amendment to Tolstoy's definition is in order. His definition of art is only strengthened if we recognize the possibility of collective, improvisatory artworks such as those produced by the Grateful Dead. Art is not necessarily created by "one man"; the music of the Grateful Dead was created collectively by several people. Furthermore, it makes sense to leave off the qualifier "consciously." Grateful Dead performances were by design not consciously planned, often reaching their artistic peak when the collective stumbled upon something stunning, when "the music played the band," as it were. Instead of using set lists, the Grateful Dead chose songs by experimenting together until a pulse, rhythm, phrase or riff emerged from the group, suggesting a song. Their collective, improvisatory musical works communicate feeling like any other artwork.

Goin' Down the Road Feelin' Bad

These changes to Tolstoy's definition aside, it's not difficult to find examples of feelings the Grateful Dead handed on to its audience. In her band biography *Sweet Chaos: The Grateful Dead's American Adventure* [New York: Clarkson Potter, 1998), Sarah Brightman mentions the trauma in Jerry Garcia's life and its connection to the emotions expressed in the songs from the album *American Beauty*:

> Jerry Garcia's mother was killed in an automobile accident while the band was recording *American Beauty*, and the heartbreak on that record, most evident in 'Broke-down Palace,' according to [lyricist Robert] Hunter, is traceable to Jerry's sadness. (*Sweet Chaos*, p. 184)

Garcia's father died by drowning when Jerry was only five, and Brightman finds the echoes of emotions from his father's death in the same song: "'River gonna take me / Sing me sweet and sleepy / Sing me sweet and sleepy / all the way back home' begins the fourth stanza of "Broke-down Palace," which was nearly always sung in a lilting whisper, as if by a child who is courting death" (p. 184).

Joy and Spiritual Union

The emotions communicated through the music were not typically sad ones, however. As any fan of the Grateful Dead will confirm, the emotion most commonly experienced at a Dead show was a kind of ecstatic joy. Joe McIntire, one of the band's managers, said "One of the most important parts of Jerry [Garcia] was that he wanted to create joy" (Robert Greenfield, *Dark Star: An Oral Biography of Jerry Garcia* [New York: Morrow, 1996), p. 343). Tolstoy specifically says of art that it evokes "that feeling (quite distinct from all other feelings) of joy and of spiritual union with another (the author) and with others (those who are also infected by it)" ("What Is Art?," p. 274). This feeling of joy and spiritual union with others is most often cited when the Grateful Dead and their audience speak of the experience of a Dead show. The Dead's followers not only filled stadiums, but parking lots outside, greeting each other, conversing, and generally joining together in community. The music was the force that brought people together, and one explanation of the power of the music is found in Tolstoy's claim that art delivers a particular feeling of spiritual union with the artist and all others infected with the feelings of the artist. Deadheads recognized that the vision of 'strangers stopping strangers just to shake their hand' became a reality at a Dead show. Phil Lesh, the band's bassist, said of their performance at the Human Be-In on January 14th, 1967:

> I felt as if I'd been privileged to be part of something that was bigger and more important than even music: a community of loving, peaceful people gathered together to celebrate a new form of consciousness—one that I hoped would expand to embrace the whole world. Like a Native American powwow, or the opening of some cosmic Olympiad, the Be-In created a sense of unity that was solid enough to walk on. (Phil Lesh, *Searching for the Sound* [New York: Little, Brown, 2005], p. 98)

These references to "breaking down barriers", "sense of unity" and "community" touch on what Tolstoy identifies as the function of real art: to unite people. And it unites people by joining them in feeling, removing the barriers between artist and audience, and audience members themselves. Tolstoy says that

> the recipient of a true artistic impression is so united to the artist that he feels as if the work were his own and not someone else's— as if what it expresses were just what he had long been wishing to express. A real work of art destroys, in the consciousness of the recipient, the separation between himself and the artist, nor that alone, but also between himself and all whose minds receive this

work of art. In this freeing of our personality from its separation and isolation, in this uniting of it with others, lies the chief characteristic and the great attractive force of art. ("What Is Art?," p. 275).

The Grateful Dead and audience members attest to this phenomenon. Phil Lesh refers to the "group mind" at Dead shows, where band and audience shared feelings and thoughts almost telepathically. He describes the band as "one organism," saying "we used to describe ourselves as the limbs of a drummer, or the fingers of a finger-picking guitarist" (*Sweet Chaos*, p. 50). After a long jam-packed "Alligator" on May 18th 1968, "The audience stood transfixed, barely clapping, as if some fundamental musical experience—the transformation of sound into emotion—was working its way through the collective psyche" (*Sweet Chaos*, p. 90). Even the lyrics of many of the Grateful Dead's songs suggest the connection between the band and the audience: "People joining hand in hand while the music played the band," from "The Music Never Stopped"; "would you hear my voice come through the music / Would you hold it near as it were your own," from "Ripple"; and "Think this through with me, let me know your mind," from "Uncle John's Band," to mention a few. From the point of view of both the band and the audience, barriers collapsed during Dead shows, uniting all involved in a great community.

Infection and the Greatness of Art

So on Tolstoy's account, the Grateful Dead's music is art. But does it belong among the greatest art of our time? Let's return to Tolstoy's definition of art. He says that art "infects" the audience with the feeling of the artist. This notion of infection plays an important role for Tolstoy—art is contagious. This accounts for much of its power. Tolstoy distinguishes infecting someone with feeling from simply causing someone to experience a feeling. Infection requires the contagion to travel from carrier to carrier, and in the case of art, Tolstoy says that the emotion of the artist is conveyed to the audience in such a way that the audience feels the same emotion. For Tolstoy, infection is not only required for a work to be art, but the quality of a work of art is judged on the degree of infectiousness of the feelings it communicates: "The stronger the infection, the better is the art"

("What Is Art?," p. 275). More than anything else, thinks Tolstoy, infectiousness is a function of the sincerity of the artist. The more sincere the artist's feeling, the more infectious the art. The more infectious the art, the greater it is as art.

Turning to the Grateful Dead, can we say that the members or the group as a whole sincerely experienced the feelings they communicated? It's clear from the testimony of the band members that the feelings were sincere. Phil Lesh described the experience of playing for an audience as being lost "completely in a spontaneous flood of music," which is "one of the great human joys" (*Searching,* p. 261). And the fans surely believed in the sincerity of feeling. One Deadhead thanks Jerry Garcia for teaching "that music is the outflow of the soul of the musician" (John Metzger, *Music Box Magazine,* September 1995), and another says that "his sincerity—his life's experience—certainly came through in a way few other singers did" (Walt Wrzeznewski, on jerrygarcia.com. http://jerrygarcia.com/days-between.html). From the band and from the audience, there is no question about sincerity.

The Real and the Counterfeit: The Thin Line Beyond Which You Really Can't Fake

Another way to illustrate the sincerity behind the Grateful Dead is to compare their music to insincere art. Insincere artists do not produce real art, says Tolstoy, they produce counterfeit art. Today we can look to TV melodrama, blockbuster movies, and apparently-heartfelt-but-ultimately-empty pop music for examples of insincere works. Viewed cynically, most of what counts as populist art, or works made for ordinary people, fail Tolstoy's sincerity condition because they are made for money. One imagines that the producers of such works feel the need for greed more than any emotion. To be a bit less cynical, most popular works attempt to bring pleasure, diversion or entertainment to people.

These motives are not bad in and of themselves, but according to Tolstoy they are incompatible with a work's being art. He says art is not defined as the "production of pleasing objects," nor is it defined by pleasure ("What Is Art?," p. 173). In fact, we ought to "cease to consider it as a means to pleasure, and to consider it as one of the conditions of human life" ("What Is

Art?," p. 170). Tolstoy admits that art pleases us, though. The unique feeling of "joy and spiritual union" conveyed by art must be a pleasant feeling, after all. Tolstoy recognizes this, but distinguishes between art as a means to pleasure and art as a source of pleasure. The distinction gets at the purpose behind producing the work—if the would-be-artist creates her work merely to please the audience, or as a means to pleasure, the work is not art. If, however, the artist creates her work to communicate sincere feelings of her own, her work is art, and it might happen to also please the audience. Pleasure may be a happy consequence of experiencing an artwork, but it is not the point of art.

Pleasant diversion appears to be the point of so many mass-produced works of film, television and pop music, and these tend to be the works available to most people. So from a populist standpoint, the music of the Grateful Dead is real art, whereas the majority of mass produced works are counterfeit art. There are, of course, exceptions. A film might convey emotions experienced by the director, infecting all those in the audience. A television show might convey the emotions felt by the writer, such that the day after watching it, viewers unite around the water cooler at work, sharing their "fellow feeling", as Tolstoy calls it. But how common are these occurrences and how effectively do they unite people? They fade quickly, replaced by the next television drama, or the next movie, which most likely will be a pleasant diversion. Compare these mass-produced works to the music of the Grateful Dead, and the community that formed around this music, and it should be clear that the Grateful Dead's music achieves Tolstoy's conception of art's highest goals.

High Art and Definition

In the interest of looking at populist works, we seem to have ignored those paradigm examples of what our culture deems the greatest art, namely famous works categorized as fine arts. We all know such paradigms: DaVinci's *Mona Lisa*, Beethoven's *Ninth Symphony*, Michelangelo's *David*, maybe even Tolstoy's own *War and Peace*. Ever the populist, Tolstoy addresses the effects of so-called European high-art in this way: "instead of an artistic activity aiming at transmitting the highest feelings to which humanity has attained . . . we have an activity which aims at affording the greatest enjoyment to a certain class of society" ("What Is Art?," p. 197). This class was the aristocracy—those who could afford the luxury of attending the theater, or the symphony or admission to galleries and museums. Tolstoy specifically judges Beethoven's *Ninth Symphony* as belonging "to the rank of bad art" due to the fact that it is a "long, confused and artificial production" which fails to transmit feelings that might unite people ("What Is Art?," p. 295). On the other hand, while a performance of "Dark Star" is long, and might be confusing (though not therefore confused), it is not artificial. The music of the Grateful Dead succeeds where other works fail Tolstoy's test.

Up to this point we have not questioned the truth of Tolstoy's view, but assumed its truth for the sake of argument. It's natural to wonder whether a theory of art which excludes such canonical works as Beethoven's *Ninth Symphony* can really be correct. While we aren't addressing that question here, we can say something more interesting about Tolstoy's view.

To get the point of Tolstoy's definition, we can distinguish between *descriptive* definitions and *prescriptive* ones. Descriptive definitions attempt to explain the nature of a given thing or phenomenon. So if I attempt a descriptive definition of 'art', I attempt to explain what art is, as it is commonly understood. I describe the existing category called 'art', which typically is given by one's culture. A prescriptive definition, on the other hand, attempts to explain how the defined term *should be* understood. So a prescriptive definition of 'art' is more of a *redefinition*, prescribing what ought to be considered art, not merely defining what is already considered art. Tolstoy understood that the existing cultural understanding of art did not match his definition, but he didn't see this as a flaw in his definition. Instead, he believed there was a flaw in the cultural understanding of art. He intended his definition to be prescriptive.

There's something of a San Francisco late-Sixties hippie idealism about Tolstoy's prescriptive definition of art. He wants to see our conception of art change, but he also wants to see us embrace the art of the people, particularly the art that unites people into community. And Tolstoy thought that music was special among the arts in that it is universal, capable of joining together all people. He says:

Sometimes people who are together, if not hostile to one another, are, at least estranged in mood and feeling, till perhaps a story, a performance, a picture or even a building, but oftenest of all music, unites them all as by an electric flash, and in place of their former isolation or even enmity they are all conscious of union and mutual love. Each is glad that another feels what he feels; glad of the communion established not only between him and all present but also with all now living who will yet share the same impression; and, more than that, he feels the mysterious gladness of a communion which, reaching beyond the grave, unites us with all men of the past who have been moved by the same feelings and with all men of the future who will yet be touched by them. ("What Is Art?," p. 287)

The Grateful Dead supplied us with that "electric flash" and Deadheads past, present, and future have felt joined to each other and to the band in "mysterious gladness." The music reaches "beyond the grave" and unites us with those in the past who have been moved and those in the future who will be touched by the songs of the Dead. As for Tolstoy, he already had the long, shaggy beard so common among Deadheads. If he simply traded in his predominantly black wardrobe for tie-dyes, he easily could have been mistaken for a nineteenth-century Deadhead.

8

He's Gone and Nothing's Gonna Bring Him Back: The Dead, the dead, and the Grateful Dead

JOHN UGLIETTA

Imagine this news flash:

> The estate of Jerry Garcia sues to prohibit use of the Grateful Dead name because Garcia's heirs plan to reform the group with a new line-up. Madonna, looking for a new image, has announced her acceptance of the offer to sing for the band. The remaining members of the band will be chosen in an American Idol-like television competition to be called "Who wants to be one of the Dead?" Marketing analysts say the band has tremendous earning potential.

Don't worry. It really hasn't happened. But what if it did? Would this group be the Grateful Dead? What if they toured a lot and developed a following of fashionable, expensively-dressed teeny-boppers, would these fans be "Deadheads"? Would these changes simply be another shift in style like ones the band had experienced before (perhaps like the one that came with Workingman's Dead or after Touch of Grey hit the pop charts?) What is it that made (or makes) the Grateful Dead the Grateful Dead?

The answer to this last question may be more complicated than it appears at first. You might say, isn't it just the people in the band that make it the band that it is? But think about it. The Grateful Dead has changed members many times.

Early on they added Mickey Hart to the band, and the band has had more keyboard players than Spinal Tap had drummers. Pigpen started out as the keyboard player. However, fairly early on Tom Constanten joined the band only to drop out a few years later. His short stay may have been a better choice than it seems, as the other keyboard players did not fare so well. Pigpen passed away in 1973. Keith Godchaux took over the keyboards around 1971 when he and his wife Donna Jean joined the band. Both left the band in 1979, and Keith followed in Pigpen's path, dying that same year. Brent Mydland joined the band but fell to the same fate, dying in 1990. Bruce Hornsby toured beside Vince Welnick in the early Nineties as the two shared the stage at the keyboards. However Hornsby never recorded with the band and left after a few years. Like Constanten, this may have been the best choice he ever made as he appears, for the moment, to have escaped the curse that seems to follow keyboard players for the Grateful Dead. Welnick has not been so lucky; he passed away in 2006. With each change behind the keyboard, the Grateful Dead took on a slightly different character but somehow remained the Grateful Dead.

However after the passing of Jerry Garcia, things were different. The band stopped playing for a while, and later regrouped but under the name "The Other Ones" and ultimately "The Dead." The name change seemed critical; without Jerry the band just was not the Grateful Dead anymore. But why? How could they add Hart, Constanten, Godchaux, Mydland, and Welnick, and over the same time, lose Pigpen, Constanten, Godchaux, and Mydland and stay the same band but lose Garcia and become a different band?

What Is the Grateful Dead?

The history of the band raises a question about the identity of the Grateful Dead. What does it mean to say that a group is what (or who) it is? The 2006 New York Yankees have no players in common with the 1934 Yankees. Is it still the same team? Why do people say that the Yankees have won the World Series so many times when it has been a different group of players every time? Corporations lose their entire management team but remain the same corporation. If Bill Gates died, Microsoft executives would not feel the need to disband and reincorporate under a new name, perhaps "Microguys" or "The Soft."

When discussing identity, the ancient Greek philosopher, Aristotle, drew a helpful distinction between two types of properties that a thing might have. He distinguished between accidental properties and essential properties. It is the essential ones that make the thing what it is. Suppose I think about something like my car. It has many qualities or properties, one of which is that it is dirty or needs to be washed. Being dirty is an accidental property of my car. It happens to be dirty now, but if I washed it, it would still be the same car. While if I melted the car down and formed it into a solid metal block, it seems like it would no longer be my car, or any car at all; it would lose the properties essential to making it a car. The essential properties, or the essence, of some thing determine if something is one of this type of thing. So what is the essence of a thing like the Grateful Dead?

Grateful Dead Inc.?

The contemporary American philosopher Peter French claims that there's an identity of groups like corporations beyond their membership that resides in the internal structure of the organization. For groups or organizations like Microsoft or perhaps the Yankees, the essence of the group resides in the internal structure of the group. So the Yankees may be able to change third basemen and managers and perhaps even stadiums and remain the Yankees as long as the team retains the same structure or relationship between these. They need to have a third baseman and a manager and a stadium, and they need to play baseball, but they could have different people or places doing all this. If the manager and all the players left and five musicians put on pinstripe uniforms and played concerts in the outfield at Yankee Stadium, they would not be the same New York Yankees. The change in the structure of the organization would destroy the essence of the baseball team. Was the Grateful Dead the same type of organization as the Yankees?

Examples from other music groups are not very helpful on this question. Van Halen got rid of David Lee Roth and hired Sammy Hagar. Yet they still called themselves Van Halen. However I would guess that Paul Simon could not hire Sammy Hagar and tour with him as "Simon and Garfunkel." You might be tempted to think this would not work because Art Garfunkel's name is part of the name of the act. Before jumping to that conclusion, you might consider the Glenn Miller

Orchestra, which has continued to perform for decades after the loss of Glenn Miller. (And, I would bet, long after any of the musicians who played with Glenn retired.)

For the moment, let's suppose there was some simple, distinct, organizational feature of the Grateful Dead. Would this be enough to establish the identity or the essence of the band? Whatever the organizational feature was, someone else could adopt it (just the way the Yankees can change people). Now suppose I round up a handful of friends, and we decide to adopt this structure. We don't know exactly which were the essential structural features, so we just adopt them all. We each take up the role of one of the members of the Grateful Dead. We play the same songs. We even dress like them and start calling each other by their names. Suppose we even get pretty good and sound just like them. While this might make us a true band, even a band *like* the Grateful Dead, it would not make us *the* Grateful Dead. Something seems to be missing, even if we copy all of the organizational features of the band, and it looks like what is missing is some sort of connection to the actual Grateful Dead. Perhaps internal structure could be part of the essence, but it does not seem to be all there is to the essence of a group like the Grateful Dead.

All bands may not be of the same type. Some may be essentially determined by their structure. (Although perhaps not entirely, as my friends and I could not make ourselves the Glenn Miller Orchestra or the New York Yankees either.) Even for the Grateful Dead, the structure of their organization might not be an accidental feature. If the Grateful Dead gave up music, and the same members formed a defense-contracting firm making weapons of mass destruction, it is not obvious that they still would be the Grateful Dead. What else could the essential properties be?

Made of the Same Stuff

One rather obvious candidate for an essential property is to be made of the same stuff, that is, to share the very same physical substance. It seems rather natural to think that if some item continues to be made of the same physical stuff, it will continue to be the same thing. So if I take my car, remember—the dirty one, drive it to another place, sell it to another person who names it

Silver (even though it is green) and thinks it will take him to another dimension, it's still the same car. Here the idea is that the identity of the car is determined by its physical make-up—so its essence is captured in the fact that it has all the same parts as it always did. When the new owner hops in and with a hardy "Hi, ho, Silver, away" turns the key and heads for the Eighth Dimension, he's surrounded by the very same metal, plastic, and rubber (and whatever else) particles that used to surround me when I quietly sat in the car and headed off to the donut shop.

This would suggest that the Grateful Dead would remain the Grateful Dead as long as they were composed of the same physical substance (and might explain why my friends and I could not be the Yankees or the Grateful Dead). The physical substance seems to be the members, so this takes us right back to our initial thought that it is the members that make up the identity of the band. Now the idea runs into some obvious troubles right away. By any reasonable account, the Grateful Dead remained the Grateful Dead, for example, when they added Mickey Hart to the band and when Pigpen left the band, but these both changed the physical make-up of the band. Exact physical identity seems too strong for band identity.

Exact physical identity may be too strong for cars as well. Suppose we are following our favorite band around the country in our 1964 VW bus. One day a tire blows out, and we buy another one to replace it. The VW no longer has exactly the same physical make-up as it did, but it is still the same VW. Now imagine that over the course of the summer or maybe a couple of summers, we have piece by piece, had to replace a substantial amount of the VW. Don't we still think it is the same VW bus? What if over a few more years, we end up changing all of the parts, again, one piece at a time? It seems that when the physical change is gradual, identity may not be lost, and it remains the same VW.

The issue becomes more confusing if we imagine that two other people have been following the same band around the country, and they have picked up our discarded parts. Being more clever mechanics than we are, they have repaired these parts and assembled them into a VW bus of their own. Now which one is the original—ours with the new parts or theirs with the old parts? The confusion alone may suggest that physical make-up isn't the essential property we were after. The VW case may even send us back toward our earlier ideas of structure or organization. (Is that what made the VW the same?) In any case, it seems that bands, perhaps like VW's, can undergo some physical changes without losing their identity, and that a concept of band identity will need to allow for this.

How is the VW with all new parts like a group of guys in a band? While changes in personnel bring changes in the physical make-up of the band, we might also note that the physical make-up of each individual band member would change over time. This may be less obvious. There are, of course, the usual comings and goings of beards, moustaches, and long hair, not to mention gains and losses in weight. We could even go so far as to note what the scientists tell us, that our bodies continuously lose dead cells and generate new ones to replace them. Over the course of thirty or forty years, not just the guys in the Grateful Dead (who, on occasion, may have been killing off cells faster than the rest of us), but all of us have probably "turned over" most all of our cells, making for a very different physical make-up. Yet we don't think this has changed our identities. As with the VW, the gradual nature of the change seems to allow for some constant connection between stages of a person or VW even when its physical make-up changes substantially.

Heart (or Liver) and Soul

We still need to describe the essential connection between different stages of the same thing. Here it seems important to note that people, or at least most people, seem different than chairs or rocks or even VWs. We usually think of these other items in entirely physical terms. This leaves little to serve as an essential property except some physical feature. However, people, again most people, seem different. Consider what happened to Phil Lesh. In 1998, Phil had a liver transplant. Who was he after the liver transplant? He was Phil Lesh when he went into the operating room with his original liver, and he still seemed to be Phil Lesh when he left the operating room with what used to be someone else's liver. The liver is a pretty big organ. So Phil lost a lot of the original Phil, he also gained something that was part of someone else. I would guess that very few people now think Phil is no longer Phil, or even no longer just Phil—now some combination of Phil and the liver donor with partial ownership of the donor's house, car, and bank account. We have already discussed the apparent failings of a theory of identity that relied purely on constancy of physical substance. But what about a different sort of transplant? What if Phil had a brain transplant? Would this be different? Would he still be Phil Lesh? We don't know what would happen if someone had a brain transplant, but what if Phil came out of the brain transplant, and he was no longer talking and acting like Phil. Instead he talked and acted like the person who donated the brain. Now who would he be?

Whether a person's mind or soul or spirit is somehow housed in the brain or just is the brain is a difficult question to answer. Lucky for us, we don't need to answer it here. If we have concerns about whether it will still be Phil after the brain transplant, but not after the liver transplant, it is probably because we think that something like the change I described might happen. We probably think that Phil's personality, whether we think it is a mind, soul or spirit, just might leave his body and go with the brain that is being removed. If we didn't think this, and Phil would leave the operation talking and acting like he did before the transplant, then the brain transplant would seem just like the liver transplant. It would be nothing to be afraid of, or perhaps it would be more accurate to say there would be plenty to be afraid of if you had to have your brain transplanted, but you would not be afraid of losing your identity.

From Livers to Locke

If we fear that changing the brain might alter one's identity while changing the liver wouldn't, this fear might suggest that there is something about an individual's mind that is essential to his identity. If the mind goes, you're no longer the same person, and perhaps you're no person at all. A person's identity seems to require some sort of psychological connection. So when Phil leaves the liver operation, he still acts like Phil and remembers the things he has done, and he still is Phil. In the 1690s (so easily mistaken for the 1960s), John Locke claimed that the mental connection that is essential for maintaining the identity of a person was a connection in memory. Roughly, on a theory like this, Phil is the same person after the operation because he can still remember the experiences he had, as Phil, before the operation.

You may be wondering why anyone in the late seventeenth century was thinking about brain transplants. Of course, the truth is that they were not. For some thinkers, the important question was if a person dies and his soul goes to heaven (or worse), will the soul in heaven still be him? Notice that if it is not still the same you that ends up in heaven or hell, then you would not have the same concern for what comes after death, be it good or bad.

Many philosophers have noted shortcomings of the simple memory theory. The most commonly noted problem has to do with memory failures. If by some strange happening, Phil were to forget a part of his childhood, the theory would seem to suggest that he had lost the connection to that younger version of himself, making him a different person from that boyhood Phil. A number of philosophers have refined the memory theory. The aim seems to be to describe a continuous consciousness. Let's see if the general idea of a psychological connection can help us figure out the group identity.

Surrendering Your Own Little Trip

Could the band maintain some kind of psychological connection over time? While it may be easy to imagine a continuing consciousness in a person, one might wonder if there could be such a thing in a group. It is something like this type of group consciousness that I want to suggest made the Grateful Dead *the* Grateful Dead. First, I should clear up a few things so this does not sound more mysterious than it has to. It seems reasonable to expect that a group composed of people would possess features like individual people, yet not quite the same. While there may be no unified consciousness of a group, there could still be a unity seen in a group spirit. This could be something metaphysically mystical like a group mind or consciousness or something more recognizable like the spirit that unites much larger groups—for example, the national pride that unites a group of people into a nation, say, Poles or Americans, or a region, Southerners, or some other group like Hippies. This spirit may be difficult to discover or describe clearly. The Grateful Dead was a much smaller and more intimate group, and the collection of sentiments and dispositions that united them was stronger and more substantial. It involved, as Phil Lesh described it, a blending and meshing of members of the group. And as Jerry Garcia said this came from "surrendering your own little trip."

Was Jerry Garcia the Soul of the Grateful Dead?

If the Grateful Dead was still itself before Jerry died and was no longer the Grateful Dead after he died, was Jerry Garcia the spirit or soul of the Grateful Dead? I think the answer is no. Once again, it is more complicated than that. If Jerry alone had been the essential part of the group, then why wouldn't he have taken this with him when he performed with others? If he were all that was required to conjure the Grateful Dead, the band would have sprung up whenever he was there, the way that Chuck Berry and his band are the same act no matter who fills out the band around Chuck. So, back in 1965, the Warlocks probably were an early Grateful Dead, while the early New Riders of the Purple Sage (even in 1969) were not the Grateful Dead.

The Grateful Dead was, even in its essential features, a group. Yet the group remained personal in that something about the relation between the unique members, or at least some of them, was essential to the identity of the band. This does not seem surprising given that the Grateful Dead was always about coming together in the music, so much so that this coming together infuses their very form. The spirit of the Grateful Dead was a dynamic entity, created by the union of some of the members just as the musical experience they created could not be had alone.

My guess is that the soul of the Grateful Dead was bigger than Jerry Garcia, but I should add, not as big as the whole group. Right to the end, not all of the members were essential to the survival of the group spirit. I won't go further on this point but will leave it to readers to suggest, ponder, and, I bet, disagree on the answer to which members were essential to keep this spirit alive.

However we characterize the spirit that was generated between the essential members of the band, this spirit was lost with the death of Jerry Garcia. At this point the band members faced a choice. They could recognize that the spirit that animated the band had been lost or they could change the very nature of the band and turn the Grateful Dead into something else. In short, they could have made the band into something like the Yankees or the Glenn Miller Orchestra (or Microsoft? Or GM?).

It may seem as if the choice put them in control of their identity. Perhaps an entity can control its identity sometimes, but it can also be beyond control. Think of how hard Prince tried not to be Prince—and never succeeded. Personally, I don't think they could control the identity of the Grateful Dead after Jerry died. Had they tried to carry on as the Grateful Dead, they would have failed. That they could recognize this loss seems like further evidence that there had been a unique group spirit.

So it seems the Grateful Dead is gone forever. Well, maybe. Unless what I heard was true. I heard some fan from Stanford had gotten hold of some of Jerry's skin tissue from a medical test Jerry had in the late 1970s. They say he cloned some of the cells, and that he has been secretly raising a new Jerry. He ought to be just about old enough to join the band soon. What should we call them?

Set One—Who's to Guide You?

Ethical Questions in the Lyrics of the Grateful Dead

9

A Touch of Grey: Gratefully Dead?

RANDALL E. AUXIER

Tuning Up

DALE: Jerry had a diabetic coma, he came close to dying a couple of times and the Dead Heads were like "oh no, he's not gonna die." When he did die, I wasn't expecting anything like that, I'd just seen him. And I figured they'd go on, and even when he died I figured, well, what are they gonna do? Are they gonna go on? Where are the Dead Heads gonna go?

ROBBIE: They were adrift for a while I do believe.

CORY: I never saw the Grateful Dead . . . I always wished I'd lived in the Sixties, it's pretty much the best you're gonna see, even going to see a pseudo-Grateful Dead show. . . . But really the kids that do that, no matter what machine is making money off that, they're gonna find somewhere that they can go and gather, and be together, and do what it is they do and experiment and socialize.

ROBBIE: There were a lot of hangers-out, you know, back in the day, like now, only more so. Some of them had indeterminate functions, if you know what I'm saying.

Live Dead

So here's the thing. I couldn't help being intrigued when, after a stint as The Other Ones, the band started touring again as just The Dead. No longer Grateful? Jerry was gone (and Pigpen, and

Keith, and Brent). It set me to thinking when Jerry died. It set a
lot of us to thinking, even those who normally don't, and even
a few who no longer *can*. I saw some of my Deadhead friends
who hadn't had a thought in *years* suddenly entertain one, han-
dling ideas like those gorillas handled that Samsonite luggage
on the old TV commercial (poor Samson, after Delilah and that
haircut, and the jawbone and all those Philistines, now he's
reduced to a proper adjective for ugly plastic luggage, but I
digress[1]). So I had friends who were way past thinking, even
primate thoughts, so they just had to whistle through their teeth
and spit. Something was over. The shoe was on the hand that
fits, and that's all there really was to it, as the poet said.[2]

But I'm not much of a poet. I want to think about this.
Hopefully I'm not past doing that much. I read a lot of shit about
death and life after it, and it occurs to me that if you want proof
of life after death, look around you. Most of the people you
know, among the "living," are probably good evidence that life
after death really happens. There was this story about the
Buddha. A woman whose child died makes a long journey to
seek out the Enlightened One. On finding him she throws herself at his feet, "Master my child is dead. I have heard that you
have the power to bring the dead back to life. I beg of you,
please restore my child." The Buddha looks upon her with compassion. "I will restore your child to you, but first you must do
something for me." The mother says she will do anything.
"Return to your village and bring back to me a person who has
never known pain like yours." The mother quickly agrees and
rushes off toward her village. A disciple says "Master, when she
returns, will you really restore her child?" The Buddha says, "she
will not return."

And there you have it, the First Noble Truth: Life sucks. It
truly blows. Not just a little bit either. You want life after death?
Well, let me put it this way: if that woman came knocking on
your door, would you be joining her for the return trip? If so,
just wait. Just mark time and have a fatty. Your time is coming.

---

[1] What seems like a digression in music can become your main riff.

[2] The poet is Robert Hunter, of course. I hope he won't mind my weave of his lyrics
with what I have to say. Apparently Jerry Garcia wrote the line in "A Touch of Grey"
that said "Light a candle, curse the glare." One is tempted to see Hunter and Garcia
together as one poet.

And, as the poet said, "you will get by, you *will* survive"—until you don't. The poet's other half didn't. He's gone. Sort of.

Sound Check

ROBBIE: We used to hire bass players if they got a new Jazz Bass and a Fender amp, it's like "You're in, it doesn't matter, you're in, baby."

CORY: There's that unwritten rule—do it to the grave.

The Epistemic Bassist

Philosophers have "epistemic principles." They like fancy words for simple things to make them sound smart. The first epistemic principle was invented by the first father whose four-year-old kid discovered the meaning of the word "why." After about six patient answers to the repeated question "why," he said to the seventh "because I say so." Presto, epistemic principle: *I know what I know because I just know it*. Philosophers have managed to turn this simple answer into a formula they call "justified true belief," and they have some explanations of it that are longer than any jam by the Dead, but it comes down to a single riff in the end. "Because I say so . . . and I'm so very smart and you're so very stoned." I need a principle for my little creation here, and I don't like "justified true belief," so I will state my own, without the nuances: *I trust Phil*. Not because he shares a name with a disciple and a groundhog. Not because his name means "brotherly love." I trust Phil because he plays the bass, and he is very smart.

Now there are lots of types of "smart." There is the visceral smart of Pigpen, just somehow knows what to play, can make up lyrics on the spot; there is Jerry's utterly frenetic genius, which defies description; there is Billy's and Mickey's grinding groove; Bobby's way of matching the chords to the groove with razor thin response time. These are all kinds of smart, and not just in music. If you look around you, you'll find co-workers and classmates who do the same things in their lives that these fellows have done on stage.

Then there is Phil. Phil sees the Whole. Nay, Phil *creates* the Whole from its parts. It's a fact that bass players are the true masters of the whole sound. They have to be both musically and rhythmically astute, but most of all they have to hear what everyone else is doing and weave it into one sound. Bass players share a secret fellowship, a sort of *gnosis* peculiar to their breed, a kind of smart that is hard for others to recognize or understand: the art of the whole sound. Bass players don't actually *believe* in musical epistemology, they are practitioners of musical metaphysics. More on metaphysics later.

The story of Phil's induction into the band is a case in point, how the bass player creates the whole sound. In 1965, The Warlocks were a hot band, but the guy on bass could not cut it, as Jerry said to Phil "we have to tell him what notes to play." Jerry continued "I know you're a musician—you can pick up this instrument so easy" (Phil Lesh, *Searching for the Sound: My Life with the Grateful Dead* [New York: Back Bay, 2005], p. 46). What Jerry knew (and Jerry knew so many things) was that Phil heard the whole, grasped it, understood it. The fact that Phil had never touched a bass guitar was irrelevant. Like Jerry, I know a bass player when I see one too, whether he actually *plays* bass or not. It isn't as mystical as it sounds. It's a way of seeing and a way of hearing the world—in *relation*. It isn't hard to recognize if you know what to look for.

Phil writes a book like he plays, like a bass player. A linear narrative adapted to the whole that it will finally become. There are controversies about many events in the career of The Dead, but even if everything else reported by others is sincere and true from its own perspective, in all disputed matters you should still trust Phil. He knows enough to remain silent where nothing ought to be said, just as he knows what notes *not* to play. And he knows how to say what he does say in the warm light of the Whole. So Phil is my epistemic principle because he is the maker of Dead metaphysics. I know what I know because I hear it with my own ears, but most of all, because Phil says so. If you don't trust Phil, go read another essay. This one will just piss you off. But I have two more reasons for trusting Phil. I'll save those for later.

First Set: Acoustic

DALE: Death is final to me. . . . It's a very nice thought, and hope, that there's a reward at the end of everything. Gives you something to look forward to, something to keep you in a straight line. . . . But I think that we created God. It gives us somebody to blame, somebody to go to when we're in despair and hurt.

ROBBIE: I have the more Buddhist view, that the ego is in fact demolished, that your sense of self, there's no such thing once the big black nothingness comes, so you're not aware of it. There's nothing to fear other than cashing out too soon, the effect it might have on those left behind. I do think that the universal spirit well, where all souls conglomerate and are regenerated. . . . there's no energy created or wasted, it just changes, that holds true throughout all known creation. They say that the human body at the instant of death, lightens by twenty-one grams, I don't know, but possibly that's the spirit essence. All religions have some basis like that. But I do think that modern ethics and morality have been devised over time by man to help control man, because man is only this far above the animal. Man is a dangerous creature because now he's got technology, but barely has control of his bestial instinct. That's why we see the world is in the shape it's in today.

CORY: I wouldn't mind reincarnation. I don't want to remember being me exactly, but I wouldn't mind living again having some sort of sense of the way I was. To learn from my past and be an old soul, I would like that. . . . It's a damned romantic idea.

ROBBIE: Still, when I go to bed at night I say an Our Father, because it's expedient. The jury is completely out as far as I'm concerned on religion.

DALE: I haven't been to confession in a long time, not looking forward to that. I *have* had many pure thoughts today, though.

Immortality: Not that Cool

Philosophers, real people, and probably gorillas with luggage, have been wondering about whether we really *die* when we die for as long as there has been luggage (which predates Samson, and even Nimrod, but maybe not all the "mighty men of old"[3]). When Pigpen died in 1973, Jerry said "That mother-fucker—now *he knows*" (Lesh, *Searching for the Sound*, p. 213). Socrates, who looked a lot like Jerry, was condemned to death for riffing with the boys when the rich folks were trying to sleep (or some other trumped up charge), and so if you can picture this, there he is, sitting around with a couple of those guys, Simias and Cebes, and those two are bitching and whining about his impending demise. The dialogue Plato wrote about this is called *Phaedo*, nevermind why. And they are freaked out that Socrates is there with them today, but tomorrow he won't be, so they discuss all the theories people have about whether we survive death in some way or another.

There are reincarnation theories and immortal soul theories and what not, but it kind of comes down to whether there is something eternal about *us*, some essence-of-you that *pre-exists* your earthly life and that's *why* it has a shot of *post-existing* it. I know this is kind of strange, but go with me for a minute here.

You're sitting there thinking, "Well, sure, I didn't *always* exist, but I'm sort of hoping I always *will* from now on." And Socrates is saying "you are *so* screwed, dude, if you're thinking that." Any idiot can see that *if* you got created at some point, and that's *all* you are, the stuff that *got* created, you are going to be in a world of hurt trying to convince yourself *that* lasts forever. I mean, let's say you think *you* started when your parents did the nasty (I know you don't want to think about that—man, I hope you don't—I mean, *I* don't even want to think about your parents

---

[3] And there is some totally wild shit in Genesis 6. I can't resist; I tried and failed. You have to check this out, Genesis 6:1-4: "When man began to multiply on the face of the land and daughters were born to them, the sons of God saw that the daughters of man were so fair. And they took as their wives any they chose. Then the LORD said, 'My Spirit shall not abide in man forever, for he is flesh: his days shall be 120 years.' The Nephilim were on the earth in those days, and also afterward, when the sons of God came in to the daughters of man and they bore children to them. These were the mighty men who were of old, the men of renown." I don't know what was going on here, but anyone can see that this is about the limits of our time on earth, and that works with what I'm saying in this essay. You've got a situation where the "sons of God" are getting it on with "the daughters of men" because they are such righteous babes, and it's looking like the Summer of Love or Woodstock around there, all to the music of a band called The Nephilim, and nobody even knows who they *were*. I wonder why I've never heard a sermon about Genesis 6. Let this little piece of prose be *my* sermon on Genesis 6. We'll see if anyone answers the altar call. Didn't the Nephilim play Woodstock? Or the Grateful Nephilim? CSN&Y: Crosby, Stills, Nephilim and Young? I honestly can't remember.

doing it, let alone think about *you* thinking about that; just chill for a minute, this is going somewhere, I swear). So, you were nowhere at all before that unthinkable night when they did dirty deed, right? And so, *what*, pray tell, do you think is going to outlast the final passage of protoplasm to dust? Do you honestly think your folks getting their (much younger) rocks off is of eternal significance? Did they create your *soul?* Do they have such power? Do *you?* Come on. You just won the Sperm & Egg State Lottery. No, dude, you're going to have to come up with an answer as to *where* you were before the nasty night, or you're toast in the long run. If your folks created your soul, or if you don't *have* one, you're history when you die. That's Socrates's point to his friends with the funny names (better than "Pigpen" though).

So let's say you think *God* created you. I know you don't think that, because if you did, you'd be reading *Mel Gibson's Passion and Philosophy* instead of *The Grateful Dead and Philosophy*. But I'm hoping there's just one person who reads this and seriously believes God created him or her, all special-like. (I am going to so totally fuck with your head if you think that.) So let's say, just for shits and giggles, God did it, God created your soul. So, that means God foresaw your entire pathetic existence—you, and me, and Pigpen, and Jerry, and that woman who never came back to collect on the Buddha's promise, and her child. I'm stealing a lick from a philosopher named David Hume here (see Hume, *Dialogues Concerning Natural Religion* [New York: Hafner, 1948, originally 1779]). You've got two big problems at least, and my bottom dollar is riding on the odds that you can't solve them.

First, how much do you trust this God? If He couldn't do any better for you than what you've got now and what you're looking forward to from here, which is nothing less than the deaths of many you hold dear followed by your own, probably in great pain, despair and misery, and then the eventual destruction of all you hold dear, then either it's all a fairly cruel joke or this God of yours just can't do any better. I mean, how do you know He wouldn't pop you right back out of existence just as easy as He popped you in? Or maybe sustaining your existence just isn't a serious priority for Him, or maybe He's too busy or having a bad hair day? How do you know? Phil can't help you with this; he's just the bass player. I trust Phil, but God has some explaining to do.

Second, let's say your God exists outside of time, in *eternity*, whatever *that* is. How is an eternal being going to create something that exists in time, like your skinny ass? I mean, if you really existed in His mind from the beginning, and you always *will* exist in His mind, what are you doing down *here?* Wasn't it good enough to Be in eternity, as one of God's ideas (if not one of his *better* ones—I mean Gandhi and Mother Theresa and Jesus and Buddha were pretty good ideas God had, but you're not in the top ten-thousand, if you don't mind my pointing it out)? Wouldn't it be better to hang *there*, at God's eternal pad, than to be sent on a very bad beer run without enough money to get yourself back with the goods? Welcome to your life. This is the beer run. So are you being punished? Tested? I'm paraphrasing Hume here but the point is easy enough. Either your sorry existence among the living calls God's motives into question (in which case your immortality is looking pretty shaky, since you can't trust Him), or God can't do much better than to bring you into the universe whenever the planets align and your parents co-operate, and even then He may not be *able* to hold onto you forever, for all you know. This is what philosophers call "the problem of evil," and what I just laid on you is called an "inconsistent triad." Here it is in "philosophese."

Not all of the following can be simultaneously true:

1. God is all-powerful.
2. God is perfectly good.
3. Evil exists.

Take your pick, but at most you can have two of these. They might all be wrong, but for my money, door number three is pretty hard to resist. I've seen what's behind door number three. So have you, or you will soon enough. That was Buddha's point about Life Sucking. It may be part of the reason he doesn't talk about God. It's also part of the reason he didn't think it would be all that *good* if you live forever, and what's even sadder is for you to deceive yourself into thinking you *want* that, immortal life. Buddha says that you really *don't* want to develop a case of the immortality munchies, because that sort of hankering could get your ass reincarnated, and then you're stuck here all over again. The Enlightened One called this the cycles of "samsara," not to be confused with Samsonite, although they really aren't that different. Think of samsara as bad luggage, sort of an ugly yellow color, and your whole essence is inside the luggage, and there are gorillas tossing you around, and then they finally wreck the suitcase and you get out. Then you stupidly think: "Wish I had another piece of luggage to get into." And the *wish* is all that even holds you in existence. Just say no, dude. This is a very bad trip. And like an idiot, you keep on wishing, and then you get into another piece of Samsonite, and you do it over and over because you just can't learn your lesson. That's the immortality munchies, and if you didn't already *have* a raging case of them, you wouldn't be here *now*. And unlike the baggage handlers at O'Hare, the gorillas never go on strike.[4] That's Buddha's Second Noble Truth, which is called the Cycles of Samsara, or in my terms, the Samsonite Scenario.

Phil talks about how Billy used to get the munchies. They'd be on their way home from a gig and Billy would "drum irrepressibly on my shoulder as he sat behind me in Jerry's car, while chanting 'Red Rab-bit, Red Rab-bit!' the name of an Automat-style food kiosk we'd always hit . . ." (Lesh, *Searching for the Sound*, p. 60). I see no serious problem with the actual munchies. It's such a small part of the bigger problem, but a lot of Buddhists decide to try fasting just to make sure things don't get out of hand with the Red Rabbit thing. But Buddha liked to eat well enough, so go on to the automat and don't worry about that.

So you've got two of the wisest people who ever lived, Socrates and Buddha, telling you that death is a release from your Samsonite Scenario, something to be welcomed, not dreaded, and their advice is "ok, you're free, so don't screw it up and come back." But that's not quite Phil's advice, and I trust Phil. Socrates and Buddha didn't play the bass.

Second Set: Twin Lead Guitars

CORY: Ever since the whole thing began, people have been trying to describe it, trying to communicate what it is that's in their head, and nobody can do it. People have

---

[4] I wonder how the baggage handlers' union felt about that old Samsonite commercial with the gorillas. I also wonder how Diane Fosse felt about it. I admit that I bought the luggage, but I got used at a garage sale. There was nothing inside. That would have made the Buddha happy. But gorillas are going to be harmed in this essay. I love and respect and revere gorillas, I prefer them to human company, so please don't rag on me for the way I'm going to use them as a metaphor. It's just a metaphor, okay?

been trying and people will continue to try . . . to describe the Dead experience, to describe the way they feel, how it is that Brent's keyboards sounded that night, and exactly what it is, you know man . . . people try, and part of it is that they're too fucked up, part of it is that you can't grasp it.

ROBBIE: There's a certain level of mysticism to grounding in electronics. If you read a paper by the RANE Company on grounding, even those guys who are very good at what they do, have posited that there is some element of mysticism to ground problems and ground looping, you know, once again, Phil was an electronic music academic in his younger years . . . the sixty-cycle hum, it's *found sound.* Since we all went almost all digital, the nasty sixty-cycle hum is greatly reduced, but it comes out of old guitar amps a lot.

CORY: My sixty-cycle hum would be the past, it always comes back. Sometimes it comes back as a physical thing or a person who has an idea or something that they require you to address or absolve yourself for, and probably my fear of the present and the future becoming the past would be my sixty-cycle hum. And what I make out of it is that while I'm busy thinking about that and worrying about it, other stuff happens and the next thing becomes and occurs and it takes over just like that. . . . Karma, I don't think it's this thing that if you do something to me, that something is going to happen to you, because something or somebody knows that you did something to me and needs to happen to you. I think it's just a name for something that already was happening, because people notice whenever *they* feel bad about doing something, and something comes back to them very soon after that, well, karma got me there.

ROBBIE: Why do these old guys, like horrible dictators who collaborated with the Nazis or the Vichy government in France, and somehow they live to be ninety, but they go to their deaths shaking in their boots, 'cause they be worried. I often imagine those guys, like wow, that'd be scary. They never admitted it, but they know deep in their hearts that they were complicit in the deaths of, say, a lot of Jewish children or Argentinean dissenters or whatever. I believe there's a special place in hell for them.

An Everlasting Jam

So in case you are getting seriously bummed out, hold on. You may be grateful yet. In the Western world, we haven't really been able to heed the Buddha's advice. It is just so engrained in us that we must *personally* be of eternal significance that we keep trying to find ways around the Samsonite Scenario. So along comes this little dude named Immanuel Kant (1724–1804) and he is way smart. He figured out that you can't really *know* whether you have a soul that lives forever, but you can't quite help *thinking* you do. It's more than a suspicion in the back of your mind, it's something that if you *don't* think it might be true, you can't very well think about anything else. So you go on thinking you are Immortal, whether you want to or not. And you also think about two other things. Kant puts "God" and "Freedom" in the same three-piece jam band with "Immortality," that he calls The Postulates.[5] God is the drummer, Freedom plays lead, and Immortality is on bass, of course. And Kant is going to use Buddha's law of karma for some new and different advice.

Buddha's Third Noble Truth is the Law of Karma. This often gets expressed as the law of cause and effect, but that isn't quite right. Cause and effect is just something like, if you drink like Pigpen, don't be surprised when your liver gives out. That's not Buddha's point. It would be closer to say "what goes around comes around," but not necessarily in the ways you expect or understand. For Kant, while he doesn't use these exact words, karma comes down to the problem of "finitude," which means *not* knowing what you absolutely *need* to know in order to do things right. You don't know there's a God, you don't know if you are really free, and you don't know if your life has everlasting significance, but if you don't *believe* these things, life isn't

---

[5] The two main works I am drawing on are Kant's *Critique of Practical Reason* and *The Groundwork of the Metaphysics of Morals*. This is not light reading, but it may be worth the effort.

really worth living. But life *is* worth living, and it doesn't have
to totally suck. That's how The Postulates get their start. Kant's
point is that there *should be* a very cool band like that, even if
there isn't one. I'll leave the drums and lead aside and just give
you the bass line.

So *why*, Kant asks, would you think you want to live forever?
Why is that so all-fired important to you? The answer is *not*
"Well, life is pretty good, so I don't want it to end." Kant says
that's not really it at all. When you are on the right path—and
believe me, for Kant and for Buddha, the "right path" is the
noble eight-fold path (which is Buddha's Fourth Noble Truth—
it just has eight parts, more like Motown octet with back-up
singers than a jam trio), when you're *on* it, you want to keep on
doing what you're doing. It's the zone. It's a jam you don't ever
want to end, because, just like Phil, you're learning *how* to play
the bass *as* you're playing it. Here is what that's like, in Phil's
words:

> After playing a wrong note, for instance, I would quickly resolve it
> to a proper note –but then I took to repeating my mistakes (a sim-
> ple matter, since the music was built out of repeating modules or
> strophes [read, "Samsara"]) in order to resolve them differently each
> time. I soon began to see the dissonances caused by wrong notes,
> or right notes in the wrong place, as opportunities rather than lia-
> bilities—new ways to create tension and release, the lifeblood of
> music. (Lesh, *Searching for the Sound*, p. 53)

You don't need to get all worked up over the monotony of
"repeating modules" if you see them as opportunities for creativity rather than as a drone of one damn life after another. The
West has always looked to creativity for solace in the face of
death. But here is Kant's point: once you figure out what Phil
knows, you won't have any reason to *want* the music to end.
You may suck at the bass now, but you will want to keep per-
fecting your technique, your understanding, and most of all,
contributing your own bass line to God's sweet groove and
Freedom's screaming lead. But for all the world it *looks* like the
music is going to end and someone will have to pay the piper.
So in your imagination you say, "no, I will play on forever, and
I don't care if I ever get paid." That's Kant's bass line. You live
as if it will never end. And hey, maybe it won't. Can't ever be
sure.

Drum Solo

DALE: If I lived forever, I'd outlive all my friends, I'd outlive all my family members, I'd be waiting for the end. I don't think I would want to live forever, although I'm not in a hurry to die. We always want to go a little bit further, we don't want to end it and we hope that it won't, you know, I wouldn't want to, really, outlive my children. . . . It's very hard to let go. . . . The house isn't there anymore, that I grew up in, my folks, the people who raised me, all of that is gone. . . . I'd like to be very old when I go, that's what I want to die of, old age . . . Do I look for despair, do I look for hope? Sometimes the lights all shining on me, and other times I can barely see. I will get by, I will survive. . . Despite the despair you have to look forward and you have to keep going, you don't give up, or I don't. I can't just lay and wallow in sorrow and misery. It's always gonna be there and it's gonna bounce back around. . . . But you can't give up and you've gotta keep going. . . . there are other people who depend on me, and it's not just me. . . .

Four-String Metaphysics

So how does it work, I mean, how do you make up a bass line that doesn't suck? The first thing you have to remember is that it's not all about you, it's about other people too. Phil describes it like this:

> During the [Acid] Test itself [at the Fillmore West], the acoustic space of the hall was finely sculptured and very dense—it was very much a sonic "landscape," [this is your life, your chance to create] with solid objects here, open spaces there, paths of least resistance (for sound). One could wander from an area dominated by the Thunder Machine, traversing a space populated by disembodied voices carrying on so many simultaneous conversations (almost like being in Neal [Cassady]'s head) to a space in front of the stage where the music was pretty obviously being played by the band. However, the so-called nonmusical sounds from the other regions would come stealing in, sometimes masking the music being played. (*Searching for the Sound*, pp. 70–71)

That's your life, in a nutshell and seen as a whole, a serious Acid Test. You'll want to avoid the Thunder Machine most of the time, but it's always there, so you might as well get used to it.

Your band is the people you know and live with and create with. The question is whether you're going to recognize the opportunities and do something worth doing amidst all the confusion. Phil goes on:

> These experiences set off some interesting trains of thought for me: Why couldn't noise, or speech, or sounds that weren't made up of a series of harmonics be part of musical thought, musical discourse, especially if used rhythmically? We had already begun experimenting with feedback . . . and one of our favorite tricks became fading down to a sixty-cycle hum (normally the bane of a musician's existence) and using that as our fundamental tone to generate harmonic music.

So Phil is saying, take a look at what you might have overlooked, even something you despise, and create around it—for example, *death* is a pretty atrocious sixty-cycle hum. Phil finishes the thought with a flourish:

> The main event at the Fillmore, however, was the manifestation of the group mind in a large crowd. For the first time, the physical, luminous, and sonic spaces were unified—the dancers moving, the musical sound breathing, the lights pulsing—as one being, limited only by the inscrutable laws of probability. At the end, after eternities of ecstatic ego loss, a voice was heard asking, "Who's in charge here?" (*Searching for the Sound*, p. 71)

Of course, it was a cop (not the Thunder Machine) who asked the question that brought *ecstasy* (which means getting outside yourself) to an end for *this* manifestation of the group mind—and the cops don't *mean* to be cosmic gorillas, but that's sort of their job. The gorillas always show up, say "get back in your own suitcase" and it's no big deal. They can bring time back to eternity, but they *can't* take eternity away from those who have been to that place. I mean, you were out of your suitcase, and with all the others who were out of theirs, and the gorillas can't take that away from you. And this is the second reason I trust Phil. He understands the relationship between space, time, light, eternity, mind, and body, all in terms of creative opportunities and the group mind. We enact these opportunities by acting together *well*, and we have to make up the rules as we go, before we can really even learn what they are (or what they were).

But there's a catch. Phil is not riffing to the same beat as I. Kant and The Postulates. The Postulates are not very open to creativity. They are at the mercy of whatever groove God lays down, and they stay inside the established harmonics, and inside their luggage. The Postulates don't like mistakes, and they don't see them as opportunities to make up new relationships. Mistakes are just bad (m'kay?) as far as they can see, and they are awfully afraid of dissonance. So they have lots of rules about how to play the God, Freedom and Immortality minuet and trio. The main rule is called the "Categorical Imperative," which says that you *have to* think of each and every act of yours as a sort of "law of action," and you have to be able to desire that each action could be a *universal* law, and if any dissonance (contradiction) shows up anywhere, you shouldn't do what you are doing. There isn't a lot of room for individual creativity when such rules are laid down, not much room for context and nuance, and so the group mind becomes more like the Borg than like the Acid Test. Phil doesn't do gigs with I. Kant and The Postulates—they look more like the gorillas than brothers and sisters.

I. Kant and The Postulates have had a lot of commercial success, plenty of platinum recordings, they get played on Fox News and all the Clear Channel stations. But every record has the same beat, and that beat numbs the senses after a while. As the poet said,

> I see you've got your list out, say your piece and get out
> Guess I get the gist of it, but it's alright
> Sorry that you feel that way, the only thing there is to say
> Every silver lining's got a touch of grey

Third Set: Getting a Little Looser

Dale: I'm not sure how many other people I've influenced in my life. I have children, and without me, they wouldn't exist, so that might . . . I'd like to think He had something, if there is a God. I haven't discovered a cure for cancer, or I haven't done any great thing in my life. I'm sure there's times, if He's up there. He shakes His head, but life is very valuable, all life, to me, and IF he created me, damned good idea.

Cory: I'm at a point with people and animals that I have to draw the line, so as not to allow myself to be taken advantage of.

Robbie: Getting your energy ripped off, that's what we used to call that.

Dale: Did I think Jerry was a God? Did I worship Jerry? Uh, yes, he was someone to follow, although we didn't know exactly what we were following. When he died, we were hoping that either Phil or Bobby or somebody would take the reins and we would have someone else to lead us.

Robbie: That's what the Dead were about all along, is metamorphosis, rebirth and resurrection . . . ultimately it was always about the spirit of the music.

Of Monkeys and Engineers, or Guerilla Gorillas

So how do you get around the gorillas? The first thing you have to accept is that God may be the ultimate gorilla—maybe not, but maybe so. You just can't be sure, but if you're going to make your life something beautiful, something worth living and dying for, you'll need to develop an understanding with God. If He wants to play in your band, He will have to listen to everybody and try to adjust His groove to how the whole sound—and light and space and bodies—are all gyrating. He is invited to the Acid Test, but only if He plays well with others. If He wants to be a gorilla and start smiting the Samsonite all over the place, well, we'll have to become guerilla gorillas. There is a way to beat God at His own game. And Phil knows how to do it, which is the final reason I trust him.

There was another philosopher named Alfred North Whitehead (1862–1947) who is pretty much on the same page as Phil.[6] Whitehead said, there is something even *God* doesn't

---

[6] I say Whitehead is on the same page as Phil, but he wrote philosophy like Jerry played guitar. Most people don't get it, but for those who do, it's an amazing cosmic jam. The book I'm drawing from is Whitehead longest jam, *Process and Reality* (New York: Macmillan, 1929) which is a strange trip and thanks for all the fish, if you get my drift. Pick it up and don't worry if you don't understand it, just sit back and take it in. It's interesting. In 1978 a pair of well-meaning scholars named Donald Sherburne and David Ray Griffin did a "corrected edition" of *Process and Reality*, which is sort of like going

know, which is what it's like to have just *your* perspective on the whole cosmos. Sure, God knows what it's like to be you, *and* everybody else, but God doesn't know what it's like to be *just* you, and *nobody* else. That's your hook line, your signature lick, that's your advantage. It may not seem like much, but think about this: if there is something that it is like to be *just* you, then there is something about *being* just you that even God can't contribute to the Acid Test *without* you. God needs *you*, and maybe more than you need God. That's why your skinny ass is *here*. Whitehead calls this your "self-creativity." Whitehead thinks God can't get free of the gorillas *Himself*, and he is trying like hell to get a little help from his friends, which is why He creates them. So maybe you're not one His better ideas. But you're certainly not his worst idea—I mean surely Hitler was the worst idea God ever had. Jerry was an excellent idea, and you might be a pretty good idea, all things considered. It sort of depends on what you do. What God needs, apparently, according to Whitehead, is a guerilla army of co-creators, so that the cosmos can have a serious Rave, and the gorillas eventually give up.

The real gorillas are evil and chaos, and they suck because they are trying to unmake everything we are making. They have an easier time of screwing everything up when we stay in our luggage. It seems like they do a lot of damage, but they can't win. The reason is that they can't unmake anything unless we *make it first*. The gorillas are reactive because they *can't* be proactive. And here is Whitehead's ace in the hole: Even if they tear down everything you made, they can't ever undo the fact that you *made* it. When we make music, even God can't unmake it—it happened, and even if God could erase every trace of what we made, *He* would still remember that we made it. If He willed Himself to forget us and our music, He would remember *willing* that. Whitehead calls this the "objective immortality of the past." It just means that whatever has once been done, always *will have been* done, and whatever value those jams had, that value affects everything that comes after it in some way, and even God can't undo it. Of course, there really

---

back through a live recording of the Grateful Dead and electronically correcting all their mistakes—which would not be a wise thing to do. The new edition is very clean, but if you want the original recording of Whitehead, you need to find an old copy, before 1978.

isn't any reason to think God would *want* to undo it, and there are lots of reasons to think that God is doing all that can be done to help us make up the coolest shit. But even if God is the ultimate gorilla, He's gonna have to reckon with your bass line—forever.

Unscheduled Jam

CORY: Sometimes I think that heaven or hell is not only in your mind, but it's simultaneous with life. If you feel that you're doing good, and you're doing everything in your power to be what you believe is right and do what you believe is right, you have high, clear mental stability there, and you feel good about yourself and it's just heaven. However, if you're this seedy, awful, nasty mother-fucker . . . or even if you're just an asshole, you go around raining on people every day . . . all it takes is one person to cross your path in the wrong way, and set you off, and then you're going to be cross with the next person you see too, and that might ruin their day, and they might ruin the next person's day, and that will come back to you because maybe you might ruin somebody's day that comes back around to you that very same day, and this person is pissed off at you because of something that somebody else did, because of something that somebody else did because of something that you did.

Gratitude

When Phil plays the bass, he is acting, and even God can't undo what he's doing. I. Kant and The Postulates can bitch about the mistakes if they want, but they can't fix them. Might as well learn to see the beauty in dissonance as moan and weep over what can't be changed. Kant and his band are so uptight about what God *might* think of them that they miss out on their own lives, and that is *un*grateful. God needs more than our best guess about His ultimate rules. He needs us to grow, to try things, and most of all to learn gratitude for the chance to add a line to the Acid Test.

I know that Phil knows this, because he learned it from Jerry, among others. Here's how Phil describes Jerry's life, as a whole:

His many gifts, his delight in life, and his gusto for experience were balanced by an endearing humility of spirit and an almost obsessive refusal to take himself seriously . . . he never failed to deftly skewer ballooning egos. It was the warmth of his heart that just pulled everybody in. Even though, like most of us, he didn't suffer fools gladly, there was room there for just about every-damn-body. (*Searching for the Sound*, p. 320)

The gorillas can't get you here. You don't need any Samsonite, and you don't even have to trust God that it all works out for the best. You got to play in the band, and nobody can take that away from you. The word I was looking for, the one that started me thinking, I found when Phil describes when he almost died himself. Recovering from his liver transplant, Phil says:

It all comes home to me when, midway through my first week of recovery, Jill wheels me outside the hospital front door to see a stunning sunset. I break down completely in a flood of *gratitude*; deep down inside, I haven't been sure if I'd see anything so beautiful ever again. I now know the simple joys of being alive—breathing, seeing, hearing—are infinitely precious, and I'll never take them for granted again. (*Searching for the Sound*, p. 330)

This is no "paint by number morning sky," as the poet said, this is the genuine article. *That* was the word I was wondering about: *gratitude*, as in grateful, as in Grateful Dead. I am pretty sure that some people never learn gratitude. I hope to God I'm not one of them, but I trust Phil because my epistemic principle says, in its final formulation: "Know gratitude when you see it." Jerry and Pigpen and the others may be gone, but their Gratitude lives. Now it makes sense to me why the fellows dropped "Grateful" from the name. We are all Dead already, we were born dead. But we aren't screwed, because the part that is really up to *us* is the gratitude, and some of us *get that* and some of us *don't*. When you help somebody *get that* who doesn't already get it, you are kicking the ass of every gorilla. The ones who get it make beautiful things, and they don't bother to blame God when it doesn't *seem* to last. The beautiful things *do* last. No gorilla can take that sunset away from Phil, even if "the rent is in arrears and the dog has not been fed in years," as the poet said. And, my friend, *no* asshole can take the bass out of your hands, as long as *you* don't let him. Play your riff, right *now*, and the cosmos will just have to deal with it. That's my riff at least.[7]

Encore

ROBBIE: All the notes are still out there. The Dead would agree with that.[8]

---

[7] I want to thank my wise friend Danny Dolinger for teaching me that genuine gratitude is just as hard to learn as compassion, and my parents for buying me that Dan Electro bass guitar when I was twelve, even though they knew I would use it to play that god-awful rock'n'roll.

[8] I wanted to improvise a chapter, find a riff and take it all the way home. without knowing where it would lead. So I wrote this whole chapter and left spaces for others to improvise. And these are a couple of guys from the band I play in, Cory Powell and Dale Groves, plus another guy I *wish* I played with, Robbie Stokes. I wanted a conversational jam with people who really had the right Head for the Dead, and I wanted them from different generations, different stages on the path, you know? So my young friend Cory, he's twenty-two and plays lead guitar in our group, the Bone Dry River Band. He learned to play by listening to Jerry. He has a young body, but an old soul. Dale is the BDRB drummer. We call him Teaser—nevermind why (use your imagination). Like me, Dale has a touch of grey, but only a touch, and he has followed the Dead since 1980, going to over 140 shows. He's been through plenty and has come out grateful and still with the rhythm in him. Robbie Stokes is a fantastic musician who collaborated with the Dead and Mickey Hart and about everybody else at some point. Check him out at www.robcoaudio.com. Robbie is in his late fifties (he must be living right, because he doesn't look it). I'm lucky to be able to call him up and get that close to the Dead themselves. So I gathered all three of them at The Mix Cafe/Alchemy Sound in Carterville, Illinois, on February 19th, 2007. My friend Jon Pluskota recorded our conversation. Check them out: www.themixcafe.com. The dialogue you see in this essay is from that night, which I ran like a jam session. I will try to get the whole conversation up on a website and link to it from The Mix Cafe website.

10

Me and My Uncle . . . and Thomas Hobbes: On the Ethics of Leaving His Dead Ass There by the Side of the Road

JOHANNES BULHOF

It's an odd fact that the Grateful Dead played the song "Me and My Uncle" in concert more than any other, reportedly more than six hundred times. Were the song the band's most popular, this would be easy to explain, but in fact, it is hardly known among the Un-Dead. And while it is instantly recognized by Deadheads, few would place the song among their all-time favorites.

The song's being played so frequently is made even more odd by the fact that it seems out of character lyrically for the band and for its followers. It's not a song dealing with some facet of drug use (like "Trucking," "Casey Jones," "Sugar Magnolia," or many others). It's not a reflection on life from an alternative perspective (such as "Playing in the Band," "Box of Rain," "Scarlet Begonias," or my personal favorite, "Eyes of the World"). Unlike other Grateful Dead staples, it is not a traditional blues song, nor one suited to jazz riffs.

Instead, the song seems to be from the folk music tradition, and the Dead were certainly influenced by the folk tradition. Many folk songs tell the tale of a life gone bad, as does "Me and My Uncle." When they do, however, it is usually with some lament (such as "Mama Tried" or "Wharf Rat"). The lesson is not only to learn from their wrongdoing, but usually also to feel compassion for the person doing the wrong. They are stories from which we can learn to lead a better life, and feel sympathy for our fellow human beings.

"Me and My Uncle," on the other hand, is a story about cheating, theft, and murder. It's told without any regret, or any attempt to feel any compassion at the murder's situation. On the contrary, as Bob Weir sings the song, the murderer only has contempt for his victims, leaving his beloved uncle's "dead ass there by the side of the road." Weir sings that the nephew "loves the cowboys" that he just killed and robbed, "loves their gold" that he just stole, and loves his uncle, whom he has just murdered. Such love is only ironic. It is, as Friedrich Nietzsche points out in *The Genealogy of Morals*, love that is self-love, the way a great bird of prey loves the lamb he just ate. It is love that loves things that only help the lover, not the beloved.

Initially, one may wonder about the author of the song. Usually, a song of this nature is a traditional ballad, one whose author has been lost to the sands of time, one whose lyrics have been changed over and over, so that, in truth, there is no "author," but a long succession of authors. Such is not the case with "Me and My Uncle," although apparently the author was lost in another way. The songwriter was John Phillips, of "Mamas and Papas" fame, who wrote the song one drunken night in 1962, in the company of Judy Collins among others. He was so drunk that he forgot he wrote it. When Collins put the song on one of her records, and attributed it to Phillips, Phillips had no idea why she had done so. Collins had made a cassette recording of the song, and so the song made its way from Phillips, to Collins, who put a live version of the song on an album, to "a hippie named Curly Jim," to Bob Weir, to the Grateful Dead.[1]

Perhaps closely looking at a song which was written in a drunken haze is a mistake. It would be easy to read into the song far more than its writer intended. Indeed, it would be hard not to. Is this merely a western tale about gambling, drinking, and murder? I think not. In this essay, I will show that the song is best understood as a lesson in morality, warning us of the irra-tionality of pure self-interest. As such, it's in a long line of philo-sophical analyses focused on the rationality of moral behavior, and in a long line of ironic literature.

---

[1] Liner notes for "Phillips 66," Blair Jackson, *Going Down the Road* (New York: Harmony, 1992), p. 269.

I'm Beggin' You Don't Murder Me: A Sordid Tale of Death

The song tells a story. A man and his uncle are riding horses to Texas from southern Colorado, and they stop in Santa Fe. They stop for a drink in a bar and find drunk cowboys with plenty of cash. They start a game of cards, and the uncle begins winning the cowboy's money. They think the uncle is cheating, and call him on it. The singer of the song professes shock. His uncle is as honest as he is, he says, and he is "as honest as a Denver man can be." Violence then starts. In the version sung by the Grateful Dead, one of the cowboys starts to draw his gun. The singer of the song then draws his own gun, and shoots not just the man who drew on his uncle, but "another who never saw." The uncle grabs all the money while everyone's attention is directed elsewhere, and the two escape, apparently changing plans, as they now head for Mexico. In and of itself, this suggests that the singer knows what they did was illegal. Mexico is where outlaws go, to avoid being arrested. It was thus not a case of self-defense, but of theft and murder.

The song then takes an ironic turn. The singer professes a "love" of the cowboys, of their gold, and of his uncle, "God rest his soul," he sings. This is the first we learn that the uncle is dead. The singer then attributes his knowledge of how to live to his uncle, in the critical part of the song. The uncle "taught me good, Lord, taught me all I know. Taught me so well, I grabbed that gold, and I left his dead ass there by the side of the road." Not only did the uncle teach him how to live, but by his uncle's lessons, ones he learned so well, he murders his uncle, and steals the loot for himself.

This does not make for the traditional "manly western." In traditional westerns, and even in the alternative "anti-hero" versions, the star is always a good, if flawed, man. In "Me and My Uncle," the singer is a self-depicted murderer and thief, not once, but twice. In both cases of murder, theft was the motive. This was not killing for an honorable cause, but, in the first case, shooting people who could not defend themselves and who had done no wrong, and in the second, killing a family member to whom he was close solely for the money. There are western songs, books and movies that display a character doing evil.

Classically, these present a tragic flaw, and, as in classical tragedies, death of the anti-hero is always at the end of the movie—"The Wild Bunch" and "Butch Cassidy and the Sundance Kid" come to mind. If the hero lives, he fights for good. If the hero dies, he fought for evil, even though he usually has endearing qualities.

But in this song, the hero fights for evil, but at the end, he is not dead. Quite the contrary, he seems to be alive and well, singing of how he loves his gold, and how he killed those men to get it. One may well imagine he made his way to Mexico, for singing this happy song while waiting to be executed for crimes committed would seem very strange. Even somewhere in Mexico, the song seems strange. Most murderers and thieves do not want others to know that they are murderers and thieves. Oh, someone might sing this if they want others to fear them, like some gangsta rap songs. This song, however, in no way inspires fear. The story of the song, therefore, is not the classic western tale. What, then, is it?

Let us focus first on the lessons that uncle taught his nephew. First, we may ask, did the uncle cheat? The singer claims his uncle did not, but adds that the reason he knows the uncle did not is that the uncle is as honest as the singer. By the end of the song, however, we discover that the singer is not honest at all. If, in fact, the uncle is as honest as the nephew, we can justly conclude that the uncle is not honest, either. Indeed, if the uncle taught the nephew everything the nephew knew, and the nephew is dishonest, it seems clear that the nephew learned his dishonesty from his uncle. This will be the key to the song. But initially, since both are dishonest, there is every reason to think the uncle did in fact cheat.

The uncle's dishonest ways, stealing the money, are replicated by the nephew, when the nephew steals the gold at the end of the song. This replication of dishonest ways is exactly what the nephew refers to as the lessons he learned from his uncle. This lesson seems to be: take what you want for yourself. There is an important additional point to the lesson. In the first case, the pair get away with their murder and theft, and in the last case, the nephew does the same. The lesson the uncle taught the nephew is: take what you can get for yourself as long as you can get away with it.

Some Folks Trust to Reason, Others Trust to Might

At this stage, philosophy rears its head. The question of our lives, and the principle question of philosophy since the times of Plato and Socrates, is how should we live our lives? Should we orient ourselves towards fame, power and fortune? Or should we aim for the moral life? It's the question that shapes the philosopher Socrates, as described by his student Plato through his many dialogues. Plato is justly famous for many philosophical views, but the central question for him was the one about ethics. Almost all of Plato's dialogues in one way or another address this issue.

In American society today, this question is not unusual, though we think we have the answer. We all think that we ought to live a moral life, though there seems to be a difference of opinion as to what constitutes the moral life. This commitment to the moral life is only on the surface. Ask any class of college students to list their principle goals, and the vast majority will list "to be rich" at the top. They orient their lives and their studies to achieve financial power.

This is not unlike many young men during Socrates's time, though the aim was of a different sort, or rather, with a different emphasis. In Ancient times, political power was the path to fame and fortune. The students of Plato's day aimed at political power through the art ("techne") of persuasive speaking. In the Classical Age, Athens was a democracy, but not like the U.S. today. There was no representative democracy. There, democracy was direct. The first six thousand free men assembled voted on everything. The people themselves decided on matters trivial and deep, all the way to the power of war. The people had to vote for war, and they even voted on who would lead their armies. In this environment, the power to speak persuasively was the key to political power, and political power was the key to fame and fortune. So the best and the brightest of Athens studied the art of persuasive speaking, so that they could pursue what they thought they ought to pursue, power.

Socrates was deeply disturbed by this. The young people of his day, Plato describes Socrates as saying, show an "eagerness to possess as much wealth, reputation and honors as possible, while you do not care for nor give thought to wisdom and truth" (*Apology*, line 29e). In Plato's masterpiece, *The Republic*, Plato describes Socrates as making an argument designed to show them that this was the wrong way to live. To introduce the discussion, Plato describes a discussion between Socrates and an Athenian aristocrat named Thrasymachus. In the middle of Book I, Thrasymachus makes what was for the Greeks and for Socrates a shocking claim: that Justice is not a virtue, but a vice. It is not clear from the dialogue whether Thrasymachus actually believes this view, but in defending it, he makes the following claim: "A just man always gets less than an unjust one" (*Republic I*, line 343d). An unjust business partner, for example, cheats and hence gets more out of the partnership. An unjust person cheats on his taxes, and thus gets more money than the just person. A just person in his acting honorably can get the ire of those who want him to cheat, too. The advantages of justice, Thrasymachus argues, flow not from justice itself, but from the appearance of justice. That is, if everyone thinks you are a just man, then you get all benefits of a just life, for those benefits only come from how others treat you.

This argument can be expanded in many ways, but it shows us the central difficulty of ethics: Why is it rational to be just, when it appears that being just frequently gets us less of what we want? For us today, this question is no less relevant. When I ask my classes, if they could get away with acting unjustly, so that neither God nor man would punish their unjust actions, who would still act justly, the response is overwhelming. The vast majority admit that they would act unjustly, putting the majority view in agreement with Thrasymachus. Justice might be good for society, but it does not seem good for the individual. Let us pause for a moment to see how this ties into "Me and My Uncle." The singer acts unjustly, gets the gold, *and gets away with it!* If Thrasymachus (and the majority of people) are right, the writer has merely done what he ought, done what he rationally should to get what he wants.

Your Back Might Need Protection: The Disturbing, Brilliant Hobbes

Many, many philosophers attempt to show, like Plato, that this view is wrong. One of the first philosophers after the Dark Ages to approach this question from a non-religious perspective was

Thomas Hobbes. Hobbes begins with the assumption that we all want security and the means of a "commodious living." By this, Hobbes does not necessarily mean that we want to be rich (though of course, some do) but that we all want to live comfortably. He also assumes that we are rational beings, capable of using reason to fulfill our self-interested desires. We may have other desires which are altruistic, such as the desire to see our families others live well, too, but no one can deny that everyone has self-interested desires.

Hobbes further asserts that humans are basically equal in mind and in body. To be sure, some people are stronger than others, some are faster than others, and some are smarter than others. Nonetheless, even "the weakest has strength enough to kill the strongest" (Thomas Hobbes. *Leviathan* [New York: Penguin, 1985], p. 183). With the advent of modern weapons, this is obvious. The gun has frequently been called "the great equalizer." But even before, as Hobbes points out, the weak can group together, and eliminate anyone. Were that not enough, the strongest among us is weak when they sleep. Strength in mind is even more even, according to Hobbes. It is mere vanity that makes people think that one is smarter than another, but the truth is revealed by the fact that everyone thinks they are smarter than the person next to them, showing a kind of equality. We might notice that no similar claim is ever made in relation to physical strength.

From equality, Hobbes argues, comes equal hope of attaining our ends. Let us suppose that there is something that two people want, but that they can nevertheless not share, for example a bag of gold. Reason can show each person how to get what he wants. Because of the equality, a person can think "I can take the bag of gold from him." Reason then realizes the problem: the other person will be angry, and not merely allow the other person to take what he wants also. So reason can come up with the solution: to accomplish her end, she endeavors "to destroy, or subdue on another" (*Leviathan*, p. 184). Reason then drives us to be enemies. We can expect, as Hobbes writes, that if we possess something of value, others will come and try to take it from us, and we can expect that they may try to take our lives, too, to be assured that they will get our stuff.

For Hobbes's argument to work, we need not all think like this. All we need to understand is that there are some people out there who think like this. There are some people who will use force to get the things they desire. It will become important to the argument that we cannot always tell who those people are. It may well be that your best friend, or perhaps your own nephew, when recognizing their opportunity, kills you and takes the gold.

This is not caused by an inherent greediness. It is caused by reason, and the fact that we have desires for things we cannot share. Both of these conditions are indisputable. It is not irrational behavior, nor some flaw in character that drives humans to become enemies. On the contrary, reason itself drives us to become enemies.

Anyone who has been to a Grateful Dead show knows that many people are not like this, that humans are capable of sharing even that which cannot in principle be shared (hat tip to the Deadhead who shared his beer, his herb, and a turkey leg with me, Manor Downs, 7/31/82). Unfortunately for man, for the argument to work, Hobbes does not need everyone, or even most people, to be like this. The first stage of Hobbes's argument showed that everyone has the ability to use force to get what they want. The second stage showed that there are some people who will use force to take what they want. This is, of course, a fact of life in the big city in contemporary society.

The next stage of the argument is that reason dictates to us that the best way to survive is to strike first. Nothing is so reasonable as anticipation (*Leviathan*, p. 184). He who strikes second will most likely be dead. This changes the whole dynamic, and makes us all enemies of everyone, and makes co-operation impossible. Suppose we were in a place with twenty people, at least one of which is acting perfectly self-interestedly, but none of us knows who. If we allow someone to get close to us, he may be the one who kills us, and takes our gold. If we shoot second, it will be too late, as that person will have shot first, and we will be dead. The far safer recourse, reason tells us, is to take no chances, and shoot first. We might kill the wrong person, but at least we will know we will be alive. So anticipation becomes the rational course of action.

Reason also leads me to conclude that everyone else knows everything I do, and reasons as well as me. So I know that each person in this group is reasoning exactly as I am. So now let us suppose someone comes close to me. Not only do I have reason to strike first, but she knows I have reason to strike her first! As she knows this, her own reason drives her to strike first. Quickly, only one of us will be left standing. Now notice: she may have meant me no harm! Not only could I not take that chance, but I know if she is rational she has every reason to strike me first. She does not wish me harm, nor to steal my stuff, but she wishes for her security, and she knows to preserve her life she must strike first, too. It's easy to see that the same reasoning applies to all twenty people in the community, and so everyone will be the enemy of everyone. Co-operation becomes rationally impossible, as we can trust no one. Without a power to keep us in awe, to enforce the law, chaos reigns.

We can see this in many communities (think New Orleans after Katrina), but it must also give us pause to recognize that there are other communities which work just fine without the threat of violence (think Rainbow community). There must be more to the story, but that would have to wait for another essay. For the moment, let us focus on the lesson learned. Rational self-interest drives us to be enemies.

Now let's suppose that in our community, some people are family. Let us suppose that one person is, say, the uncle of someone else. How does that change things? Well, if the nephew is rationally self-interested, it changes nothing! It will still be in his interest to get the gold, and it will still be in his interest to destroy or subdue his uncle to get it. What of the uncle? He should have rationally realized that he was in danger, and struck first. It was the uncle who did not act in his rational self-interest, and paid for it with his life and his gold.

Once I Was the Student, Now I Am the Master

Let us return to the song, and let us focus on what the uncle taught the nephew. The uncle taught him "everything I know." What does he know? He knows how to kill, how to steal, and how to cheat. In short, the nephew knows how to act in a perfectly self-interested manner. He loves his uncle, he loves the cowboys and he loves their gold all because they have helped his own personal self-interest. His love is perfectly self-interested. He did not learn selfless love of others, the importance of community, or any other virtue useful for living peacefully with other. We must then assume he learned his self-love from his uncle, as this is all he knows, and his uncle taught him all he knows.

Unfortunately for his uncle, his uncle did not see what rationally follows from rational self-interest: that everyone is an enemy to everyone, that his nephew is now his enemy. The student learned the lesson better than the teacher. In a Hobbesian world, reason leads us to one man standing. In our song, we are also left with one man standing. This is not by accident. The lesson we are to learn from both is the same: rational self-interest is communally irrational. The lesson to learn from the song is the lesson the uncle should have learned, namely where his reasoning was leading him, to his death, and to the death of cooperation and community. If we learn his lesson, we then do not act in a rational self-interested manner, nor should we teach such behavior to our friends and family. Pretty deep for a drunken ramble.

11

Buddhism through the Eyes of the Dead

PAUL GASS

The San Francisco Bay Area in the 1960s was an epicenter for cultural change. The Grateful Dead were caught up in and were a motive force for that change. The city already had a long history as a haven of outsiders when many of the Beat writers, including Lawrence Ferlinghetti, Gary Snyder, and Michael McClure, made San Francisco their home. Ferlinghetti's bookstore became a meeting place for young people with a literary bent. The Beats (a name with obvious musical allusions that has other significance as well) are best known for Jack Kerouac's *On the Road* and Allen Ginsberg's poem, "Howl." The Beats took the freedom of Bebop Jazz as inspiration and developed not only a new literary style but challenged what they saw as the hypocrisy of 1950s middle American values. This throwing off of convention, which included such challenges as Ginsberg's frank depictions of human sexuality in "Howl," would be central to the cultural revolution of the 1960s.

Jerry Garcia, Ron "Pigpen" McKernan, Bob Weir, Bill Kreutzman, and Phil Lesh came together in the context of this creative and experimental setting. Mother McCree's Uptown Jug Champions, then the Warlocks, who soon became the Grateful Dead, played at poetry readings, sharing the stage with many of the Beat poets. The Grateful Dead's social circle included Ken Kesey, one of the next generation of writers emerging in the area. Kesey discovered the recreational use of LSD through his participation in an experiment covertly sponsored by the CIA and began sharing that experience through what would come to be called the Acid Tests. The Acid Tests, festivals of multimedia participation art, featured poetry readings, light shows, day-glo art, and music provided by the Grateful Dead, all designed to accompany a collective acid trip. In this scene, the Grateful Dead developed their extended improvisations and set structure to enhance and guide the audiences' trips. Much of the Grateful Dead's connection to their audience developed in these wild scenes where the audience was part of the show, which is why, as Jerry explains, he paid to get in.

The poster art used to advertise concerts and other events in the San Francisco area was an integral part of the counter-culture scene. The posters advertising some of the acid trips show the importance of the literary influence by giving Ginsberg and Neal Cassady top billing. The poster announcing the Human Be-In of 1967, a huge gathering of the new counterculture, listed the Buddha on the bill along with the Beat poets; whereas, the musical participants were listed as "All San Francisco Rock and Roll Bands," not mentioning the Dead by name. The Be-In began with Ginsberg, Snyder, and McClure leading the crowd in chanting and included poetry readings by Ferlinghetti, McClure, Ginsberg, and Snyder, alternated with music sets by the Grateful Dead and other San Francisco bands.

The Beats, the Buddha, and the Dead

Many of the beat writers looked to Asian religions and philosophies, particularly Buddhism, for inspiration. Kerouac was impressed with Snyder's Zen Buddhist courage and calm mind and recounted their travels in *Dharma Bums*. Ginsberg went on to create the Naropa Institute, a Buddhist writing program, in Boulder, Colorado. Neal Cassady bridged the Beat generation and the new cultural movement. He was 'on the road' with Kerouac and 'on the bus' with Kesey. Jerry Garcia described a special connection with Neal Cassady:

> Neal represented a model to me of how far you could take it in an individual way, in the sense that you weren't going to *have* a work, you were going to *be* the work. . . . I was oscillating at the time. I had originally been an art student and was wavering between one-man-one-work or being involved in something that was dynamic and ongoing and didn't necessarily stay any one way—and, also, something in which you weren't the only contributing factor. I decided to go with what was dynamic and with what more than

one mind was involved with. The decision I came to was to be involved in a group thing, namely the Grateful Dead, and I'm still involved in it.[1]

There were connections to Buddhist ways of thinking within the Grateful Dead's extended family as well. Lyricist Peter Zimels, also known as Peter Monk, was already a Buddhist monk when he began his collaboration with the Grateful Dead and served as a sort of spiritual leader for the Grateful Dead's extended family.

In the midst of all these influences, it is not surprising to find Buddhist themes throughout the Grateful Dead's oeuvre. The chorus of "Eyes of the World" invites listeners to achieve enlightenment and to discover their own Buddha nature:

> Wake up to find out
> that you are the eyes of the world
> but the heart has its beaches
> its homeland and thoughts of its own
> Wake now, discover that
> you are the song that
> the morning brings
> but the heart has it seasons
> its evenings
> and songs of its own

Enlightenment is an awakening to a deeper truth. The title 'Buddha' means 'the awoken one'. Siddhartha Gautama, the Buddha, discovered that there is a deeper reality behind the appearances that we normally accept as real. He explained that conventional truths about the world of our ordinary experiences are understood by our ordinary minds, but ultimate truth can only be understood by a purer mind, the state of our mind achieved through meditation.

The Buddha's Discovery

The Four Noble Truths are a central tenet of Buddhism. The first is that our life and the continuous cycle of life, death, and

---

[1] Paul Perry, *On the Bus* (New York: Thunder's Mouth, 1996), p. x.

rebirth, known as reincarnation, is suffering (or dukkha). The second is that there is a cause of that suffering, namely karma, which is much like a natural law that guides reincarnation. Third, there is an escape from that suffering: nirvana, a state outside of the cycle of reincarnation. Fourth, there is a path to that relief: the Buddha's teaching of the middle way, which comes to be called dharma.

The Grateful Dead's lyrics often investigate themes of suffering, such as the sorrow of facing death and separation from friends in "Black Peter" or the poor dog's hunger in "Touch of Grey." But the Buddhist notion of dukkha includes more. Even things that bring pleasure, like listening to music or enjoying good food, lead to pain. This is either because they are missed when they end or because in excess the pleasure becomes too much, as in the pain from eating too much or the physical damage from listening to music that is too loud. Even the love we feel for those closest to us will bring pain through the separation of death. Nothing in this world, not even our own life, will last. Suffering comes from the fact that everything is impermanent, and our awareness of our own impermanence causes the deepest sense of dukkha. We cling to a sense of self-identity and believe there is a permanent self or soul that persists not only through this life but through our many reincarnations. But ultimately, there is nothing there to cling to, and this becomes the root of our suffering. We detect this disjointedness between perception and reality and feel an uneasiness because things are misaligned.

Karma acts like a natural law. Our past deeds, good and bad, cause our present rebirth and experiences. Certain actions, which qualify as complete, create the seed for a rebirth and govern the conditions of a life. But our belief in a self gives rise to our desires and actions which cause us to accrue more karmic debt. This debt must be worked off through the continuing cycle of birth, death, and rebirth.

Nirvana, the escape from suffering, is a complete absence of ordinary experience and the cessation of the cycle of reincarnation. The path to nirvana is to follow the dharma, the teachings of the Buddha. While other Indian schools of thought see enlightenment as gaining an understanding of our deepest selves and deepest nature, Buddhism calls us to discover there is no self. At a conventional level, the self consists of a body and a mind, but both of these are impermanent.

We come to this belief in a self because of the way we experience life, but according to the analysis of Buddhist philosophy, the self is really the temporary aggregate of five characteristics that come together to form this illusion: form is the physical body; sensation is the experiences we have through our senses; perception is our judgment of feelings or moods; volition or disposition is our will and what we desire; consciousness is a self-reflective awareness of the others. According to Buddhist philosophy, all of these states are constantly changing, and all things constantly pass in and out of existence at a rate faster than humans can perceive. Our false belief in the self is due to the fact that these aggregates overlap and do not go out of existence at the same time. Such an ephemeral sense of self is alluded to in "Attics of My Life":

> In the Attics of my life
> Full of cloudy dreams unreal
> Full of tastes no tongue can know
> And lights no eye can see
> When there was no ear to hear
> You sang to me
> I have spent my life
> Seeking all that's still unsung
> Bent my ear to hear the tune
> And closed my eyes to see
> When there were no strings to play
> You played to me . . .
> In the secret space of dreams
> Where I dreaming lay amazed
> When the secrets are all told
> And the petals all unfold
> When there was no dream of mine
> You dreamed of me.

We naturally feel that there is a self that has experiences, but Buddhism calls us to abandon this, ultimately false, view.

The idea that there is no self may seem unsettling, but there are parallels in the drug experiences that the Grateful Dead's music accompanied. Albert Hoffman, the discoverer of LSD, described his second trip as involving a complete loss of self: "My ego was suspended somewhere in space and I saw my

body lying dead on the sofa."[2] Ken Babbs, a member of the
Grateful Dead's extended family, explains that psychedelic
drugs can lead to another kind of awareness, in which ordinary
feelings such as fear are experienced differently. The experience
"doesn't get rid of fear but gives another way to look at it. It's
not as scary as you thought."[3] Some saw experimentation with
LSD as part of a religious quest. Others describe the Grateful
Dead's music as having similar effects. Grateful Dead performances can be spiritual experiences involving, "a transformation
of ordinary consciousness into an extraordinary state that was
essentially ineffable or indescribable, beyond a euphoric sense
of well-being and connectedness with others."[4] As Mikey Hart
puts it, the Grateful Dead were in the "transportation business—
we move minds."[5] Jerry Garcia explains:

> When we get on stage, what we really want to happen is, we want
> to be transformed from ordinary players to extraordinary ones, like
> forces of a larger consciousness. And the audience wants to be
> transformed from whatever ordinary reality they may be in to
> something a little wider, something that enlarges them.[6]

It is not just particular songs that carry the spiritual significance,
the structure of live performance itself can lead to a religious
experience. As one Deadhead describes it,

> There was something about their music . . . that came to symbol-
> ize something more. They really seemed to open up some kind of
> interior space that was very refreshing and satisfying to have access
> to. Listening to their music I was able to lose myself to a greater
> extent than with any other kind of music or any other experience
> . . . . The Grateful Dead symbolized some sort of nexus of
> expanded experiences of consciousness.[7]

---

[2] Martin A. Lee and Bruce Shlain. *Acid Dreams: The Complete Social History of LSD: The CIA, The Sixties, and Beyond* (New York: Grove, 1992), p. xix.

[3] Paul Perry. *On the Bus* (New York: Thunder's Mouth, 1996), p. xv.

[4] Shan C. Sutton. "The Deadhead Community: Popular Religion in Contemporary American Culture" in Rebecca G. Adams and Robert Sardiello, eds., *Deadhead Social Science* (New York: Altamira, 2000), p. 115.

[5] Dennis McNally. "The Dead at Warner Bros," *The Grateful Dead: The Golden Road* (Warner Bros., 2001), p. 10.

[6] "The Deadhead Community," p. 116.

[7] Robin Sylvan. *Traces of the Spirit* (New York: New York University Press, 2002), pp. 94–95.

Emptiness

Buddhist philosophers use an analogy (modernized here) to help explain how the self arises from the five aggregates. Imagine the sights at a Grateful Dead show during Space when the audience holds up lighters and creates a twinkling light show. Imagine that it begins with the flame from just one lighter. That initial flame is used to light the next lighter and then the next, and so on, except in this case, as the flame ignites the next lighter, imagine that it is extinguished from the previous lighter. The flame, then, is passed from lighter to lighter. In some way there is a connection: it is the same flame that moves from one lighter to the next but there is no sameness at all to the flame which is constantly changing. The flame is like the self. It is constantly changing: flickering, growing, moving with the breeze. In fact, it is never the same flame. It is continually burning different fuel. Just as the flame moves from one lighter to the next, the self moves from one incarnation to the next. This analogy can be extended to explain nirvana. It doesn't make sense to ask where the flame goes when it is extinguished from the last lighter. Likewise, it doesn't make sense to ask where the self goes when nirvana is achieved.

This view connects with the Buddhist notion of emptiness. Buddhist philosophy not only denies the existence of the self but holds that nothing has independent existence. All experience, what we would call experience of the ordinary world, is said to be conditioned, meaning that every event, every thought, every physical object depends for its existence on some prior cause or condition—nothing has independent existence. Physical phenomena are just as fleeting as mental experiences. Living things are born, grow, decay, and die. Even inanimate objects are governed by this cycle. For example, a boulder or stone which may seem to last forever will erode to sand or be subsumed in lava. The entire solar system came together, and astronomy gives a timeline of the sun's expansion and eventual decline. We may not live long enough to recognize the coming and going of phenomena, but we are aware things are not going to last. This is not to deny the existence of physical objects but to assert that all phenomena come to be through what is called dependent arising. That is, all things come from prior existing causes. One physical phenomenon causes another which sets

up the conditions for another and so on. Because all phenomena come to be from prior conditions, they are empty.

Our preoccupation with conventional truth and sense experience distracts us from ultimate truth. Meditation and the practice
of mindfulness is a way of clearing the mind and eliminating distraction so that we may come to understand emptiness. It
requires directing ones thoughts and concentration until one can
increase the amount of time between thoughts and clear the
mind. This calm allows for deeper insights into reality. It is as
though the mind is, in actuality, a very deep pool. Perceptions,
desires, and ideas stir the water. As the water is stirred it becomes
murky. The practice of meditation shifts our attention away from
sensory experience to a more subtle truth. By training the mind
to shift attention away from external stimuli, the mind becomes
clearer. In that state we can perceive the greater truth. As in "Eyes
of the World," we come to see through the mind's eye.

Meditation on emptiness helps us abandon the false view of
the self and the sensations and desires that accompany it. The
self is really just a concentrated sphere of the action of karma.
Just as gravity causes a distortion of space, karma causes a distortion in the realm of experience. An accumulation of the
action of karma causes the five aggregates that we experience
as a self. Because there is no self, there is no "I" that is reading a book or listening to music; instead, this bundle of the five
aggregates is experiencing reading or listening to music.

The view that we are left with is much like a song. We
think of a musical composition as an entity, a thing, but really
it is a succession of instances of sound that have pitch and
timbre. One instance comes and goes and is succeeded by the
next. These successive instances come so quickly as to give
the song a sense of independent existence, but it is really a
construction of our experience. Buddhist philosophy sees all
existence much like that song. Our body, our surroundings,
and our thoughts are all just momentary manifestations of
karma. They are disjointed and disappear as quickly as they
come to be.

Analyzing Emptiness

The analogy of the flame is useful to help us get our minds
around the idea of emptiness, but it does not suffice as a philo-

sophical explanation. However, a more precise explanation of emptiness is problematic and the source of an extensive debate among and within the different schools of thought in Buddhism. Some schools interpret emptiness as applying only to certain types of things and hold that some things aren't empty at all; for example, there must be something unconditioned that carries karmic debt throughout various lives. Other schools hold that the dharmas, the karmic forces that create the universe and serve as the source for conventional beliefs, are unconditioned and arise independently and are thus not empty. Within Mahayana Buddhism, one of the central figures in this debate, Nagarjuna, attempts to show that emptiness is really the central teaching of the Buddha.

Mahayana Buddhism derives its name, which means greater vehicle, from the idea that nirvana should be achieved *en masse* rather than individually. Bodhisattvas, or Buddhas to be, vow to remain in the cycle of rebirth until all sentient beings pass into nirvana. Bodhisattvas have incredible spiritual powers and can choose their future incarnations.[8] One of the central images of Mahayana Buddhism is also found in "Eyes of the World":

> There comes a redeemer
> and he slowly, too, fades away
> There follows a wagon behind him
> that's loaded with clay
> and the seeds that were silent
> all burst into bloom and decay
> The night comes so quiet
> and it's close on the heels of the day.

The redeemer is a bodhisattva bringing all sentient beings to nirvana in a great wagon. Their karmic seeds burst into bloom and decay, extinguishing their karmic debt and ending the cycle of rebirth. The bodhisattva fades away into nirvana like the Buddha but does so more slowly, over the course of many incarnations.

---

[8] Tenzin Gyatso, the Fourteenth Dalai Lama, the incarnation of Avalokiteshvara, the Bodhisattva of Compassion, is perhaps the best known bodhisattva in the West.

Nagarjuna argues against those who take emptiness too far, as well as those who establish it as an ultimate truth. The first position undermines much of Buddhist thought because it can lead to nihilism, the denial of all truth and all values. The second position gives emptiness the status of an unconditioned or absolute truth. That view is self-contradictory, the equivalent of holding the position that all truths are empty except the assertion that all truths are empty. He tries to forge a middle path, which comes to be called the Madhyamaka, that holds on to the distinction between conventional and ultimate truths but doesn't assert that emptiness is *really* an ultimate truth. Nagarjuna argues that emptiness is an ultimate truth only in comparison to conventional truths. Its meaning, or truth, does not come from convention. But the idea of emptiness is empty as well. To hold on to emptiness as an absolute truth left for us by the Buddha, he warns, is to go very far astray from the path.

However, Nagarjuna adds as much to the difficulty of defining emptiness as he resolves, and the problem becomes a difficulty of interpreting Nagarjuna's philosophy. But perhaps the best interpretation is to use a Mahayana idea and view emptiness as an expedient means. They explain that the Buddha lived a long time and addressed many sorts of audiences. Centuries later, the sayings attributed to the Buddha, the Sutras, did not present one coherent picture. They held that the Sutras were tailored to the audience. Some Sutras are an expedient means to serve the needs of a particular audience and help them advance along the path towards enlightenment.

In this way, the belief in emptiness as an absolute truth is an expedient means to help us develop our understanding of ultimate truth. But this belief must be recognized as empty as one comes to a deeper understanding. Again relying on an analogy, the idea of emptiness as an expedient means to reach nirvana is compared to using a boat to cross a river. When one has reached the other side, the boat is no longer needed and is left behind. When enlightened, one no longer needs the doctrine of emptiness and shouldn't hold on to it. The analogy is often extended to say that when one looks back, one finds there was no boat, and there was no river. Viewed through the eyes of the Dead this is reflected in the lyrics from "Dupree's Diamond Blues":

Son, you'll never get far,
I'll tell you the reason if you want to know,
'cause child of mine,
there isn't really very far to go.

12

Blind Hope: Wharf Rat, Levinas, and the Face of August West

STEPHEN STERN

Faces

Here's my philosophical story, for now. I write a lot about faces and stories, which at first made writing about "Wharf Rat" ideal. August West has a story to tell. I wanted to listen, so that I could tell you a story about August West in relation to Emmanuel Levinas. But when I started writing, I felt strange. It seems strange to be writing about two faces I have never faced and perhaps stranger to write these faces into facing one another, Emmanuel Levinas and August West. And what about the faces of the Grateful Dead and your face that is reading this? There are lots of faces intersecting in this paper. However, I don't see anyone facing one another at this intersection. Nonetheless, in writing it I am introducing lots of faces to one another, figuratively speaking. (In fairness to me, I have faced the Grateful Dead. I've looked into all their faces many times. But I doubt they ever looked into my face while playing before me. Plus, we're not facing one another now.) Do you think its odd that I'm writing and introducing faces for so many who are faceless to me, to whom I am faceless, and are faceless to one another? I do. But that's my job. I am philosopher who defaces the very faces I emphasize. I de-face with the written word.

More often than not, the written word pulls me or takes me away from the face of the other, such as your face. Even if the written word introduces me or shows me the way to the other's face, the written word is still beyond facing the other. While writing or reading, I am not facing others' faces. Sometimes I

read out loud in front of groups, such as students. They're looking at me, but I'm not looking at them while reading. I guess I'm
trying to say that I have never faced anyone while reading or
writing. Although, I have faced others while reciting written
works. But that's not happening here. This is a philosophical
work in progress. It's not ready for recitation. I don't think I'd
ever want to recite it anyway.

Reciting philosophy for others normally isn't very entertaining
or engaging for the listener. I don't know about you, but I often
space out when people recite a long philosophical passage. It's
hard to focus. (I wonder if you're still even reading. I can't tell.
I'm writing.) Traditional philosophy often doesn't come with
faces and stories, even when it has a traditional narrative structure. And I find it easier to focus when someone is telling a good
story. I do feel engaged when I recite a philosophical passage,
but I'm not sure what's engaging me; the passage, the audience,
both? I don't know. But when reciting, I often find the audience
spacing out, not in the way I would at a "Dead" show. But in the
way the Peanuts characters spaced out when the teacher spoke.
Writing or reciting philosophy is nothing like the Grateful Dead
singing "Wharf Rat," or August West telling me his story.
Philosophy is not at its best when recited.

Philosophy is often best when read or discussed. I like philosophical discussion. Yet, philosophically, I often exile myself to
the written word, like right now, which isn't a real discussion
with the kind of give and take and unpredictability that comes
with a conversation or a good story. (For example, I normally
do not know the end of a discussion at the beginning of the
conversation. But when writing, such as in this piece, which you
are just beginning, I often know the ending in advance.)

This is a strange place to write, taking something unabstract,
like someone's story, and making it abstract. Here I am about
to take something oral, a song, which sings or plays the story
of August West, and use it to explicate themes from the notable
twentieth-century philosopher Emmanuel Levinas. I wonder if
am I committing violence against August West and to those
who play his story, not to mention Emmanuel Levinas, who
desperately tries to get us to look up from the text and see or
hear the other's face. On the other hand, by using Levinas,
August West is being introduced to those beyond the story
played by the Grateful Dead, and by using August West,

Levinas is being introduced to many beyond his philosophy. Whatever. If I'm committing violence by defacing these folks so as to introduce you to them, I'm not sure I really care. I'm listening to "Wharf Rat" as I write. That's my story. Let's start the introductions.

The Face of August West

Hi, that's "Wharf Rat." As you can see, he's sitting way down by the docks, where he is blind and dirty. He just asked the narrator for a dime.

Wharf rat down[1]
way down
down, down by the docks of the city,
Blind and dirty
asked me for a dime—
Dime for a cup of coffee
I got no dime but
I got time to hear his story.

Unfortunately, the narrator only has an ear to give. "Wharf Rat" would probably rather have the dime. I don't know about you, but when I'm really hungry, thirsty, and feeling rat-like, I'd rather first eat, drink, and then tell my story. But what can the guy do when he doesn't have a dime? The narrator seems to assume that offering an ear is the next best thing to a dime. Maybe. I'd like to hear his story, especially who named him "Wharf Rat."

Does the narrator name August West "Wharf Rat" or was it socially assigned to August West? I don't think August West would choose such a name, not because I don't like it. But he does not say he is "Wharf Rat," but August West. "My name is August West." So, who named him "Wharf Rat"? I don't know, but calling someone a "rat" sounds Nazi-like to me; this takes us to Emmanuel Levinas when he served four years in a Nazi concentration camp.

---

[1] The lyrics written by Robert Hunter begin "Wharf Rat down," although the line was most often sung by Jerry Garcia as "Old man down."

The Face of Emmanuel Levinas

The Nazis saw Levinas as a rat, not even rat, actually, but vermin. Rats where higher up on the Nazi caste structure, which means "Wharf rat" had more social rights than Emmanuel Levinas. Levinas was considered vermin by the Nazis and treated like vermin when he was in a Nazi prisoner-of-war camp for four years where sllave labor was performed. He was a French Jewish prisoner of war. And Nazi ideology designated the Jews as vermin. On the other hand, Levinas claims that his French uniform kept him out of a murder camp, such as Auschwitz. Nevertheless, p.o.w. labor slaves were not safe from being worked to death. August West, though, surely would have been gassed if he were a Jew. His blindness would have excluded him from a work detail. But compared to Levinas, West has some security. Levinas wasn't allowed to ask a passerby for dime. Asking for a dime would most likely have ended in Levinas's murder. In fact, those who passed him didn't even give an ear for his story. When a passerby's eyes gazed upon him, the eyes stripped Levinas of his human skin (Emmanuel Levinas, *Difficult Freedom*, pp. 152–53). But they do share some things, such as love from women.

More than My Wine, More than My Maker

In the midst of his rat-like existence, West has love, as did Levinas when he was vermin. West loves Pearly Baker best, more than his wine and more than his maker, which he claims is not his friend. I like that he claims his maker is no friend. What kind of maker would give creation a "Wharf Rat" existence? Not a friendly one. Yet, August West does not deny the existence of his maker, or God. Nor does he say he is not a friend to God, but that God is not friendly to him. Thus, West is with God, but this raises the question as to whether God is with him. It looks as if West finds God with him, but that God is not friendly to him. This is juxtaposed with Pearly Baker, who is not present, but has West's love and we later find that West believes that Baker is true to him. God, who may be present, is not friendly to him and Baker who is not present is true to West. Does Pearly Baker give West hope in the midst of his unfriendly God? Strangely, Levinas is in a similar bind.

Levinas loved his wife and daughter, yet they were not present for his four-year enslavement. But his love for them and hope that they were alive gave him hope. Perhaps this hope, which presupposes that his wife and daughter were true or committed to him, kept him going in his relations with his unfriendly God that was either eclipsed by the Nazis or not. Either way (from West's understanding of God) West provides us with insight for Levinas; some human commitments for one another may be more reliable than our understanding of God as friendly. (It's hard to imagine a friendly God in a Nazi Concentration Camp.)

For example, a family of five was murdered on a Florida interstate. The mother's last gesture was to clutch her two boys, to protect them, to love them and to hold them. In other words, her life ended in commitment for her boys. We might ask where the friendly God was as this family was executed. There's no certain answer. But what is certain is the mother's commitment to her children. Levinas, in contrast to West, might say that traces of God are found in the mother's commitment to her children, but are traces found when one is committed to one who is not present, such as a wife, or Pearly Baker? Or, is one merely blind to be so committed or to trust in the commitment of one who is not present? Perhaps, hope is found in West's blindness, for it blinds one to hopeless surroundings.

Brother Can You Spare a Dime?

West states that people said he would come to no good and that "Pearly believed *them*." Both West and Levinas did come to "no good." I don't mean socially speaking where others judge one's success, I mean personally. I don't know anyone who desires to live like a blind, "wharf rat," or vermin. The names imply living in filth. The names also raise the question of social responsibility and how come no one has more than a dime to help West move beyond the wharf? For example, when my students ask me how come most of the non-Nazi average Germans didn't do anything for the Jews, I ask them how come we're not doing anything for those who live in destitution within our midst? I wonder if someday our grandchildren will look at us in horror over the fate of those we allow to suffer. I suspect when most of us see someone like West, we look at him as the average German looked at Levinas in a slave labor camp. Levinas writes, ". . . the other men . . . who had dealings with us or gave us work or orders . . . and the children and women who passed by and sometimes raised their eyes—stripped us of our human skin. We were subhuman, a gang of apes" (*Freedom*, pp. 152–53). It's no wonder one might find hope in a lack of presence in such a circumstance. Certainly, one does not find it in one's present rat like existence. In such a place, one must, I imagine, turn to one's "estate of memory."[2] In this estate, West and Levinas find their future, which is built from the women in their past. In their past from which they hope for a future, we find their hope that they "come to good," not "no good," as others prophesized West's future.

Some Other Fucker's Crime

West is not responsible for a large part of his fate, but he responsible for becoming more than his fate. The part for which he's not responsible is when he had to pay for "some other fucker's crime." West doesn't tell us the crime. But like him, Levinas also pays for "some other fucker's crime." The crime is Nazi Germany and the silence of many of his neighbors—for which he paid, which raises this question. Aren't the "Wharf Rats" of the world paying for our silence and our aversion to "Wharf Rats," which is essentially to strip one (a "Wharf Rat") of one's human skin? The very name "Wharf Rat" is such a stripping of the other. It's no wonder that West spent the other half of his life "stumbling around drunk on burgundy wine."

West tells our narrator that one day "I'll get back on my feet . . . The good Lord willing, 'cause I know the life I'm livin's no good. I'll get a new start live [and] live the life I should." What does West mean by the life he should? Who is responsible for his life? In one respect it's West, in another respect it's us, the listeners to his story. West cannot tell us to take responsibility for his life. He could tell us, but what purpose would it serve? But his call to us, through the narrator relaying his story, immediately obligates us to him. In other words, the minute we hear West's call for a dime, we find ourselves responding to and for him. We are responsible. A question for us is: Why aren't we

---

[2] Here I am playing with the title of Ilona Karmel's Novel on the Holocaust, *An Estate of Memory.*

taking responsibility for those who suffer such misfortune? This doesn't mean we should all comb the wharfs for West like people, it means we need to continue to build better communal infrastructures so that the Wests of the world are helped to come out from under the wharf. Fortunately, our narrator takes some responsibility by showing him respect through listening to his story. As Levinas writes: "I am never absolved with respect to others" (*Outside the Subject,* p. 44). Without help, how does a blind person find their way out from under the wharf? Without help, how does a slave laborer liberate him or herself from bondage? We are often on our own—as are West and Levinas in their circumstances. But this fact does not necessarily absolve us from helping, being helpful or responsible.

Levinas explains that we do not choose our responsibility, although we may choose to exercise it. Another way to understand this is to replace the word 'responsibility' with the word 'helper' or 'helpful'. We do not choose when we are identified as a helper for another. For example, if a mother or father hears her or his child scream for help, or if you hear a stranger call out for help, the mother or father or you have been identified as a helper. You didn't choose this assignment, the other who calls for help chose you. Levinas writes: "To hear a voice speaking to you is *ipso facto* to accept obligation toward the one speaking. . . . Consciousness is the urgency of a destination leading to the other person and not an eternal return to self" (Emmanuel Levinas, *Nine Talmudic Readings,* p. 48).

In other words, for example, when a mother hears her baby cry for help, she finds herself obligated to the baby. The baby has assigned her this obligation. In fact, a mother becomes conscious of being a mother when she gives birth, when her baby is before her. She cannot be conscious of being a mother before having a baby, for she is not a mother. The identity of motherhood is a response to having a baby. It's upsetting when a mother does not accept this identity, such as when a mother rejects her baby and returns to herself (for example, when Susan Smith had her kids drowned in a lake) which helps contextualize the following question. The question for the one whom the other called is whether or not one will be helpful or walk away. The Germans who walked by Levinas walked away, just as many most likely walked away from "Wharf Rat" without even extending him an ear for his story. Those who walk away are free to walk away, but they may be accused of being self-centered or egotistical, so to speak.

The ego is not the author of the other's call for help, but one's ego often compels one to walk away from a call. In fact, without being called, we would be unable to discuss our egos, for the ego is realized or visible in one's response for the call, not the call itself. We might go so far as to say one's ego is born out of hearing the other's call. It would not make sense to speak of a person without children as having a parental ego. Another way of saying this is that we do not consciously walk by someone, ignore someone, or not respond to someone if we have not first been called by someone. We might go so far as to say that one's concern for oneself originates in the call from the other. When a parent hands his or her baby to the spouse who has just come home, we can imagine the one parent saying, "I just need some time for myself." In other words, "I need some space for myself where I am not taking hands on responsibility for our child." Concern for oneself is a type of response for the call of the other, like a baby whose very presence is a call for a parent to be responsible for its life. Concerning oneself with oneself is a response for the other, maybe a necessary response for the other and oneself. But to concern oneself with oneself is to step away from others who are demanding one's response, just like the parent who hands off his or her baby to the other parent. Levinas writes: "Responsibility for the creature—a being of which the ego was not the author—which establishes the ego. To be a self is to be responsible beyond what one has oneself done" (*Readings,* p. 49). This raises the question, Do we create ourselves out of our response to others?

I've Got Time to Hear His Story

The narrator of West's story strikes us a sensitive person. We come to this conclusion, because even though he does not have a dime for West, he gives West his time, time for West to tell his story. This provides West with community, maybe not the desired results of what a dime might bring, but certainly the narrator saves West from isolation. If the narrator just walked by, we would not think of him as being sensitive to West. But because he stops and listens, which is a response for West, we are able to conclude the narrator is a nice person. Listening is the narrator's way of taking responsibility for "Wharf Rat." And the minute the narrator starts to listen, we find that this man under the wharf is not a rat, but August West, just as when we read Levinas's account of his internment in a Nazi p.o.w. camp where slave labor was performed, Levinas ceases to be a sub-ape, becomes a human being. Treating West as a human, not a rat, is one way of helping West get on his feet and to fly away from out under the wharf. Before leaving West, the narrator reassures West that Pearly Buck has been true to him.

The narrator then gets up and walks away and becomes concerned for himself. He tell us,

> I got up and wandered
> Wandered downtown
> nowhere to go
> just to hang around
> I got a girl
> named Bonny Lee
> I know that girl's been true to me
> I know she's been
> I'm sure she's been
> true to me.

Through talking to West, we find the narrator comes face to face with his hope, that there is someone for him, someone who has been true to him, responsible for him, so to speak. Her name is Bobby Lee. Perhaps in such responsibility we find traces of God and a way to contest West's claim that God is not friendly to him.

Although God may not be a friend to West, the narrator is his friend. But then, what does West expect from God? God's presence in his life? Maybe, through our narrator's response for him, August West found traces of God's presence. Levinas writes: "The coming to mind of God is always linked, in my analyses, to the responsibility for the other person and all religious affectivity signifies in its concreteness a relation to others. . ." By listening to West's story from Levinas's understanding of God, perhaps West is introduced to friendly traces of God, which are not found in God's presence, but in a human gesture for another. In other words, our narrator gives the "Wharf Rat" community and from this we do not find a "Wharf Rat," but find ourselves face to face with August West. It's here that divine hope may be found, with the other, such as Pearly Buck and Bobby Lee, who liberates one from one's self, from isolation, so to speak. In the end, even if for a short moment, our narrator liberated August West from isolation. But for his life, it is Pearly Buck who liberates August West from himself and those of us who treat him like a wharf rat.

For Levinas, the war ended and he was reintroduced to and liberated from slave-like isolation by his wife, his daughter, and some of French society. Perhaps, I misspoke at the beginning of this chapter. I do not find that August West and Emmanuel Levinas have been defaced. Instead, I have responded to them and for you. In the intersections of this paper, we find ourselves communing. For this, I thank the Grateful Dead for introducing me to August West and, thus, revealing traces of divine hope.

13
Eyes of the World: Santayana's Ontology Set to Music

JESSICA WAHMAN

I first saw the connection between the American philosopher George Santayana and "Eyes of the World" back in graduate school when a summer day, a Dead bootleg, and a touch of serendipity all converged into philosophical inspiration. It was the late 1990s, and I was at the formidable "dissertation stage" of the process, barely getting by financially, totally unsure of my future in the profession, and having trouble writing. My project was on Santayana's naturalism, and I knew, intellectually, what I wanted to say, but otherwise I was just kind of stuck. What mattered in this highly technical project? To me, to my life, or to anyone? The question was immobilizing.

But I had, for the moment, been able to put all that aside. I was on my way back from the beach with my friend Steve, and it was one of those beautiful afternoons when you forget your troubles and burdens and just drive, not much caring where you're going. I had the second set of Nassau Coliseum '90 playing, with Jerry Garcia and guest artist Branford Marsalis trading phrases on guitar and saxophone. As we drove, a warm breeze wafted in through the open windows and blended with the lilting tones, bearing them gently back out into the world. Steve was a recent Dead convert, thanks to an excellent local cover band (and despite the fact that he had never seen the Dead perform themselves), and was listening intently to the songs, each of them new to him. As I chirped along, semi-consciously, he asked me the meaning of the lyrics.

"Eyes of the World? Heck if I know"

I had rarely given much thought to parsing an entire Robert Hunter tune; it seemed nearly impossible to do anyway, given Hunter's quixotic style. I instead tended to focus on isolated poignant phrases, like one of my favorites from "Scarlet Begonias": "Once in awhile you can get shown the light in the strangest of places if you look at it right!" (That one has carried me through more than one challenging scenario.) But now I had to really listen. It's often the case that, when we view an art form vicariously through the perspective of another, we find something new in what was all too familiar, and Steve's fresh ears were just the point of refraction I needed. Who knows whether it was in explaining the lyrics to my friend, or listening to them with my dissertation on a mental back-burner, but as I examined Hunter's words in this strange way I was indeed shown the light. "Steve!" I shouted, "I know this! This is Santayana's philosophy!"

Why had I never seen it before this moment? My interest in Santayana had the same roots as my love of the Grateful Dead. Each articulated a world I felt I inhabited: one paradoxically fatalistic and free; intensely spiritual and yet naturally grounded; friendly enough to animal life, but basically irrational and unconcerned with human progress. Santayana is relatively unknown today, and his outlook has always run contrary to the dominant forms of thinking in academic philosophy. I wrote (and continue to write) on Santayana's naturalism because his vision of reality resonates deeply with my own sensibilities and yet seems to be lacking in contemporary philosophical circles. I chose his work for my dissertation because I felt it was important to get his voice back into the mix. And here again, in Robert Hunter's lyrics, I had discovered that same voice. In "Eyes of the World" an awakened spirit is liberated to wander imaginatively, yet is tethered to its physical host and is thus but a part of the inevitable life-and-death cycle of nature. "Eyes" is a lyrical manifestation of Santayana's ontology—his understanding of reality and the place of subjective experience in the natural world—that at the same time illuminates a pervasive attitude expressed in the Dead's music and embraced by its fans.

What Do Those Lyrics Mean Anyway?

One of the reasons I tend to focus on isolated phrases is that the lyrics to Grateful Dead tunes can be so hard to figure out. Robert Hunter's, in particular, often seem more like a string of free associations than a coherent tale. Of course, this is one reason why the songs are so intriguing. Like a Freudian inkblot, Hunter's poetic imagery makes general suggestions to our unconscious minds, and what the words prompt is as varied as the individuals who listen to them. Not too surprisingly, then, in the foreword and afterword to *The Complete Annotated Grateful Dead Lyrics*, both Robert Hunter and John Barlow explain that their verses offer no singular meaning. In other words, neither lyricist is deliberately sending a message that one is supposed to "get" (David Dodd, *The Complete Annotated Grateful Dead Lyrics* [New York: Free Press, 2005]). The interpretations of the audience contribute as much to the meaning as do the words and music that inspire those associations.[1] In that light, I do not intend to claim that this is *the* meaning of "Eyes of the World," nor is it the only worldview to be found in the Dead's music or in the attitudes of Deadheads.

On the other hand, I can't draw just any conclusion I would like about what the songs mean. If I were to argue that "Eyes" is about the war in Iraq or nuclear proliferation, I would have my work cut out for me making connections. The music and lyrics, due to their specific content, suggest some feelings and ideas more than others. As a result, there is philosophical value in analyzing how they could, in this case, prompt me to see connections to Santayana's ontology. In short, there is a specific text to be interpreted, however rich it is in possibilities, and what follows is my explanation of what I discover to be objectively present in the work.

---

[1] The mutual contribution of artist and audience extends to the performances themselves. In our recent interview, Bob Weir explained that the music actually *happens* at a point of triangulation between the performers and the audience: "You know, assuming that the singer or singers are watching a movie when they're singing, and the people in the audience are watching a movie when they're listening, where that movie occurs is somewhere between them—that azimuth between the audience and the singer—and that's where the moment happens."

George Santayana's World

Before I delve into the hermeneutic possibilities of "Eyes," I will explain some of Santayana's ontology, for, as he once wrote, one "must study Santayanese as a special language" in order to make sense of his rhetoric.[2]

Naturalism, in philosophy, generally affirms that there is but one existing world, with nothing supernatural to account for. This is the world of our everyday experiences and also the subject matter of our sciences. Santayana is a naturalist in this sense, which is important to keep in mind when we consider that he carves reality into four different "realms of being": matter, essence, truth, and spirit. These four realms are not separate worlds nor separate kinds of things, but distinct aspects of a single world that he finds important to distinguish from one another.

Matter, to begin with, indicates the actual substance of all existence. This fundamental stuff, he claims, is not directly accessible to either our perception or comprehension; instead matter takes on a variety of forms by which we interpret it. These forms, often referred to by Santayana as nature's "garments," populate the realm of essence. They do not exist in a substantial sense, but they account for the fact that matter *appears*, or is given, to us in a variety of different ways. Essences, however, are not merely perceptual; they also account for our ability to think abstractly, as when a concept presents itself to our mind. We use these appearances to make sense out of the world when we are practically engaged in it, and they become the objects of our aesthetic pleasure during times of play and reverie. Some essences truly describe the world, while others do not (a unicorn might be an example of the latter, as would a square circle), and this distinguishes the realm of truth as a subset of the realm of essence.

The point that essences are the only objects that we can directly and consciously experience brings me to the fourth category, "spirit," Santayana's term for conscious awareness.

---

[2] George Santayana, *Letters of George Santayana, 1921–1927.* Book Three, Volume V of *The Works of George Santayana* (Cambridge, Massachusetts: MIT Press, 2002), pp. 118–19.

Santayana does not use "spirit" to indicate anything like a substantial soul or life force, only the actual "light of awareness" itself. This is the sense of consciousness referred to when we talk of losing, regaining, or being in an altered state of consciousness. It is a natural phenomenon that renders us aware of our surroundings. By contrast, Santayana reserves the term "psyche" for soul, by which he indicates the natural structure and habits of a living organism, including those aspects that give rise to consciousness. A human psyche is a wholly physical function, a general operating principle of the organism, and, like the rest of matter, is not something we can be directly aware of. As a result, spirit is a product of psyche but is far from identical with it.

You Are the Eyes of the World, But . . .

Wake up to find out that you are the eyes of the world
But the heart has its beaches, its homeland and thoughts of
    its own.

The chorus to "Eyes of the World" effectively presents the crux of Santayana's distinction between psyche and spirit. The "heart"—psyche or soul—is fully embedded in the material world and has its own agenda and interests, most of which never reach our awareness. Any organism, by virtue of being alive, has a psyche, an organizing function geared toward survival, self-maintenance, and reproduction. A psyche becomes sentient, or aware of its surroundings, only when it becomes a sufficiently complex kind of system. In an evolutionary sense, psyche is much older than spirit. Its habits are the result of eons of adaptation to surrounding conditions. At some point in evolutionary history consciousness emerges, and, for the first time, nature becomes aware of itself. Consciousness is, Santayana claims, nature's only witness. Spirit alone sees and is, therefore, the eyes of the world.

This unique vantage point has implications for subjective existence, whether we are talking about knowledge of the world or of ourselves. We awake into a world of visions, sounds, and other sensory wonders, but we are cut off from that direct organic connection with our origins. The alienation of spirit from nature is a condition that humans have long tried to address, not only in philosophy but religion and psychology as well.[3] Many of these accounts bemoan the connection that has been lost, and some offer attempts at reunion, at a oneness with the universe. But "Eyes" takes another approach, and in this way reflects Santayana's attitude as well. Garcia's playful melody does not mourn the separation between the heart and mind, between psyche and spirit, it celebrates it. This dual existence is the fundamental condition of human life, and there is joy to be found in its mysteries.

Winter's Summer Home (the Natural Cycles of the World)

There comes a redeemer and he slowly, too, fades away
And there follows his wagon behind him that's loaded with clay
And the seeds that were silent all burst into bloom and decay
And night comes so quiet, it's close on the heels of the day.

Santayana notes in one of his later essays that, due to our unique phenomenal vantage point and the caprices of nature, life is a carnival: vibrant, spontaneous, and comic. But it also is determined by material necessities—our bodily needs and physical laws—and is therefore inevitably limited. A recurring theme in Santayana's philosophy is the acceptance of mortality. Life, generally, is a cycle of growth, death, and renewal; when each season begins again, it also begins anew, creating new souls and discarding the old. A single life, therefore, is a passing appearance on the world stage, and each conscious spirit is but a brief illumination surrounded by long darkness.

The cycles of nature and the mortality of all living things is given special attention in the second verse of "Eyes of the World." The redeemer is likely a Christ figure, but he does not ensure salvation in the form of immortality. Fully and solely human, he has his historical moment and withdraws, dragging along his body—his "clay"—and dying with it. These lines are followed by images of genesis, blossoming, and destruction, the spark of a day in its ephemeral beauty, silently giving way to

---

[3] Existential alienation makes an appearance also in art, literature, poetry, drama, and so forth. Something so fundamental to the human condition cannot help but pop up in a wide variety of forms.

nightfall. Similarly, the span of our soul's existence is a summer habitation flanked on either side by the fundamentally inhospitable conditions of winter, and each life is an inevitably short but vibrant moment that ends in sleep.

If we know we're going to die, and we believe that nothing follows this eventuality—no heaven or hell, no reincarnation, no unity with a cosmic consciousness—the issue becomes what to do with the time that we are given. One possibility would be to immerse oneself in a greater historical project or utopian vision and thereby earn eternity as a momentary cog in a grand political system. But Santayana resists the temptations of immortality in any form and focuses his attention squarely on the value of the present life for its own sake. Once we recognize nature and its compelling rhythms as the ultimate source of our being, the most appropriate response—as any Deadhead could tell us—is to dance. As Santayana notes: "The art of life is to keep step with the celestial orchestra that beats the measure of our career and gives the cue for our exits and our entrances (Santayana, "Carnival," *Soliloquies in England and Later Soliloquies* [New York: Scribner's, 1922], p. 144).

Our mortality is a simple fact, neither tragic nor evil, and our lifetime, to the extent of our possibilities, is an interval for artistry. Living well means getting in tune with nature by piously heeding its commands and graciously embracing what is offered. Accepting our fate and honoring our parentage, we will do well if we enjoy the carnival while we are in town.

The Spiritual Life

Right outside this lazy summer home
You ain't got time to call your soul a critic, no.

Viewing nature as the appropriate object of our piety has significant connotations for spirituality, and no theme in Santayana's philosophy is more relevant to a comparison with "Eyes of the World" than his notion of the spiritual life. The phrase is a bit misleading, for Santayana denies that a spiritual attitude can constitute an entire life; it is more like the mind taking a holiday from everyday concerns. In *Realms of Being*, Santayana offers a description of the natural conditions of spiritual life that makes for a useful comparison with "Eyes." He notes:

> It is so simple to exist, to be what one is for no reason, to engulf
> all questions and answers in the rush of being that sustains them.
> Henceforth nature and spirit can play together like mother and
> child, each marvelously pleasant to the other, yet deeply unintelli-
> gible; for as she created him she knew not how, merely by smiling
> in her dreams, so in awaking and smiling back he somehow under-
> stands her; at least he is all the understanding she has of herself.
> (Santayana, *Realms of Being* [New York: Scribner's, 1942], p. xix)

Psyche, as a part of matter, is portrayed by Santayana as blind,
groping "her" way through the world. Consciousness, he
claims, was likely produced as an adaptation, a means for the
organism to focus its attention and to prepare for the future by
imagining alternative possibilities. And practically speaking, this
is what we do. But this adaptation produced an accidental and
beneficial phenomenon, the capacity for daydreams and for
wonder. Psyche's offspring, spirit, is thoroughly visionary.
Though we are tied to a specific time and place and limited by
our material conditions, our minds can wander to the farthest
reaches of the universe and the outer limits of logical possibility. In those times when we are able to put aside concern for
our physical and psychological needs, spirit can play freely in
the realm of essence.

As conscious beings we can take two different perspectives
toward the forms that we perceive. When our concerns are practical, we treat the objects of our awareness as instruments,
which we utilize for the purposes of making sense of our surroundings and getting things accomplished. In a basic sense,
when we need to pound in a nail, we don't concern ourselves
with whether or not a hammer is aesthetically pleasing. On the
other hand, we are always capable of stepping back and appreciating the world just as it presents itself to us. When we notice
a sunset, catch the smell of autumn leaves, or stop and listen to
the sound of crickets on a summer night, we are engaged in a
spiritual reflection on existence. In these moments, our relationship between ourselves and the world becomes one of play
instead of work. We aren't concerned with solving problems, we
aren't judging, we just *are*. And of course, the best season for
playing is summer. The weather is accommodating, or too hot
for labor, and nature is fully alive after spring's rebirth, offering
treats for all the senses. Our psyches can relax their critical vig-

ilance for the time being, and spirits are liberated to appreciate the passing moment. In the long lazy days of summer, our thoughts may be carried wherever our inclinations take us, borne on the wind like the wings of a nuthatch.

The spiritual life is not, however, limited to appreciating the pleasures of the passing moment. It is most fully realized, Santayana claims, in contemplative reflection on aesthetic forms, in other words, in engagement with works of art. These forms take on a variety of shapes—plastic, literary, musical—but each elevates and focuses our attention on some important *quality* of life, and in this way the arts can provide us with insight into ourselves and our situations. And I would suggest that no one knows this aspect of the spiritual life better than a Deadhead at a show. Everything from the parking lot scene to the concert itself amounts to a holiday from everyday existence, a celebration for all the senses, and an opportunity to appreciate life in the here and now. But above all, there is a bounteous play of essences at work in the artistry of the Grateful Dead.

There are a lot of reasons to go to a rock concert. Some music puts you in a certain mood—jubilant, enraged, energized, melancholy—and sometimes there's just a great beat to dance to. But at a Dead show, in addition to these qualities, there is significant attention to auditory form. Whether in the acoustic jams in the middle of each song or the more free-form experimentation of Drums and Space, the qualitative character of the sound is itself a primary focus of the music. The Grateful Dead played for over twenty-five years, and they endlessly repeated many of the same songs. Fans didn't enjoy this only because the songs were well-known. As with performances of jazz standards, the familiarity of the basic structure of the tune allows the audience to focus on what is *different* each time, on the nuances of the choices made by the musicians. In other words, it elevates our attention to the "shape" the music is taking.

And of course, no Dead show would be complete without the visual forms. In addition to the eye-catching bubbles, beach balls, and tie-dyes in the audience, even sound can take on visual characteristics when perception is altered and heightened, sometimes with the assistance of psychedelic substances. Tripping Deadheads have been known to say that they could *see* Jerry's notes flying off the fretboard. I don't believe one has to be "on" anything to enjoy even the visual aspects of a show; the music itself can put you into a highly sensitized perceptual state, even if it alone does not induce literal hallucinations. But it's no coincidence that the drugs of choice for Deadheads tend to be hallucinogens (mushrooms, LSD) rather than mood alterers like cocaine or heroin. These substances accentuate perceptual awareness and can spark insight (for good or ill) based on those perceptions.[4] Santayana might have seen such experimentation as an indulgence rather than an opportunity for contemplation. However, while the hedonistic aspects no doubt exist, I would argue that we miss the point if we see these experiences as mere debauchery.[5] A Grateful Dead concert is a carnival of forms, and we are invited join in the festival.

World Traveling

Sometimes we live no particular way but our own
And sometimes we visit your country and live in your home
Sometimes we ride on your horses, sometimes we walk alone
Sometimes the songs that we hear are just songs of our own.

During his life, Santayana traveled widely and resided in many different cultural climates. From his Spanish birth to his New England upbringing, his extended stays in England, Paris, and Rome, and a trip to the Middle East, he was very much a citizen of the world who appreciated the wealth of possible forms of human society. Yet at the same time, he seemed to himself always a visitor (he even titled part of his autobiography, *My Host, the World*) and felt at home, not in any specific geographical location, but in his own spiritual solitude. Santayana infused his general attitude toward life into his philosophy, and both his cosmopolitanism and detachment—themes expressed in these final lines of "Eyes of the World"—are evident throughout his work.

---

[4] Before it became illegal, LSD was used in psychotherapy, among other things, as a means of helping the patient tap into her unconscious mind. The practice was and is controversial, but there are still proponents of this therapeutic use of the drug.
[5] For a more detailed explanation of the balance between the intellectual and hedonistic aspects of a Dead show, see Chapter 5 in this volume.

In the preface to what is perhaps his most famous book, *Scepticism and Animal Faith*, Santayana remarks that his description of the universe is but one of many possible accounts, and that "it is foolish heat in a patriot to insist that only his native language is intelligible or right" (*Scepticism and Animal Faith* [New York: Dover, 1955], p. vi). Because, he claims, we can access material existence only by way of essences, all of our knowledge of nature is indirect and approximate. And because nature supports a wide variety of living beings, each with its unique perspective, the interpretations of existence will be as varied as those who perceive it. Santayana's ontology, therefore, is a portrait of his native landscape, which he composes both for his own self-knowledge and for others who may recognize the terrain. In giving this descriptive sort of account, he recognizes that there are many ways to make sense of the world and that others have a legitimate claim to their own views. He defends his position, but does not expect that his arguments should compel us to universal agreement; if someone disagrees, he says, "let him clean better, if he can, the windows of his soul" (pp. vi–vii). Those with whom his philosophy would resonate are spirits who can sympathize with his vision.

Ultimately, however, Santayana regarded each conscious spirit as being isolated and alone. If our sentiments about the universe do resonate with one another, it's not because they sound the same note but because they "*soliloquize in harmony*" (Santayana, "Cross-Lights," *Soliloquies in England*, p. 27). Each consciousness is a universe unto itself, experiencing the world in its own particular way. We can never directly access other people's private subjective states, but if they are feeling hospitable, they may share with us what life is like for them. The other person's home is never my own, but, as the last verses of "Eyes" suggest, I may be invited to visit, and the descriptions others give me of their sense of reality are the horses that carry my imagination off to explore these regions for myself. These are fortunate moments of friendship; much of the time, however, we walk a solitary path. But this needn't be cause for despair. We don't always have to agree or even to understand each other. Sometimes it's enough just to try to understand ourselves.

Santayana, the Grateful Dead, and
Self-Knowledge

In the end, the entire project of this essay has been a reflexive endeavor. By this, I mean that the common themes I have discovered in "Eyes of the World" and Santayana's ontology refer back to the very process of comparing them. In Robert Hunter and Santayana I discovered a sympathetic harmony of isolated subjects, and in my appreciation of the worlds that they inhabit, I resonate with both of them as well. Their words serve as promptings to my subconscious psyche, and the meanings that emerge are the aesthetic reflections that characterize the life of my spirit.

And in that original moment, that idle summer afternoon when inspiration sparked all these connections, I didn't just find out what Santayana and "Eyes of the World" had in common. In actuality, both acted as a mirror that illuminated to me something about myself. I then knew why I was writing on Santayana and why a Grateful Dead concert was, for me, a spiritual celebration. I saw my own lived experience in this panoply of essences springing from a deeply natural source and realized how this view helped me to find beauty in the varieties of life and rejuvenation in the fullest experience of the present moment. Comparing "Eyes of the World" and Santayana's philosophy became an opportunity for self-knowledge, helping me to clean the windows of my soul and understand a little of the song my heart was singing.

Set Two—What Shall We Say? Shall We Call It by a Name?

The Nature of Nature and Knowledge

14

Thoreau-ing Stones: Wildness at the End of the Natural World

ALLEN THOMPSON

"Throwing Stones" is first an unsettling song, evoking a sense that we sit on the very edge of catastrophe. As the status quo of corrupting socio-economic forces drives morally blind politicians to advance policies that mete out only injustices upon the undeserving, the song portrays a sense not only of great *human* tragedy but also a sense of an unspeakable *ecological* tragedy. The world is in chaos, it seems, and all will be consumed and destroyed, as we hear in the repeating chorus, "Ashes, ashes, all fall down . . . Ashes, ashes, all fall down . . ."

We find ourselves in a profoundly existential moment (for me this becomes clear when Bobby sings, "the future's here, we are it, we are on our own.") As we stare, perhaps enraged, into an apocalyptic future of political ineptitude and environmental disaster we may each ask ourselves, "Here we are. Now what can I do?" If you look around, there are many good answers to this question, things that each of us can do, things we *should* do, as informed consumers and citizens. (Check out, for example, *Worldchanging: A User's Guide for the Twenty-First Century*, by Alex Steffen [Abrams, 2006] or www.worldchanging.com.)

But there's another and still appropriate response, often unappreciated and overlooked, an embodied response to our existential moment: dance and dance wildly, becoming again (if only while the music plays) wild. At least this is the view I will defend, for "in wildness," says Henry David Thoreau, "is the preservation of the world."

Environmental, Political or Apolitical?

In 1982, when Barlow and Weir were writing "Throwing Stones," the notion that human beings could be responsible for bringing about what is effectively a permanent change to the Earth's basic atmospheric conditions was only speculative and, in fact, quite an incredible idea. People in the ecological movement (one of the many social movements born in the 1960s) had worked hard to focus the public's attention on a handful of crucial environmental problems, including chemical pollution, nuclear weapons and power, acid rain, ozone depletion, and deforestation. What appeared to be the most pressing environmental concern by the early 1980s was the loss of species and wilderness areas—generally, the loss of global biodiversity.

Not until the late 1980s did the possibility that human beings could be responsible for global warming begin to be taken seriously. (Perhaps this came with the testimony on June 23rd 1988 before the Senate Committee on Energy and Natural Resources by the director of NASA's Goddard Institute, James Hansen, who stated that he was ninety-nine percent certain global warming was already under way.) Of course, all that has changed. Today there is an overwhelming scientific consensus that global warming is very real, very dangerous, and largely anthropogenic (caused by human beings). Hansen's most recent assessment is that we have less than ten years before we pass a point of no return (James Hansen, "The Threat to the Planet," *New York Review of Books*, July 13th, 2006). This is not a problem for future generations. The future's here, we are it, we are on our own.

The issues of species loss, deforestation, and global warming had barely been pulled apart when the Grateful Dead held a press conference on September 14th 1988 to announce that they were on a campaign to help save the world's tropical rainforests. Proceeds from a benefit concert at Madison Square Garden (9/24/88) would be donated to three environmental groups the band admired for their direct action: Greenpeace, Cultural Survival, and the Rainforest Action Network.

During the press conference, the boys were asked specifically about environmentalism and the lyrics of "Throwing Stones." In a characteristic wisecrack, Jerry cuts off the question and says to Bobby, "See, you never should have written that song. Our one political song!" (Bobby replies, "It's not political!

It's apolitical!"—a claim I will return to later.) The question continues, "There's a song called Throwing Stones. Does that have anything to do with your environmental consciousness?" To which Weir replies, "Not really. That's just barely articulated rage at the way things are going in general." (Garcia: "This is just the beginning of our series of gripe, y'know.")

But there's a very reasonable idea, discussed in certain schools of literary criticism and by post-modernist philosophers, that the acknowledged intentions of an author or artist cannot possibly exhaust meaningful interpretation of their work (see Roland Barthes, "The Death of the Author" in *Image Music Text* [New York: Hill and Wang, 1977], pp. 142–48). And Bobby didn't write the lyrics of "Throwing Stones" alone, anyway. What might John Barlow say?

In any case, the position I defend is that "Throwing Stones" expresses the feeling of an existential crisis that many environmentally conscious people today experience in the face of anthropogenic global warming. Further, I believe that "Throwing Stones" can be interpreted in such a way as to articulate one appropriate moral response to the threat of an environmental catastrophe that is well beyond the moral responsibility of any one person. On my view, this response is intellectually rooted in ideas of the American naturalist Henry David Thoreau, the work of beat poet and bio-regionalist Gary Snyder, and a particular version of the environmental philosophy known as deep ecology. This response, I claim, can be found not only in the lyrics of "Throwing Stones" but also embodied in the music of the Grateful Dead itself and, perhaps most importantly, in the physical response of Deadheads to that music, that is to say, in our dancing.[1]

Home for You and Me

Picture a bright blue ball just spinning, spinning free,
Dizzy with eternity.
Paint it with a skin of sky, brush in some clouds and sea,
Call it home for you and me.

---

[1] "We started out playing for dancers in the ballrooms of San Francisco in the late 1960s. And that's really what we've always thought of ourselves as, as a—essentially a dance band" (Phil Lesh, interview with Carson Tucker, May 2005).

According to the best estimates of our natural sciences, the Earth is about four and a half billion years old and the first forms of life appeared about three billion years ago. Then, about one billion years ago, multi-cellular organisms began to fill the seas eventually evolving into more than ten million different species of living things, including human beings, that is, you and me. The first traces of modern human beings date as far back as ninety thousand years ago. So, just to gain a little perspective, this means that modern human beings have been around for only about 0.002% of the history of Earth and for only 0.003% of the history of all life on Earth. The ancient Greek culture that produced those pillars of Western philosophy, Plato and Aristotle, was integrated into what would later become the Roman Empire about twenty-two hundred years ago. Then Christopher Columbus "discovered" America about five hundred years ago.

If we date the Industrial Revolution to 1850 (actually, this dates the start of what's often called the Second Industrial Revolution), then with the use of external and internal combustion engines we can locate the beginning of widespread consumption of fossil fuels, the practice that powered the creation of our modern world, about one hundred fifty-seven years ago. Since that time, carbon dioxide has been pouring out of tail pipes and power plants and into the Earth's atmosphere at an ever-increasing rate. (Consider also, just for fun, it was a mere sixty-four years ago that LSD was discovered and only forty-two years ago that the Grateful Dead was formed.) With the ability to convert what remains of the dinosaurs into a cheap and apparently endless supply of energy, economies of the northern industrialized nations began to soar, along with atmospheric concentrations of carbon dioxide and other greenhouse gases.

Although predictive models vary, there is wide consensus that human-induced global warming is very likely to bring tremendous change to life as we know it. First, global warming almost undoubtedly will result in a significant amount of human suffering and injustice. If something drastic is not done soon to curb greenhouse gas emissions, warmer oceans and melting ice sheets will cause sea levels to rise dramatically enough to flood coastal cities worldwide, displacing hundreds of millions of people and upsetting the social and economic structures that otherwise would be called upon to help mitigate the suffering. As isotherms migrate toward the poles, tropical diseases like malaria will plague societies completely unaccustomed and unequipped to deal with them. Recently, top British climate scientists predicted that by 2100, one-third of the planet's land surface might be affected by extreme drought rendering agriculture virtually impossible—compared to between one and three percent today (Michael McCarthy, "The Century of Drought," *The Independent*, October 4th, 2006). And if temperatures rise enough to trigger various positive feedback loops, such as melting frozen methane hydrates, then, in the words of NASA scientist James Hansen, "all bets are off."

Further, if we grant what many environmentalists hold, that species and ecosystems are morally considerable for their own sake (and not just as a resource for human beings), anthropogenic global warming obviously is morally objectionable. Current predictions regarding worldwide loss of plant and animal species due to climate change range from twenty to sixty percent, due largely to the loss of habitat. This is a loss of global biodiversity simply unprecedented since the last mass extinction, which occurred between the Paleocene and the Eocene epochs, about fifty-five million years ago. During the entire history of life on Earth there have been at least five mass extinctions. It is widely believed that we are now in the sixth and the only one caused by the activity of human beings. The impending loss of so many forms of life, the loss of so many irreplaceable ecosystems, and of course the concomitant sum of human suffering and injustice all add up to provide good reason for believing that anthropogenic global warming is an impending moral tragedy.

However, many environmentalists share yet another intuition of moral horror at the prospect of global warming. In addition to the obvious evils discussed above it seems as though something *even more* is at stake, that we're not only facing destruction *in* the world, but we're facing destruction *of* the world. Not unlike the threat of nuclear holocaust during the Cold War, global warming has aroused profound concerns about the future of humanity and the planet as a whole. Indeed, environmental writer Bill McKibben has argued that anthropogenic climate change is tantamount to the very *end of nature* (Bill McKibben, *The End of Nature* [New York: Anchor Books, 1989]).

The End of Nature

A peaceful place or so it looks from space,
A closer look reveals the human race.
Full of hope, full of grace, is the human face,
But afraid we may lay our home to waste.

It's a provocative idea, that global warming is the end of nature. Today we face the possibility that the environment will be destroyed, but no individual will be responsible. Yet it's difficult to think clearly about the threat posed by global warming. The moral philosopher Dale Jamieson has claimed that the dominant system of values in western society leaves us feeling confused when we try to think about the ethical issues connected with global warming (Jamieson, "Ethics, Public Policy, and Global Warming," *Science, Technology, and Human Values.* 17:2, pp. 139–153). But putting ethical issues aside for a moment, I wonder what we mean when we say that global warming will destroy the natural environment? What *is* the end of nature?

It's common to think of nature as everything that is not a human being or not made by human beings. In this sense, the meaning of "nature," as in "the natural world," just is the world independent of human beings. McKibben's idea is that global warming is causing the end of this world; anthropogenic global warming amounts to very the end of nature. His argument is not complex: "We have changed the atmosphere, and thus we are changing the weather. By changing the weather we make every spot on Earth man-made and artificial. We have deprived nature of its independence, and that is fatal to its meaning. Nature's independence *is* its meaning; without it there is nothing but us" (*End of Nature*, p. 58). Because of human intervention, largely through the burning of fossil fuels for energy, nothing in the natural world is as it would be without human activity. So everything has, in a certain sense, become an artifact. Nature has literally been destroyed and we now live, McKibben claims, in a post-natural world (*End of Nature*, p. 60).

However plausible this argument may sound, the force of McKibben's conclusion is not clear. What could it mean to say we have come to the end of nature? In a leading journal of the field, *Environmental Ethics*, Steven Vogel offered what appears to be a decisive criticism of McKibben's argument (or, at least the straightforward reading of it). Are human beings natural or not? The transformations that *other* living organisms effect upon the natural world do not destroy nature because other organisms are a *part* of nature. In McKibben's view, only *human* activity can destroy nature because human beings are precisely *not* part of nature. Vogel rightly identifies that in order to get his thesis off the ground, McKibben must be read as a metaphysical dualist, advancing the view that human beings simply do not exist as a part of the natural world (Steven Vogel "Environmental Philosophy After the End of Nature," *Environmental Ethics* 24 [2002], pp. 22–24).

But this leads to the unpalatable implication that human beings are somehow *outside* of nature; we are in some sense *super*natural. This is a position at odds with both how most environmentalists would like to think about a human-nature relationship and the framework of scientific naturalism, the dominant worldview that currently maintains, for example, that human beings are the product of a natural process of biological evolution. As a result, either McKibben's position implies an implausible metaphysical thesis or depends upon equivocating over the meaning of "nature." "The problem," Vogel writes, "is that neither meaning allows us to distinguish between those human actions that 'violate' nature and those that are in some way in 'harmony' with it: either we violate it *all the time* or violations of it are *logically impossible*" (*Environmental Philosophy*, p. 27).

So when McKibben claims baldly that human-induced climate change has brought about the end of nature, his argument appears to face an insurmountable problem. Human beings can't bring about the end of nature unless we are somehow supernatural. On the other hand, if human beings are a part of nature, then it is no more possible for us to bring about the end of nature than it would be for dolphins, say, or mice to bring about the end of nature. Which is to say it's impossible. Although his argument may not be philosophically sophisticated, McKibben's intuition of moral horror about global warming is good—even if anthropogenic global warming is not *actually* the end of nature, it still does *feel as though we are responsible* for the end of nature. This produces a horrible feeling of fear. But what, exactly, are we afraid of?

An Ordering of Impermanence

There's a fear down here we can't forget,
Hasn't got a name just yet.
Always awake, always around,
Singing ashes, ashes all fall down.[2]

Suppose we tried to understand McKibben's claim about the end of nature another way—we are not causing the end of the *world of nature*, but we may be bringing about the end of *wild* nature. In two well-known essays, "Walking" and "Wild Apples," Thoreau articulated a distinction between nature as wild and self-willed on one hand, and the civilizing tendencies of human domination on the other. (*The Essays of Henry D. Thoreau* [New York: North Point, 2002]). No one has done more to develop or apply this distinction than Gary Snyder, in his collection of essays called *The Practice of the Wild* (San Francisco: North Point, 1990). While Snyder's able discussion ranges over many provocative ideas, his basic drive is toward a reframing of the current environmental crisis. He urges us to abandon thinking about environmental problems in terms of pristine nature versus destructive human beings and to begin moving toward finding resolution to the dichotomy between *civilization* and the *wild*.

Recasting the environmental problem this way puts it right where it belongs, at the center of our own being. *Wild* nature is not, by definition, the non-human. Rather, it is the whole natural world, including humans. "The world is nature, and in the long run inevitably wild," Snyder writes, because the wild, what he describes as that mysterious "ordering of impermanence," is the very "process and essence of nature" (*Practice of the Wild*, p. 5). Humans, too, are a part of this process and thus participate in, by belonging to, a wild nature. Although this fact is something we can too easily forget, as we sit in front of our computer or

---

[2] In a phone interview with Steve Gimbel and Jessica Wahman conducted for this volume (November 30th, 2006), Weir addressed the meaning of the refrain, "Ashes, ashes, all fall down." "Well," says Weir, ". . . of course that's the nursery rhyme that the kids sing that was all about the plague, and it's just a cautionary inference that there is, you know, there *may be* a dark side to these festivities." Although the audio is unclear, Weir seems to assent to the suggestion that "the kids they dance and shake their bones" refers to people in the audience dancing and enjoying the show.

TV screen or behind the wheel of our SUV at the drive-up window, it's something we need to remember.

What does "wild" mean here? "*Wild*," Snyder tells us, "is largely defined in our dictionaries by what—from a [civilized] human standpoint—it is not," (*Practice of the Wild*, pp. 10ff). Consider entries from the *Oxford English Dictionary*:

> Of animals—not tame, undomesticated, unruly.
> Of plants—not cultivated.
> Of land—uninhabited, uncultivated.
> Of food crops—produced or yielded without cultivation.
> Of societies—uncivilized, rude, resisting constituted government.
> Of individuals—unrestrained, insubordinate, licentious, dissolute, loose.
> Of behavior—violent, destructive, cruel, unruly.
> Of behavior—artless, free, spontaneous.

"But it [the *wild*] cannot be seen by this approach for what it *is*." So Snyder turns it around:

> Of animals—free agents, each with its own endowments, living with natural systems.
> Of plants—self-propagating, self-maintaining, flourishing in accord with innate qualities.
> Of land—a place where the original and potential vegetation and fauna are intact and in full interaction and the landforms are entirely the result of non-human forces. Pristine.
> Of food crops—food supplies made available and sustainable by the natural excess and exuberance of wild plants in their growth and in the production of quantities of fruit and seeds.
> Of societies—societies whose order has grown from within and is maintained by the force of consensus and custom rather than explicit legislation. Primary cultures, which consider themselves the original and eternal inhabitants of their territory. Societies which resist economic and political domination by civilization. Societies whose economic system is in a close and sustainable relation to the local ecosystem.
> Of individuals—following local custom, style, and etiquette without concern for the standards of the metropolis or nearest trading post. Unintimidated, self-reliant, independent.
> Of behavior—fiercely resisting any oppression, confinement, or exploitation. Far-out, outrageous, "bad," admirable.
> Of behavior—artless, free, spontaneous, unconditioned. Expressive, physical, open, sexual, ecstatic.

The wild, in this sense, is not unlike the *Tao* in Chinese philosophy, that "absolute principle underlying the universe, combining within itself the principles of yin and yang and signifying the way, or code of behavior, that is in harmony with the natural order" (*Oxford American Dictionary*). The wild is not a proper object for scientific study but it is no less a part of the natural world. Indeed, Snyder has called the wild the very essence of nature.

So where are we? We are now in a position to see environmental problems, including global warming, as the product of too much human civilization. And what this diagnosis calls for is a re-wilding, a re-embracing of the wild that is—and always has been—within us. Now consider again the descriptions above, particularly Snyder's own positive characterizations of wild societies, wild individuals, and wild behaviors. Doesn't this strike you, dear reader, as a fitting account of the people, the culture, and the spirit surrounding the Grateful Dead? Ask yourself: from the band itself ("a band beyond description"), including their music, their organization, and their community and crew, from those early days in Haight-Ashbury to the legion of Deadheads (both your friends and mine), from the traveling carnival of "fireworks, calliopes, and clowns" in the parking lot to the dancers in the hallways, from that fateful day the bus came by and you got on . . . hasn't it all been directed simply at being *wild*? Isn't this your *modus operandi* as a Deadhead and why you love the Dead? It's the American dream and the last great adventure, wild and free.[3]

Dizzy with the Possibilities

If the game is lost, then we're all the same,
No one left to place or take the blame,
We can leave this place an empty stone,
Or that shining ball of blue we used to call our home.

---

[3] "I think [all of us in the band thought of Deadheads going on tour] as the last great American adventure. You can't hitchhike or run away with the circus or ride the rails anymore. Going on tour with the band, any band, really, is an adventure. There's a little uncertainty, a little danger. Generally it's a safe environment and you can extend yourself. You can explore other realities and still come back and tell the tale the next day" (Phil Lesh, interview with Carson Tucker, May 2005).

And the politicians throwin' stones
So the kids they dance and shake their bones,
And it's all too clear we're on our own,
Singing ashes, ashes, all fall down,
Ashes, ashes, all fall down.

When the environmental crisis is understood as resulting from
the fact that civilization has long been on a collision course with
wild nature, then re-identifying ourselves as wild can only be the
first step. When Thoreau says, "Give me a wildness that no civilization can endure," Snyder replies that, "It is harder to imagine
a civilization that wildness can endure, yet this is just what we
must try to do" (*Practice of the Wild*, p. 6). Reconnecting with the
wild inside ourselves—recognizing that we are as wild as anything—allows us to begin reconnecting to a *wild whole* (echoing
here the notion of "whole" implicit throughout many works of
Romantic poetry, see especially Wordsworth's "Lines Composed
a Few Miles Above Tintern Abbey" and Shelley's "Ode to the
West Wind"). This whole, of course, includes both the whole of
our human community and the whole of the natural world.
Resolving the dichotomy between civilization and wild nature
may *begin* with our wild selves but it cannot end there. We must
also reform our civilization, first by reconnecting to our earthly
humanity and then by eco-logically reconnecting a truly humane
society with the whole wild world of nature.[4]

Our current form of civilization is neither truly humane nor
ecological. Public policy regarding natural resources and
entrenched economic practices (such as not having to pay at the
pump for the cost of pollution) helped create the environmental crisis, but strong political resolve and real leadership will be
required if we are to avoid the worst. Social, economic, and
political pressures drive human activity, "commissars and pin-
strip bosses roll the dice. Any way they fall guess who gets to
pay the price? Money green or proletarian gray, selling guns [or
cars, communism, or consumerism . . .] 'stead of food today."

---

[4] See *The Ecological Life: Discovering Citizenship and a Sense of Humanity* (Lanham:
Rowman and Littlefield, 2006) where Jeremy Bendik-Keymer vigorously develops the
idea that when we are true to ourselves (what he calls our "sense of humanity") we will
find that already we are much "greener than we think." I am indebted to Bendik-Keymer
(personal correspondence) for the references to Wordsworth and Shelley.

Weir and Barlow recognized there is a political monster behind the curtain. This, in fact, is the object of their rage. But "Throwing Stones" is not a polemic issued from one side of the isle, aimed against another political party. As Bobby insisted, "Throwing Stones" is not a political song but an a-political song. It's about the evils of contemporary political practices, a polemic against any heartless powers trying to tell us what to think and leading us to lay our home to waste.[5] In addition to articulated rage about an inhumane political reality, I have tried to suggest the song is also about confronting a special kind of anxiety, an existential fear in front of global catastrophe.

So just what is that "fear down here we can't forget" that "hasn't got a name just yet?" For all previous human history, the non-human, wild world of nature provided the background conditions of our lives, largely environmental conditions over which we have had no control and for which we certainly bore no responsibility. Hurricanes, droughts, and the like were simply natural disasters or, for some, acts of God. Now we know that the fundamental conditions of the biosphere are something that, collectively, we *are* responsible for. I believe that part of our intuition of moral horror—that still unaccounted for fear we feel about changing the global climate—is an existential angst connected with the psychological burden of this responsibility. We valued *not* being responsible for conditions of the natural environment, and we have lost what we valued. Our anxiety, I believe, is over our loss of innocence. "The future's here, we are it, we are on our own. . . . So the kids they dance to shake their bones while the politicians throwin' stones, for it's all too clear we're on our own, singing ashes, ashes, all fall down."

Now I want to bring it all around. Of course, we can't undo the past. We find ourselves in a polluted world and recognize that we are collectively responsible for some of the most basic conditions of the biosphere, the conditions supporting all life

---

[5] In the interview with Gimbel and Wahman (November 30th, 2006), Bob Weir offered his understanding of the lines, "Heartless powers try to tell us what to think. If the spirit's sleeping, then the flesh is ink." "You know, basically," Weir said, "if the spirit's sleeping, then the flesh is *history*. What you've done, or not done, counts." This view is consistent with the idea that in the face of an accelerating environmental crisis, we may be equally responsible for what we do *and* for what we could, but fail, to prevent. See Allen Thompson, "Environmentalism, Moral Responsibility, and the Doctrine of Doing and Allowing," *Ethics, Place, and Environment* 9:3 (October 2006), pp. 269–278.

on Earth, our home. And there is nothing any one of us alone can do about it. This is our lot in life, the Earthly conditions during our time in existence. We need to enact good environmental policy, we need to be good environmental citizens, and so we need a fitting environmental philosophy. My view is that the right environmental philosophy will be fecund not only in regard to guiding public policy but also in the realm of personal psychology—inside, where we are able find our lives meaningful.

Although not without its detractors, deep ecology is an environmental philosophy about a fundamental transformation (or perhaps re-discovery) of the self. The version of deep ecology I have traced here has its intellectual roots in the work of Thoreau and Gary Snyder. At the center is a project of re-identifying oneself as *wild in nature.* At the end of the day, however, this is not merely an intellectual exercise. Rather, it is a lived experience of one's whole being, body and soul. Remember that you are, *you are,* an embodied animal—a small part of nature—and thus your mind-body is essentially *wild.*

So we can't go to the shows anymore (not *those* shows, anyway), with the roar of an ecstatic crowd and the amplified hiss of live psychedelic music being just *laid out* across the concert lawn, seeping through the hallways full of dancers, freaks, and friends. No, now we must face our future. So, please, I implore you: begin again today. Dig out your favorite old bootleg and clear away some furniture. Just crank up the boys, yep, really crank it up! Now DANCE and again become wild.

15

Mama Tried: Biological Determinism and the Nature-Nurture Distinction

CHUCK WARD

Fathers are usually giddy with optimism about their children's future when those children are infants. They see only golden promise. But consider the case described in the Grateful Dead song "Mississippi Half-Step Uptown Toodleloo":

> On the day that I was born
> Daddy sat down and cried
> I had the mark just as plain as day
> which could not be denied.

The song tells the story of a rambling, gambling man, and we clearly see the idea that the man's character was fixed from birth. It was clear to the guy's father—it could not be denied— that this kid was no good! How can that be? How can the fate and character of a person be fixed from birth? Don't we choose our destiny? Can't we work out the path of our life and work on the kind of person we become?

Do We Choose Who and What to Be?

It is, of course, an obvious fact that we make choices. We make mundane choices all day long: what to have for breakfast, what record to play, whether to plant petunias or mums in the window box. Occasionally we make choices that have pretty significant effects on the course of our lives: what major to pursue in school, whether to take the job offer and move the family across the country, whether to quit the job and follow the Dead on their next tour. We choose, but where do our choices come from? An answer that may seem obvious is: my choices come from me! I think about my options and choose the one that seems best to me. While this may seem like a simple and obvious way to close the issue, we have to remember that our choices can be influenced by other people too. In fact our tendencies to choose certain things have been shaped to some degree, maybe a large degree, by our upbringing.

The ancient Greek philosopher Aristotle wrote about these issues. Our choices, he said (in his book entitled *Nichomachean Ethics*) flow from our character. But our character is determined by our past choices. Making good (or bad) choices is a matter of habit. That's why children must be guided, even bribed through offers of reward and threats of punishment. If the family and community can succeed in developing good habits of thought in the child, then that person will go on to make good unbribed individual choices in the future.

But even if our character is subject to the influence of family and community, the shaping of character is no easy or automatic process. In "Mama Tried" the Grateful Dead (covering a song by Merle Haggard) told the story of a "bad seed."

> Was the only rebel child from a family meek and mild
> Mama seemed to know what lay in store
> In spite of all my Sunday learnin'
> For the bad I kept on turnin' and mama couldn't hold me
>   anymore.

> And I turned twenty-one in prison, doin' life without parole
> No one could steer me right, but mama tried, mama tried
> Mama tried to raise me better, but her pleadin' I denied
> That leaves no one but me to blame cause mama tried.

Even as a child his mother could see that trouble lay ahead. Despite this she tried to raise him to be a good person. She took him to Sunday school. She pleaded with him to make good choices. But he resisted. The lyrics suggest that no one could keep this character from going bad. By the time he turns twenty-one he is serving a life sentence in prison.

The character seems to recognize that he is himself to blame for his plight. But it is also suggested that the outcome was destined from the beginning. "Mama seemed to know what lay in store." Perhaps, like the rambler in "Mississippi Half-step Uptown Toodleloo," there was some built in tendency toward bad behavior in this person.

Signs of Things to Come

It's not uncommon to see such characters described as fated to that kind of life from the beginning. And "occult" devices such as Robert Hunter's mysterious 'mark' from "Mississippi Half-Step Uptown Toodleloo" ("I had the mark just as plain as day") have a long history in American roots music. Consider, for example, the Willie Dixon lyrics from that Muddy Waters blues classic "Hoochie Coochie Man" which tells about how a gypsy and a mysterious doctor (one of seven) foretold the character of a man before he was born.

But compare this lyrical device to the Allman Brothers' song "Rambling Man" that tells of a rambler who is the son of a rambling, gambling man that was shot for his indiscretion.

> My father was a gambler down in Georgia, Wound up on the
>   wrong side of a gun
> I was born in a Greyhound bus, Rolling down Highway 41
> Lord I was born a ramblin' man . . .

The rambling ways of this man seem also to be inborn, but in this case the character of the man may be inherited from the ill-fated father. Parental inheritance is a very different lyrical device than Robert Hunter's 'mark' from "Mississippi Half-Step Uptown Toodleloo."

Biology as Fate

The general idea that a person's basic character and personality might be subject to inheritance has very old origins. The ancient Greek philosopher Plato, while recognizing that exceptions do occur, said that there's a tendency for character traits and cognitive abilities to be passed on from parents to offspring. In the last one hundred and fifty years (beginning with the work of Gregor Mendel, Charles Darwin, and others) our understanding of inheritance in general has achieved a much higher degree of scientific sophistication. Throughout that history there have been attempts to apply our knowledge of genetics to the problem of psychological and behavioral characteristics. However, when a purely biological explanation of psychology or behavior is offered there will inevitably be counterarguments to the effect that, when it comes to psychology, environment plays a deciding role—especially the social environment. These contrary explanations form the debates over whether nature (biology) or nurture (social environment) determines a person's psychological makeup.

We often see claims in the media that scientists have found the gene for alcoholism, or the gene for homosexuality, or the gene for this or the gene for that. A few years ago, then President of Harvard University, Lawrence H. Summers, triggered a brouhaha when he suggested that innate differences in the brains of the sexes might explain why there has been fewer women of achievement, as compared to men, in mathematics, science and engineering. Back in the 1990s Richard J. Herrnstein and Charles Murray, a psychologist and political scientist respectively, created a great controversy with their book entitled *The Bell Curve*. In it they argued that (a) IQ (a measurement of intelligence) is a good predictor of the socio-economic status a person will achieve; (b) IQ is at least in part determined by genetic factors; and (c) there are real (biological, genetic) differences between the races that may explain differences in measured IQ. The conclusions that Herrnstein and Murray drew in *The Bell Curve* have been hotly debated by psychologists, biologists and social policy experts ever since.

Even more recently (and perhaps more pertinent to our rambling character from "Mississippi Half-step Uptown Toodleloo" and our convict from "Mama Tried") there has been a lot of discussion of the possibility for genetic predispositions toward violence and criminality. Some people are, so the argument goes, genetically predisposed to become criminals. The language is usually cautious. To say that someone is genetically predisposed toward criminality is not to claim that they will become a criminal for sure. Rather it is a claim that they are more likely to become one. Everyone recognizes that certain environmental factors can contribute to whether such a person actually becomes a criminal or not and that genes are one (sort of) causal factor among others. But we can say that if we look at a large population of folks, those other factors (family structure, socio-economic conditions, education, and the list goes on) will be distributed similarly among any subgroup you pick out, so we can zero in on the genetic factors. In such a population those with the "criminality gene" (one subgroup) actually become criminals at a higher rate than those without it (a different and mutually exclusive subgroup). The explanation for the difference between the groups is, of course, the genes.

Another important technique in the field of behavioral genetics is twin studies. In a recent review of the methodological and philosophical issues in this field, Erik Parens wrote a nice summary of the logic behind the most typical application of this technique.

> First, behavioral geneticists posit the fact that identical twins are 100 percent genetically similar and fraternal twins are on average only 50 percent genetically similar. Second, they make the crucial assumption that the environmental conditions for identical twins in the same home are as similar as they are for fraternal twins raised in the same home. Given that fact and assumption, they infer that the extent to which identical twins appear more similar than fraternal twins with respect to some trait indicates the magnitude of genetic influence on that trait. (Erik Parens, "Genetic Differences and Human Identities: On Why Talking about Behavioral Genetics Is Important and Difficult," *Hastings Center Report* Special Supplement 34, 2004, pp. S1–S36)

As Parens points out, these studies are used to quantify the degree of genetic influence versus environmental influence on some trait. Such studies cannot tell us what gene or genes are involved or how they work to produce the differences observed.

Biological determinism and genetic determinism as implied by such work is unsettling for a lot of people for at least two reasons. First, biological determinism challenges the idea that human beings have free will. Second, genetic determinism suggests that there is little we can do, in terms of education or social policy, to avoid or modify undesirable characteristics built into some people. Maybe this is why the father in "Mississippi Half-Step Uptown Toodleloo" sat down and cried. He knew there was nothing to be done.

Both of these worries are ill founded but, at the same time, encouraged by the very misleading way that research and results from behavioral genetics and evolutionary psychology are often presented, especially in the popular press. Such reports suggest that we can isolate the various causes of behavior and that we can, potentially manipulate them independently. These suggestions fail to recognize some real limits of philosophical and scientific analysis in seeking to understand highly complex phenomena.

Are We Free?

I've used the phrases 'biological determinism' and 'genetic determinism' a number of times. 'Determinism' is the name of a principle according to which anything that happens is the necessary result of the conditions that preceded it. This is connected to the idea that everything that happens must have a specific cause, or, more precisely, some definite set of causes. Once those causal conditions are in place the effect must happen. This principle has been central to the development of modern science. But it is related to a really old philosophical conundrum about human freedom. I'm not talking here about political freedom: freedom of speech or freedom of religion. Those issues are extremely important, to be sure. But the kind of freedom I'm talking about is different. It is the question of whether our actions and choices are genuinely up to us in the first place.

Let's suppose that at one point in your life you were faced with the choice between traveling the country following a Grateful Dead tour for several months or keeping your job and being satisfied with seeing a few local shows during that period. The choice you make could have a pretty significant effect on the future course of your life. So let's say you chose the second option. Why did that happen? Both options were available to you. And yet only one was realized. Why that one instead of the other? The obvious answer is because that is what you chose. But that just begs the question again: why did you choose that instead of the other option? Now sometimes we just act on a whim. But most of us believe we are at least capable of being the deliberate authors of our own lives. If we really are, then we have the kind of freedom I'm talking about.

So far I haven't explained why this idea involves a philosophical conundrum. To do so, think more about the process of deliberation. While sometimes we might be impulsive, at other times we are more careful in thinking through a choice, weighing pros and cons, etc. Then we reach a decision. How does that process work? Certainly the outcome of the process of deliberation depends in part on what you desire, what you like, what you are committed to, your values, your fears, and a host of other things about you. And the reason you have choices is that sometimes different options fit different sets of these things, in other words there are conflicting desires. This is pretty clear in our example above. Following the tour would satisfy a host of desires, dreams, aspirations, etc. But doing so would also require giving up a bunch of other things that you want and value. Conflict. Bummer. But the choice has been put before you, so a decision must be made somehow. That is what deliberation is about. Sorting out all that stuff. And what determines the outcome? One common philosophical answer focuses on human reason, which in this case is your ability to sort through things in a way that ultimately makes sense and, ideally, leads you to choose the option that maximizes the benefits and minimizes the costs.

But some philosophers would add that the outcome of the process ultimately depends on what you value most. Reason can only perform calculations when given some input about the various strengths of your conflicting desires. But what makes us want one thing more than another or like one thing more than another? Why do I enjoy listening to the Grateful Dead more than listening to, say, a Wagner opera (which, by the way, I don't like too much). That's a really tough question. It doesn't seem to be entirely intrinsic to the object of enjoyment. The quality of the Dead's music has something to do with it. But that cannot be the whole story because some people don't like the Grateful Dead very much and really dig Wagner (you know its true, strange as it may seem). People vary a lot when it comes to likes and dislikes, desires and values. Why is that?

I'm not convinced anyone has a really good answer to that last question. But there are a lot of partial answers, and some of them treat all these psychological facts about us "naturalistically." The basic idea of this line of thought is that while our choices and action are the result of our own desires, beliefs and values, those things come from somewhere. They have causes. In other words, while my choosing to go to a Dead show over an opera may be explained by my musical preferences, the fact that I enjoy Jerry's playing more than Pavarotti's singing can't just be a random accident. There must be specific facts that cause us to have the desires, tastes and values we happen to have. Those causes may include facts about our past experience, the kinds of things we were exposed to and how we were exposed to them—in short, the environment we grew up in. And some of it may be biological, that is to say built in.

If this is the case, then, how are we really free? It sure seems like some of the causes of our desires, beliefs and values are things that are not under our control. So we cannot be the only thing making us who we are. This is the conundrum I spoke of earlier. It seems obvious that most of us, those who have not encountered extreme bad fortune, can freely chose the course of our lives, or at least what kind of person we will be. In other words it seems obvious that we have a genuinely free will. But it seems equally obvious, at least to some philosophers, that the psychological characteristics that underlay our choices must (like everything else) have prior causes not entirely under our control. These two conclusions both seem to rest on good grounds. But they also seem to be incompatible with one another. Philosophers often refer to this as the free will versus determinism issue.

This is one of those really tough philosophical issues that may never be completely resolved. Over the centuries there have been philosophers that defend the view that human beings have free will in some pretty strict sense. Others have defended the view that we are, like everything else, subject to causal determinism and so cannot be free in the strict sense. A good many philosophers have attempted to resolve this issue by arguing that, despite surface appearances, the claim that we have free will and the claim that our thoughts and behaviors are causally determined are actually compatible with each other.

The difficulty in finding a clear and convincing resolution is due to the fact that the issues involve the concept of the 'self', a concept subject to numerous interpretations. I could take the position that I am really the author of my choices and actions, but what is the nature of this 'I' to which I am referring? For a long time (from Plato to the twentieth century) a standard view in western philosophy was that the 'I' was some non-physical soul. That approach has fewer fans these days because a lot of people are inclined to see human beings in more naturalistic terms, which is to say as organisms that are entirely part of this natural world. But it's precisely this shift away from the dualistic view of human beings as a combination of physical bodies and non-physical souls that seems to open the door to a pure determinism that leaves out free will altogether.

But even if we are purely natural, purely physical beings, there is no doubt that as physical systems we are incredibly complex. We are only beginning to understand the nature of the complex processes going on in our brains. Recently a number of philosophers, cognitive scientists and neuroscientists have tried to develop accounts of freedom of will from a naturalistic point of view that accepts both (1) that thought and behavior have a physical, neurological basis and (2) that the structure and function of human brains results from evolutionary processes.[1] Some of these efforts are beginning to work out an account that might succeed in showing how the sort of complex systems like human bodies (and brains) can produce behaviors that are consistent with both causal determinism and the idea of human beings as self-determining systems.

Nature and Nurture: Can They Be Resolved?

The apparent incompatibility with free will is not the only aspect of biological determinism that raises contentious issues. Biological determinism also occupies one pole in the so-called nature versus nurture debates. The suggestion that antisocial behavior, for example, is under strong genetic control seems to imply that efforts to prevent such behavior by managing environmental factors through social policy will have limited effects. The claims coming out of behavioral genetics and evolutionary psychology are often criticized for ignoring the importance of environmental and social or cultural factors in determining the psychology of people.

These debates involve another set of philosophical concepts. Genetic determinism is a form of reductionism. 'Reductionism' is the view that the behavior of complex systems is simply the

---

[1] See, for example, Daniel Dennett's *Freedom Evolves* (Viking, 2003), or Douglas Hofstadter's *I Am a Strange Loop* (Perseus, 2007).

result of the properties and behavior of their component parts. While this may seem to be obviously true, there are arguments against it. Some philosophers and scientists contend that in certain kinds of complex systems, the properties and behavior of the parts are determined by certain features of the larger whole. On this view causal determination (and hence explanation) does not just go from the bottom up (from parts to the whole), but can also go from the top down (from the whole to the parts). This view is variously known as holism or organicism. A common slogan used to capture this idea is the claim that the whole is more than just the sum of the parts.

Let's use an analogy to understand this distinction. Consider the generally groovy (for lack of a better term) atmosphere at a Grateful Dead concert. Why did such an atmosphere always seem to prevail at the shows? Is it just that groovy people went to the shows? While it is a plausible claim that Dead shows attracted a certain type of person, others would argue that there was something about being at a Grateful Dead concert that had an effect of the people there—and I'm not talking here about a certain chemical present in the bloodstreams of certain attendees. Being at the show made people feel in certain ways and behave in certain ways. On this view there was a two-way relation between the individuals that made up the crowd and the generally groovy atmosphere that prevailed in that crowd. The latter might be called a higher-level feature of the whole concert-event. It resulted from the characteristics and actions of the individuals there. But it also contributed to what their characteristics and actions were.

Some scientists and philosophers adopt such a holistic approach to understanding organisms, people, and social phenomena. They don't think that reductionism is the best or only way to understand such complex systems. Genetic determinism is a specific kind of reductionism. Not only does it see the properties of whole organisms as resulting, in a bottom up way, from their material components (ultimately certain kinds of molecules). It also tends to privilege DNA as being a set of master control molecules, controlling and directing the rest of the system. The criticism against this form of reductionism is that it ignores the fact that the "behavior" of genes (understood as strands of DNA) is itself regulated by other aspects of the whole organism in which they are found.

The idea of genes as master-control molecules seems quite natural. After all scientists have found specific genes that are responsible for certain diseases such as sickle-cell anemia. These cases promote the idea of genes as master-control molecules, and this idea leads to the description of genes as carrying information sufficient to build an organism. Extrapolating from simple cases of diseases caused by genetic mutations to the case of complex behaviors is a big leap. Psychological and behavioral characteristics don't result from the operation of single genes. Even if we just limit our attention to the brain, as the seat of our psychological and behavioral traits, the situation is incredibly complicated. Brains are complex systems of interacting subsystems of interacting neurons. How our brains work depends on how all these neurons are wired together. And the patterns of wiring (the interconnections of neurons) is something that emerges over time, both during embryological development and long after the birth of the child. The behavior of a complex and dynamic system like that is precisely the sort of case where the operation of parts is subject to top-down influences of the sort recognized in a holistic view. Moreover, environmental factors play a large role in the developmental process through which the system arises.

No serious scientist argues that genes are not important for explaining these processes. But a few argue that we must remember that the actions of the genes themselves are influenced by higher level features of the complex system in which they operate and environmental factors are among those that influence genetic action. None of this means that we cannot or should not seek to understand the role of genetic factors in the origin of disease and even certain kinds of behavior. But it does suggest that understanding the role of genes will always involve understanding the interaction of those factors with a complex of environmental factors. And it suggests that the idea of built in character is highly problematic.

"Just Like Mary Shelley, Just Like Frankenstein"

Earlier I compared some lyrics from "Mississippi Half-step Uptown Toodleloo," to some lyrics from Willie Dixon's "Hoochie Coochie Man" because they both use mysterious signs to represent the idea of inborn characteristics. The "occult" devices such as Robert Hunter's mark, the gypsy woman's sight, and the weird bit about the seven doctors might just be written off as residues of the superstitions of a folk culture from the past. But these lyrical devices actually work to express the mysterious nature of where our character comes from. The lyrics recognize the presence of inborn traits, but they also recognize the inherent complexity of the situation by refusing to provide a simplistic or reductive account of how such traits arise.

In "Mama Tried" the tragic character describes how his poor mother could see the writing on the wall—trouble seemed predestined. But he also says that he came to a bad end because he "denied" the pleadings of his mother. The story is ambiguous with regard to whether his fate resulted from a free choice or simply some inborn and undeniable tendency toward antisocial behavior. The lyric does not attempt to resolve this question. It simply contains the ambiguity. In attempting to understand the nature of human freedom we would do well to remain sensitive to such ambiguities. What has been offered as opposing horns of a philosophical dilemma, free will versus determinism, may not, in fact, be opposing aspects of human functioning.

Art is very good at this kind of move—at lending expression to things that are so very complicated that they don't lend themselves to clear analysis. In a recent comment the Poet Laureate of the United States, Donald Hall explained that poetry shows him "how to be able to feel in that complicated, human way when you feel more than one way at once—ways that seem contradictory but which are true both at the same time" ("This Week," ABC News. October 1st, 2006). This is the power of art. In our present context we're discussing a central aspect of human experience, the experience of thought, deliberation, choosing, and acting. Philosophers and scientists have long sought to give us analyses of these things, but their analyses reveal complexities that seem at times to contain contradictions. So we end up with the tensions between free will and determinism, genetics and environment, nature and nurture.

What art, even in the form of song lyrics, can do is express the limits of analysis. If analysis gives us concepts of nature opposed to concepts of nurture, art can remind us that these terms may not name truly separable processes. I'm not saying that art in general, or poetry in particular, provides knowledge where philosophy and science fail. I'm suggesting that art can serve as an aid and a balance in the search for understanding, by reminding us of the inherent complexity of the world and the limits of our attempts to simplify it.

16

You Don't Need Space: A Question of Musical Value

MARY MACLEOD

As the second set of a Dead concert begins, my husband is a happy camper. He knows Drums and Space are coming, and when they do, he will take great pleasure in it. This is his first mistake. Space is bad, and the correct response is displeasure.

"Come on," says Eric, "you like free jazz, so you should like Space. There's a place in music for free rock. Space gives us music relatively unhindered by conventional melodic and rhythmic constraints. It's still clearly rock, but in an interestingly abstract way, and it generates a good feeling, a good mood."

"Not for me, it doesn't. Anyway, that's not the point," say I. "The issue isn't how it happens to makes you (or me) feel. The issue is whether Space has artistic merit, musical value. Any fool who noodles around in his basement can play unconnected rock licks for twenty minutes. It's happening right now all over the world. What's special about that? I'm not saying Jerry is no better than some novice who just picked up an instrument, but the difference between them isn't really shown by Space. It's just noodling. It's too easy. And that makes it musically uninteresting."

"What's interesting," says Eric, "is how the band manages to play *together*, in sensitive ways, without the usual framework of grooves and chord progressions. There's your musicianship, your artistic value. And maybe you don't know this, but Space is actually pretty theoretical. If you're going to get all snooty, remember the connection with Modern Classical music. Bob Weir has been quite explicit about that influence."

"Even if Space is influenced by, say, Bartók," I counter, "it doesn't follow that Space has musical value. Suppose Duran Duran claim Wagner as an influence. Does that make them a good band? And, anyway, of course you're right that the band plays *together* during Space, but not in a way that takes much skill. I just don't see anything worthwhile in noodling around, together or not."

Let the Hurdy Gurdy Play

If you disagree with me, it's for one of two reasons. Unlike me, you may think Space does have artistic merit. You may even give reasons like Eric's to support your view. It's not just that you take pleasure in Space; you think any right-minded person *should* take pleasure in it, because of its interestingly abstracted character, its Classical influences, or such like. That's what my husband thinks. (This is his second mistake.)

If you disagree with me, but not because you side with Eric, then probably your view is that Eric and I are both wrong. He and I are arguing about a "should" claim, and many people think this is misguided, confused. To say a person should, or should not, take pleasure in something is just odd, goes the thought: "Eric likes Space, whereas you, Mary, don't, and that's the end of it. Neither of you is right and neither of you is wrong because there simply are no "should"s when it comes to musical enjoyment. To each his own, *et cetera*. There's no accounting for taste, and no being held accountable for it either." If this is your opinion, you have plenty of company. It's a popular view.

Crazy or on Drugs

Dead fans really do argue about Space, quite fervently. My husband is not alone; many people really enjoy Space, and some of them go so far as to think that their response is the correct one. Others find Space at best barely tolerable, can't wait for it to end, and think anyone who likes Space must be crazy or on drugs.

Deadheads who debate the merits of Space take their argument seriously, and to do so they must suppose that there is something to disagree about here, something one can be right or wrong about in this matter. If I say "I loathe Space" and Eric says "I lllove it," we haven't contradicted one another, and our claims do not express disagreement. I can agree that he likes Space, and he can agree that I dislike it. But if I say "Space is utterly lacking in musical value," and he says, "Space is musically great" then we have contradicted one another, arguably. Only one of us can be right. We hear the same music and are agreed on what—descriptively speaking—the music contains, and on how it makes each of us feel. But only one of us thinks what we hear has musical worth.

The debate has implications for what we should feel. When I say that Space has no musical value, I'm not just saying that it displeases *me*. I'm also implying that it *should* displease other listeners. Eric, when he insists that Space does have value, contradicts my "should" claim. The disagreement isn't about whether either of us does *in fact* enjoy Space. Rather, it's about whether people *should* enjoy it. On this question, Eric and I cannot both be right.

So we need to distinguish between a subjective matter—whether some kind of music gives one pleasure—and an objective matter—whether that kind of music has value and thereby demands her enjoyment. If you're among the many who think it's confused and misguided to debate the merits of Space, that's probably because you think musical preference is entirely subjective.

It's not easy to sustain that opinion, though. One can't deny that people talk as if judgments of musical value are objective. When conversation turns to the big hair bands of the Eighties, we don't restrict ourselves to "I statements." We make value judgments about the bands themselves, and probably, given our demographic, not very nice ones either. (Duran Duran are hurtin', say we, and not just because their pants are too tight.) So even if there actually are no objective truths about musical value, we do talk as if there are.

What do we mean if we say Duran Duran is a bad band? One could say that such talk is just hyperbole: people do indeed talk as if some bands are good and others bad, but all we *really mean* is that some bands we like and others we don't. On the surface, one could say, we seem to be talking about bands and their features (I'll say "properties"), but deep down we're making claims about our own subjective preferences, and nothing

more. A guy who says "Duran Duran is a bad band" is just registering his own dislike, goes the view, in a particularly
emphatic way. And when, on the surface, he attributes value to
Bob Dylan's music, here again he's really just talking about his
own feelings.

   I don't think this answer works. Do you like it when Phil
Lesh sang *Box of Rain*? Of course you do; you bought this book.
Pretty much all Dead fans love it when Phil sings *Box of Rain.*
But do we want to say he sings it *well,* that his singing has musical value? The connection between personal preferences and
claims of merit is not that close. Moreover, to press the point
one more time, we take our debates about artistic merit very
seriously, and we wouldn't, if we were just voicing our own personal preferences, nothing more. I can agree that Eric likes
Space, and he can agree that I dislike it, and still the debate goes
on.

Self-Centered to the Extreme

Some will think my position is just arrogant and untenable.
"Who are you," I'll be asked, "to go around saying what music
people should or shouldn't like? What gives you the right to
such pronouncements? Would you like to have a ban on powder blue leisure suits, too?" (Actually, yes.) "And why can't Eric
say *he's* the sheriff? Can't he claim that you, MacLeod, are the
one with mistaken emotional responses? What have you got that
he hasn't got?"

   Consider the book you're holding. It's made of paper, is rectangular, and it weighs about twelve ounces. These are all intrinsic properties of the book, which means that the book's having
these traits doesn't depend on anything other than the book. It's
made of paper (rectangular, about twelve ounces) whether we
say so or not. And we can detect these properties using our
senses. We sometimes make mistakes in our judgments about
color, shape, and such, but our senses do give us reliable information about such properties.

   I think value properties are intrinsic. Whether a piece of
music has merit or not doesn't depend on whether anyone thinks
it does. Its musical value is as much a property of the music as

its key signature or instrumentation. I also think we can detect value properties fairly reliably, some of us better than others. Take Eric and me. I have insights into musical value that he lacks; that's my answer to your challenge. What I know, and what Eric doesn't know, is that Space is without musical value. I hear the music with my ears, and Eric does too, but I also hear something he doesn't—the lack of value, the intrinsic objective badness of the music.

I also hear you snorting.

I Need a Miracle

"Don't be ridiculous," comes the response. "There's the music and what it's like, descriptively speaking. There is how you respond to it emotionally, and that's all. Either you enjoy it or you don't, and your reaction isn't a perception of a value property. Your emotional reactions aren't *of* the music at all. You react *to* the music, but emotions aren't *about* their causes in the way that sensations are."

"Moreover," my formidable opponent continues, "value properties couldn't be detected. What would the physical process of detection involve? We don't seem to have a faculty that could detect musical value. We have ears to hear music, and we have (more or less educated) feelings about the music heard. Ears and heart are all we have, when it comes to the experience of music, and neither ears nor heart is a detector of objective musical value. With what faculty are you claiming to *hear* the objective badness of Space, MacLeod? The mind's ear? The heart's ear? The heart's nose? Dubious. You'd need a miracle to pick up such a signal," concludes my foe, ripping off my sheriff's badge. "No one is right and no one is wrong in their emotional responses, and there is nothing to be right or wrong about."

Value Realists beg to differ, but the problem just pressed against them is serious. Value Realists think value properties are an irreducible part of the fabric of the world. The value of a piece of music, or art, doesn't reduce to a description of how it is, factually; it doesn't reduce to natural properties. A good piece of music may involve uncommon chord progressions or novel harmonies, but the worth of the music is something more, something basic, says the Realist: its value properties are related to but distinct from its distinctive properties. They are irreducibly evaluative.

Value properties are welcomed by those who think value judgments are objective, but there is a price to be paid. If value properties don't reduce to factual ones, you can't turn evaluative properties into properties known through the senses. In that case, then, if such properties exist, they would be unobservable—at least if by "observation" we mean sensing. You can smell coffee, taste tomatillo, see yellow, and feel warmth, but it's rather mysterious how we could have direct, immediate acquaintance with artistic beauty and moral goodness or rightness, or their deficient opposites. This makes Value Realism seem dubious.

Two Kinds of Shoulds

Value Realism, despite its problems, appeals to those who want to save the objectivity of value judgments. There may be other ways, but Value Realism is the most intuitive. If value properties really are part of the fabric of the world, it is easy to understand why someone could be either right or wrong in their value judgments and emotional responses, and what they'd be right or wrong about—the properties.

Those who think musical preference is entirely subjective will be unmoved by this point, of course. Subjectivists think people can't really be wrong in their claims about musical value because really such claims are just registering personal preference. If it's all subjective, there is no need for external truths relative to which one's musical preferences can be correct or incorrect. I, an Objectivist, counter that we *can* make errors in our judgments about musical value. So I must insist that there is an external source deciding whether our judgments are in error. Of course, Subjectivists tend to think Objectivism is arrogant and elitist, and the Value Realism that underwrites it dubious and untenable.

Unless you're a music critic or an art critic, aesthetic judgments may not matter much to you, but moral judgments probably do, so before you relegate Realism to the trash, you may want to consider recycling. With music, Subjectivism doesn't leave much of a bad taste in your mouth, but with ethics, it does. We don't think that action choices are simply a matter of personal preference. Rather, we think moral errors are possible.

There may be no errors of musical taste, but we think people can be wrong in their judgments about the moral status of actions—which kinds are morally right and which kinds wrong. We don't want to say, for example, that the moral status of torturing innocent children depends only on personal preference. We don't want to say that since Jeffrey Dahmer liked doing this, it was "right for him." It wasn't right in any way.

What was Dahmer mistaken about? The most natural and intuitive answer appeals to moral properties, and since moral subjectivism is unappealing, Moral Realism demands serious consideration. A Moral Realist thinks that actions and character traits have intrinsic moral properties. The rightness or wrongness is just built in to the action, as its own, special trait, independently of anyone's edict or opinions. And we can detect rightness or wrongness, the Realist thinks, not perfectly, but quite reliably.

Unless you're willing to say "to each his own" when it comes to moral questions, you will need to be open to Realism about moral properties. Probably you'll want to remain a Subjectivist about aesthetic judgments, and you'll be in good company. "Murder is not just a matter of taste, but art and music are" people say, suggesting that ethics is objective, and aesthetics not.

As you know, I disagree. I think aesthetic judgments are objective, too. And I would remind you again that people do earnestly debate aesthetic questions. We argue about whether a certain sculpture is ugly, whether a painting is beautiful, and we argue about whether Space is a pointless waste of musical talent. If you don't feel the force of such questions, if you deny that works of art and music have value properties, we Realists will be inclined to say you're "beauty blind."

And when Deadheads argue about the musical value of Space, about who's got it right, and who better apprehends the truth, what do *you* make of *them*? Are they just deluded? Hallucinating? (Okay, wrong question.)

Less Concern about the Deep Unreal

A few decades ago, British philosopher John Mackie argued, concerning ethical value, that people really are just deluded, "seeing things," when they take themselves to be apprehending moral properties (J.L. Mackie, *Ethics: Inventing Right and Wrong* [Harmondsworth: Penguin, 1971]). We don't and can't "see" moral goodness or badness, rightness or wrongness, if what you mean by that is something irreducibly non-factual about the acts themselves. Neither can we see aesthetic beauty or ugliness. We can only respond emotionally.

If that's right, why do we take moral and aesthetic debates so seriously? Are we making a deep error? Mackie argued that we are. We experience unpleasant emotional responses when we encounter certain kinds of actions, while other kinds please us. We then project our emotions on to the actions, as a self-absorbed child might. Mackie focused on ethics, but we can extend his points to aesthetics. In my debate with Eric over Space, for example, I make the mistake of taking my own emotions (a subjective issue) as genuine properties of the music. All ego, I project my feelings onto the world, the music, treating a non-representative emotion as an apprehension of a value property. I'm in error because there are no value properties (it's all just a matter of taste) and no value property detector (what could that be?) So the error is wrongly taking a subjective, bad (or good) feeling to be an awareness of objective badness (or goodness).

Mackie granted, quite reasonably, that ordinary talk is replete with the ascription of value properties that cannot be reduced to properties known through the senses. That's why we take the debates seriously. But, he also thought, there are no such properties. And even if there were value properties, he argued, we couldn't know them. So we're making a systematic error. It's a mistake, for example, to say that respect for persons is intrinsically wrong, *and it's also a mistake to say respect for persons is intrinsically right.* Any ascription of intrinsic evaluative properties is mistaken, but we do it all the time.

Mackie clarified his position with an analogy. We attribute color properties to objects we see, and this reflects our belief that mind-independent objects are colored on their surfaces, the belief that color as we experience it is out there in the world on the objects. This belief is false, says Mackie, and he's got science on his side; the difference between a red object and a green object isn't what we think it is. It's just a difference in which wavelengths of light each object absorbs, and which it reflects, roughly. These absorption and reflection propensities cause us to have color experiences when we perceive a Granny Smith apple and a Delicious apple, but nothing in the apples themselves resembles the qualitative character of our experiences. We really think apples have properties with the qualitative character of our color experiences, and this naivety impregnates our ways of talking. The meaning of color talk is Realist, but Realism about color properties is mistaken.

Mackie takes his cue from an eighteenth-century philosopher, David Hume, who spoke of the mind's "great propensity to spread itself on external objects, and to conjoin with them any internal impressions, which they occasion" (*Treatise of Human Nature* [Oxford: Clarendon, 1978], p. 167). He distinguished reason, which "conveys the knowledge of truth and falsehood," from taste, which "gives the sentiment of beauty and deformity, vice and virtue (*Enquiry Concerning the Principles of Morals* [Oxford: Clarendon, 1975], p. 88). Whereas reason "discovers objects as they really are in nature, without addition or diminution," taste "has a productive faculty, and gilding and staining all natural objects with the colors, borrowed from internal sentiment, raises in a manner a new creation" (*Enquiry*, p. 88). A spoonful of honey helps the medicine go down, but however nicely he puts it, Hume thinks we're deluded, too.

So There's No Accounting for Taste?

According to Value Realists, the truth makers of value judgments are value properties. As we've seen, such properties cannot be known through the senses. And they are often considered odd in themselves, quite independently of questions about how we would know them. Mackie concludes that although ordinary thought and parlance betray a commitment to Value Realism, Value Realism is mistaken, a delusion.

But if Value Realism is mistaken, are we stuck with Subjectivism, even about ethics? Must we concede that torture is "bad for us" but "good for Dahmer"? Or can we find an objective standard relative to which we can be held accountable, a standard less problematic than value properties? Can we make value judgments objective without making evaluative truths strange and unknowable?

If you get a bunch of music experts together, and seek their views on the aesthetic value of Space, you'll probably find that they disagree, even if you restrict yourself to experts in folk and rock. Their disagreements will bottom out in brute differences in feelings. Some musical experts will like Space and others won't. Some will like John Cage, or Schoenberg, and others won't. For any given piece of music, some experts will say you should like it, and others will say you shouldn't. But let's not exaggerate; often there will be some convergence of opinion.

An Aesthetic Realist will want to play up this convergence. After all, if there are irreducible value properties out there to detect, shouldn't we expect that relevant experts would reach consensus about them? And when they do, the Realist explains this as resulting from their shared apprehension of aesthetic properties.

But maybe expert agreement is what *makes* the aesthetic facts what they are. If we're looking for a standard to which we are answerable for our musical preferences, why go for freaky value properties? Why not just say that experts' opinions decide aesthetic questions by making the aesthetic facts what they are? On such a view, whether Space is good or not would depend on whether a suitably delineated group of experts side in favor of it. Their agreement in approving of Space would constitute its aesthetic merit, and not just be evidence for it.

If expert agreement is the source of aesthetic truth, problems with knowability go away. There is no great difficulty in knowing, at least in principle, whether a group of experts approves of a particular work of art or music. So if such agreement is what makes the work good, then we can, at least in principle, know whether that work is good, no miracle needed. The objectivity of aesthetic judgment is saved as well. You *should* enjoy just those works of art and music approved of by most relevant experts, and if your preferences diverge from theirs, you can be said to be in error.

Similar points hold concerning ethics. A Realist will say, for example, that killing an innocent man is intrinsically wrong; the wrongness of this act is a basic feature of the action, not dependent on anyone's attitudes towards it. But we could say instead that what makes that kind of action wrong is our widespread consensus against such killings. The Realist will treat societal agreement as *evidence* of a moral truth concerning killing, but we might instead treat such agreement is the *source* of wrongness. And if we do, we can save the objectivity of morality without taking on the knowledge problems Realists face. John Mackie endorses a variant of this position.

The position can be called "morals (or beauty) by agreement." To motivate it, philosophers talk about traffic conventions. I don't mean convention as in "wear a name tag and seek out adulterous opportunities," I mean convention as in "folks convene and reach agreement on certain questions." In the United States we've reached agreement that cars are to drive on the right side of the road. Societal agreement, codified in legislation, is what *makes* it wrong to drive on the left side. There is nothing intrinsically wrong with driving on the left; Realism about traffic "oughts" is just silly. It's entirely arbitrary which side you make people drive on; the important thing is to pick a side and stick to it. But if a society—by passing laws—makes left-side driving wrong, it is wrong for them. The societal agreement makes it wrong. Until the convention is established, there is no right or wrong side, no "ought" of traffic coordination. Traffic "oughts" come into being as the result of conventions.

Obviously there are traffic "oughts," and Realism about traffic "oughts" is silly. ("Yes, we've agreed to drive on the right side, but which side *should* we be driving on?" is a silly question.) This is what makes "oughts by agreement" so plausible when it comes to traffic. Traffic oughts are arbitrary; in Great Britain they picked the other side, and are doing just fine. But can we "pick the other side" when it comes to moral oughts, or aesthetic ones? Are societal agreements about moral policies similarly arbitrary? How about expert agreements concerning aesthetic value?

It's important to understand that such agreements have to be arbitrary for the position to work.[1] If there are no moral truths until social conventions are established, then the initial choice of social policies must be, in a moral sense, arbitrary. If killing innocents is wrong only because we've reached agreement in opposing it, then we can't turn around and say that we reached agreement in opposing it because we perceived the intrinsic wrongness of such actions. Similarly, if expert consensus is what constitutes the aesthetic value of a painting or a piece of music, we can't turn around and say that experts reached consensus because they perceived the intrinsic value of the work. And this

---

[1] For a fine discussion of this point, see Elliot Sober, *Core Questions in Philosophy* (Englewood Cliffs: Prentice Hall, 2005).

means that any kind of action could be morally required of us, even random torture and killing. Any kind could be morally forbidden, even caring for children. Any work of art could demand our approval, even a Duran Duran hit, and any work could demand our disapproval, even your favorite Dylan tune. We'd just need to reach the relevant agreements.

"But relevant experts would never agree that Duran Duran is good and Dylan bad. They're experts, so of course they will appreciate the intrinsic value of Dylan; of course they'll find little of value in Big Hair bands." You can say that, but not without reverting to Realism. There's nothing wrong with this reply, but if you make it, you've given up "aesthetic oughts by agreement." Similarly for morals by agreement. You can claim, reasonably, that no competent social group would decide in favor of random torture and killing, but if your reason for this claim is that any competent group will perceive the immorality of such a policy, again you've reverted to Realism.

"Oughts by agreement" was to provide an unproblematic source of objectivity, but when we take the view out for a ride, it threatens to lead us back to Realism. We can always opt instead to endorse Subjectivism, but then we've got the Dahmer problem. Subjectivism about Space doesn't trouble us, but Subjectivism about morals does. Maybe we should try harder to solve the problems with Realism.

17

Who Was Wise? Decision Theory in "Lady with a Fan"

STEPHEN G. DILLINGHAM

In the Grateful Dead's "Lady with a Fan," a storyteller tells of a beautiful woman who throws her fan into a lion's den. She asks a sailor and a soldier, "Which of you to gain me, tell, will risk uncertain pains of hell? I will not forgive you if you will not take the chance." The soldier, being "much too wise," declines the challenge, but the sailor is willing to try. He retrieves the fan from the lion's den and wins the affections of the lady. Given the outcome, the storyteller says, "You decide if he [the sailor] was wise."

A casual listener might be tempted to interpret this question as being merely rhetorical—of course the sailor was wise because he won the lady's affections. We hear this "all's well that ends well" type of reasoning every day from politicians, the news media, and others. But do we really expect it to be the allegorical point in a song by the Grateful Dead? This essay will take the storyteller's admonition to us at face value—we will investigate whether the sailor was indeed wise, and whether the soldier was wise to refuse the lady's challenge. We will use a philosophical approach called decision theory as our framework, and we will see that the answer may not be so simple.

Uncertain Pains of Hell

Decision theory is based upon probability, a field pioneered by Blaise Pascal and Pierre de Fermat in the mid-seventeenth century when they took an interest in trying to predict the outcomes of gambling games. The axioms and theorems of probability—

the rules that tell us how to add, multiply, or otherwise manipulate probabilities in order to get the right answer—fall solidly
in the realm of mathematics. But since the field began, philosophers have been interested in discovering how we can *interpret*
an *application* of probability statements. That is, how do the
axioms and theorems of the mathematicians apply to the real
world? What can they tell us about how events really turn out?

Philosophers have offered many views on the nature of probability statements over the last three hundred and fifty years, but
for our discussion of decision theory, we can focus on what has
come to be known as the subjectivist interpretation of probability. (This is also sometimes called the Bayesian interpretation,
after eighteenth-century mathematician Thomas Bayes. Bayes did
important work in probability, including proving a theorem that
bears his name and is used in, among other things, spam-filter-
ing algorithms for email. The subjectivist interpretation relies
heavily on Bayes's theorem, but it did not arrive on the scene
until the early twentieth century, long after Bayes's death.)

According to the subjectivists, a probability statement represents the degree of belief a person has in a certain proposition.
So if I say, "I think there is a seventy-five-percent chance that it
will rain today," I'm asserting my degree of belief about whether
or not it is going to rain. My degree of belief may or may not be
based on a particular piece of evidence (such as a recent
weather forecast). And it may or may not agree with your prediction. Maybe your degree of belief that it will rain is only fifty
percent—perhaps you heard a different forecast than I did, or
perhaps you have noticed that I predict rain more often than it
actually rains. Whatever the reason, our disagreement is okay
because our statements about the probability of rain simply
reflect our *subjective* degrees of belief. (The subjectivist account
says that if we both see enough of the same evidence, we
should start to agree, but those details would take us too far
afield here.)

People think about events with uncertain outcomes all the
time—whether it will rain, whether the Orioles will win a particular game, whether an incumbent will get re-elected, and so
on—but most normal people don't express their degrees of
belief in terms of specific numerical values. In these cases, we
can determine the numerical values we should assign by asking
about the odds at which a person would take a bet on the propo-

sition in question. If my degree of belief in the proposition that it will rain today is seventy- five percent, I ought to be willing to bet three dollars against one dollar. (Asking about betting odds is intended as a kind of thought-experiment. We aren't worried about cases where people may choose not to bet for ethical, practical, or personal reasons. The idea is to figure out the odds at which they would bet absent any of those considerations.)

Strategy, and Not Disaster

In decision theory, we try to decide whether or not to act in a certain way by evaluating the probable consequences of the action. We calculate a quantity called the *expected value* for each choice, and compare them. We assign probabilities of success and failure to each action, and assign values for each outcome. Values can be in any units we like—dollars are the obvious choice for may applications of decision theory. But the situation we are concerned with involves happiness, not wealth, so we will use arbitrary units of happiness called roses in our example. We will stipulate that an event can change our happiness level by plus or minus ten roses. Now, to calculate the expected value of an action, we multiply the probability of success by the number of roses by which our happiness would be increased. Then we multiply the probability of failure by the number of roses by which our happiness will fall if we fail. (For us, this quantity will always be negative, since we will assign negative roses to bad outcomes.) Adding the two give us the expected value. Finally, we can compare the expected values of all or our options (accepting the lady's challenge or refusing it) and choose the action with the highest expected value.

Two types of numbers will alter the expected value of the outcomes—the probability of success and the values assigned to each possible outcome. The description above may sound a little abstract. To see how different values can lead to different decisions, we will work through the decision process for the case we are interested in, varying the probabilities and outcome values.

Case 1—The Fair Bet

Let's start simple. Let's assume that the soldier doesn't really know anything about lions. Maybe he can sneak in and retrieve the fan while the lion isn't paying attention. Or maybe he can simply be quick enough to get the fan and run out to safety before the lion can catch him. Or maybe he can overcome the lion by brute force. In his career as a soldier, he has relied on stealth, speed, and strength at different times, but knowing so little about lion behavior, he calculates his odd of success as fifty-fifty.

Next the soldier must assign values to each potential outcome. If he does nothing, he will be no more or less happy than he is now, so he assigns a value of zero roses to this outcome. If he ventures into the lion's den and succeeds, he will win the lady and be very happy indeed. He values this outcome at ten roses—the maximum on our scale. On the other hand, if he fails, let us assume that he will be killed and eaten by the lion. This outcome is about as bad as it gets, so he values it at minus ten roses—the worst outcome on our scale.

Now we can calculate the expected value for both cases. If he does not take the lady's challenge, the expected value is zero. For the case where he takes up the lady's challenge, we multiply the chance of succeeding by the value obtained by succeeding and add that to the product of the chance of failure and the respective loss. This gives us five roses (fifty percent, or one half, times ten roses) for success and negative five roses (one half times minus ten roses), for a total expected value of zero. So in this case, the expected value of taking the challenge is exactly the same as that of not taking it.

From the point of view of deciding whether or not to do something, an outcome in which the expected value of acting or not acting turn out to be equal may not appear helpful. But this example is useful because it illustrates a fair bet in the context of decision theory. The odds are fifty-fifty and the pay off for the good outcome is equal (in magnitude, as measured in roses) to the loss that would be suffered under the bad outcome. Mathematically, this example is no different than deciding whether to bet a dollar on the outcome of a (fair) coin toss. But although sometimes we might accept a low-stakes bet on a coin toss or the like, risking one's life by taking an action with a zero expected value seems quite foolhardy. In a decision (or bet) with high stakes, we'd like a positive expected value, which correspond to bets that are better than fair (to us).

With the "fair bet" case as our starting point, we can adjust probabilities and outcome values and examine the results. We will start with probabilities.

Case 2—Strategy Was His Strength, and Not Disaster

This time, let's suppose that the soldier knows something about lions. He knows that they are strong, fast, and territorial, and will not take kindly to a human invader trying to retrieve a fan. So in this case, he thinks he only has a twenty-five-percent chance of success, and a seventy-five-percent likelihood of failure.

We will use the same outcome values as we did in case one—success brings ten roses worth of happiness, failure brings minus ten, and inaction brings no roses. In this case, the expected value for succeeding is two-and-a-half roses (twenty-five percent of ten); for failing, it is minus seven-and-a-half roses. So the net expected value for taking the challenge is minus five roses. The net expected value for not taking the challenge is (of course) zero, which, while not ideal, is preferable to an expected loss.

In this case, decision theory gives us a clear answer: the soldier should not take the lady's challenge. He is wise to refrain.

Case 3—Sailor's Delight

We can alter our assumptions in favor of success as well. Let us assume that during his travels, the sailor has run across lions before. He has been to circuses and exotic exhibitions, and he has met and conversed with animal tamers, zookeepers, and big-game hunters. Always on the lookout for interesting stories and new tricks that might come in handy, he has learned something about lion behavior. Based on his knowledge, he thinks he has better than a fifty-fifty chance of retrieving the lady's fan successfully. He gives himself a seventy-five-percent chance of success, and a twenty-five-percent chance of failure.

To keep things simple at this point, let's assume that the sailor places the same value on each outcome as the soldier did in the first two cases. Success is worth ten roses, failure is worth minus ten, and inaction worth nothing. So the expectation in the

case of success is now seven-and-a-half roses (seventy-five percent of ten); with minus two-and-a-half roses for the case of failure (twenty-five percent of ten). The expected value of taking
the challenge, then, is five roses, while the expected value of
doing nothing is no roses.

Under these conditions, it looks reasonable for the sailor to
take the challenge. He is still risking his life, though, so we
might still be inclined to think he is somewhat foolhardy. We
will come back to that suggestion later; for now, the point is that
taking the challenge results in a higher expected value than not
taking it.

Now let's look at a couple of cases where we alter the values assigned to the different outcomes.

Case 4—The Sailor Gives At Least a Try

Let's suppose that the sailor does not know anything about
lions. Following the same reasoning as the soldier in the first
case, he decides his chance of success is fifty percent and his
chance of failure is fifty percent. And let's further suppose that
he values success and failure as much as in the last three cases
(ten roses for success and negative ten for failure). But let's also
suppose that the sailor strongly wants to win the lady's hand
and that failing to do so would break his heart. Choosing not to
take the lady's challenge would mean he has no hope of winning her affections, so he assigns a negative value to this case
as well. He is not enough of a romantic to equate his heartbreak
with death, but it would still be pretty bad, so he assigns a value
of minus five roses.

Now, as in case 1, the expected value of accepting the lady's
challenge is zero roses. But this time, the expected value of not
accepting it is negative five roses. Based on his own preferences, it looks as if the sailor had better try to face the lion.

Case 5—But Lost at Love

As our final case, we'll consider a case in which the potential
gain and lost of are of different magnitudes. We're told that the
soldier came through many fights, but lost at love. We will
assume this means that based on his past experience, he is jaded
about the prospects of a successful relationship with the lady.

Even if he retrieved the lady's fan, he thinks it likely that something would come along to lead to a break-up. He builds this pessimism into his calculations by assigning only six roses (rather than ten) to the successful case. Being eaten by the lion is still a worst-case outcome, so he assigns minus ten roses to that case, and he assigns no roses either way to the case where he refuses the challenge. As in the original case, he gives himself fifty-fifty chances for success if he takes up the challenge.

In this example, the success case gives us three roses (one-half times six), while the failure case gives negative five. Thus, the net expected value for taking up the challenge is negative two. Refusing the challenge has an expected value of zero, making refusal the smarter choice according to decision theory.

The Storyteller Makes No Choice

Initially, the storyteller's task for us seemed relatively straightforward: either the soldier or the sailor was wise. But by considering their actions in terms of decision theory, we see that whether or not each was wise depended on how much they valued each outcome and how likely they were to succeed. Both may have been wise, or neither. The cases we described above did not exhaust all possibilities. Decision theory gives us the framework, but until we fill in the probabilities and outcome values, we can't decide who was wise.

Encore—Mysteries Dark and Vast

Metaphysical Quandaries

18

I'm Just Playin' in the Band: Stoicism, Taoism, and Freedom

MATTHEW TURNER

> Do not seek to have events happen as you want them to happen, but instead want them to happen as they do happen, and your life will go well.
>
> —Epictetus, *Encheiridion* 8

Listen to the River Sing Sweet Songs

One of the features that makes the Grateful Dead truly outstanding is their ability to improvise. Indeed, their improvisations run deep—they don't just take turns playing solos—the songs are a flexible and amorphous set of guidelines that are themselves altered and shaped in different ways at different times. This is true for different songs on different nights, and it is especially true when we look at how the songs themselves evolved over the years. Although many songs capture the Dead's approach well, I'm going to talk about "Playin' in the Band."

Typically, the song begins with the verses and the chorus, but then extends into a long, improvised jam. The point where they turn into the jam is incredible: they gently gear down with the short melody before hitting the point where the jam begins, and then all of a sudden, it's as if the music lets go. Where before the band was holding tightly to the pattern prescribed by the song, they now allow themselves to drift.

But they don't drift aimlessly—they follow the logic of the jam, each listening to the other, allowing the jam to develop where it will before bringing it slowly back into the melody that began the jam. This is especially evident in performances from the 1970s, where the jam would sometimes last for twenty or thirty minutes before coming back (if it does at all!).

One way that we can describe the appeal of jams like these is to say that there seems to be something so *free* about it. As you listen, you can close your eyes, and submerge yourself in the current, and allow it to carry you along with it. The band, also, appears to be free and open, following the music where it takes them, as opposed to following a prescribed and rigid pattern. As fun and enjoyable as this experience is, it raises an interesting philosophical question: if we're not doing anything but drifting along, how can we be said to be free?

Of course there's a straightforward sense in which we're free—there's nothing external constraining our behavior or actions—we've *chosen* to sit back and be carried along by the music. But we might also say that this sense of freedom doesn't capture what is happening when we drift along with the Dead's improvisations. We might say that when we listen to the Dead, what we do is try to get into the music as much as possible, but this has nothing to do with the moment of our choosing to listen to the music to begin with.

I can explain what's at issue by the following example. Imagine a long and powerful river that flows from the mountains to the sea. Does the river run free? We might say so if the river hasn't been dammed, diverted, or had its course otherwise altered. The metaphor of the river captures some of our sense of what is happening when we drift with the Dead: as long as that flow isn't interrupted, we drift along free from constraints. But is the river really *free*? Isn't the flow of the river simply the result of the force of gravity and the properties of the physical earth through which the river cuts? Could the river take a course other than the course that it does? If we believe that the laws of nature determine the course of physical phenomena, it's difficult to see how the river's course could be otherwise than it is. Many factors determine the river's path—the kind of earth over which it flows, the volume of water, the slope of the land, and so on.

In contrast to the river, however, when we think of ourselves as free, we not only recognize that we are free from some kinds of constraints on our actions, but also that we ourselves *do* something. That is, we don't want to think of ourselves as merely being swept along by the forces of nature, but rather that we *influence* the course of nature, through our own choices.

Given this image, what kind of freedom shall we associate with human actions? Are we like the river, or unlike the river? Many philosophers have argued that we are different from the river—that we don't simply flow along with the laws of nature. But the more that we know about the physical world and its laws, the less room there seems to be for an understanding of ourselves as meaningfully free. That is, free in the way where we influence nature out of the *choices* that are ours.

Freedom's Just Another Word For . . . ?

This problem—whether human beings are truly free or are just highly complicated machines obeying the laws of nature like everything else—is a perennial philosophical problem. There are a few broad categories of solutions to the problem, and most either ask us to accept the bleak fact that the world and everything in it is spinning out of our control, or that somehow freedom is compatible with the mechanistic universe. There have been other solutions to the problem, but these solutions typically take one of two approaches. They either deny the view that the world is deterministic—fully and necessarily determined by the laws of nature, or they attempt to redefine and reinterpret the notion of freedom.

There is one particular philosophical thread that deals with this problem of human freedom in terms of the latter solution. I call this solution the Stoic solution. This name comes from a particular kind of philosophy that was ascendant in the ancient Greek and Roman world. The Stoics shared a particular outlook on life, focusing in part on human powerlessness in the face of the events of the world. I also include the Chinese philosophical school of Taoism in this category, as well as the Enlightenment philosopher Benedict Spinoza, because their approaches to this problem of freedom closely parallel that of the traditional Stoics. When I talk about the Stoic solution to the problem, you can take me to be referring to the general way that all of these philosophers respond to this problem.

The Stoic philosophers typically held the view that there is no way to escape the fact that many of our experiences are outside of our control, but they didn't thereby conclude that we ought to throw our hands up in despair at our impotence. It is possible for us to adopt an attitude toward our own lives and our own experiences that enables us to avoid despair at the inevitability of events. This point is often put in terms of our judgments. We know that we can look at the world in different ways; one event can be judged differently. Epictetus says in the *Encheiridion*, "What upsets people is not things themselves, but their judgments about the things" (Epictetus, *Encheiridion*, in *Classics of Western Philosophy*, edited by Steven M Cahn [Indianapolis: Hackett, 2002], Section 5). What he means is that events themselves have no intrinsic value, rather it is we who ascribe value to them. This value is derived from that complex system of beliefs and desires that comprises our entire world-view. But once we realize that the world itself is indifferent to our view of it, we can understand that there's something *arbitrary* about our worldview.

Thus, each of these Stoic philosophers contends, in their own particular way, that if we understand the world truly, then much that gives rise to disappointment falls away. But at the same time, the Stoics hold that we often judge ourselves to be in control of things we are not, which appears to entail that we are not free. Nevertheless, the Stoics believe that we are free, and meaningfully free, but more like the river instead of the agents we normally take ourselves to be.

Here's an example. Face it: the Dead sometimes screwed up playing live—Jerry would forget the words, the band would stumble through a particular change, and so on. When they were on, they were really on, but they had their moments. I don't think that this ever detracted from the overall appeal and enjoyment of their music; in fact, I think that it enhanced it—it made them appear more human and more accessible. But there are times when I'm listening to a show, hearing them jam toward a particular climax, building up in anticipation of the great feeling of release that comes after the growing tension, only to have the band not be able to stick it. The experience is terribly anti-climactic.

One thing that we might say about this example is that the band, or Jerry or Bob, or whoever screwed up, and the implication is that because our experience of the song is worse than it could have been, the performance of the song is thereby worse than it could have been. In this way of describing the event, notice the direction in which responsibility lies: someone in the band is responsible because our desires were frustrated and not satisfied.

The Stoic would characterize the situation differently. Because it is outside of our control how and what the Dead play and whether or not they are successful at it, there's no point in being upset, since there's nothing we or anyone else can do about it.

This view, however, has a significant implication for what we say about human freedom. If the advice of the Stoics is that we are to understand that much is outside of our control, then we must also recognize that there is not much that we can *do* to change the world. On the Stoic view, then, the scope of our own freedom is limited, if not entirely illusory. Freedom then, ultimately means being free from misperceiving and misunderstanding the world, even though we may not be able to cause actions to happen in the way that we typically believe that we do.

This Stoic view has struck some as unreasonable, for it seems to reduce the scope of our freedom far too much. Not only that, it seems to undermine legitimate human responses to circumstances. Why shouldn't we get mad where we have a flat tire? Or if the example seems inconsequential, think of what would arouse your ire—a military draft, nuclear explosion, forced labor. How would the civil rights movement have fared if Dr. Martin Luther King and others had been content to simply not attempt to change the world directly? Is it reasonable to believe that King's frustration with institutionalized racism was his simply *seeing* the matter in the wrong way? In short, Stoicism spells quietism, and that's a philosophy of life many would just as soon do without.

I believe that the Grateful Dead's improvisational approach provides us with a concrete example of how Stoicism doesn't equal quietism, because within the confines of those particular constraints, the Dead develop something original, unique, and substantive. If such a product can lead to something valuable, it stands to reason that we might hope for something similar with regard to human action more generally. That is, we have in the Dead's approach to playing an analogue of how we might begin to structure our own lives.

People Joinin' Hand in Hand, While the Music Plays the Band

In order to understand how the Dead might provide this analogue, we should look at their general improvisational approach, and how that approach affects our understanding of what a Dead song is. We need to do this in order to get a sense of how constraints operate on and affect how the Dead play. We can understand how these constraints function by thinking a little bit about what makes a Dead song the particular song that it is.

First, most songs are easily recognizable through the lyrics or the melodies. We don't mistake "Sugaree" for "Help on the Way." But at the same time, we're aware that over the years, as the Dead played their songs, they would change and evolve in new and different ways. As an example, compare how the tune "St. Stephen" changed from when the Dead began playing it in the 1960s to when they played it during the 1970s, especially the late 1970s. The tempo and feel of the song had altered dramatically: it had slowed down and become statelier. But tempi are only one of the variations between different performances of Dead songs. Consider the riff that Jerry plays in "Tennessee Jed" that introduces the song and comes between verses. Although the riff is (almost) always recognizable as the standard riff from the song, Jerry played it differently at different times and in different points in the song. We recognize the riff as counting as a "Tennessee Jed" riff each time it occurs, without it ever having to be exactly the same.

So there's a lot of flexibility to a song, even given the particular constraints on it. To say, however, that the songs are *merely* guidelines seems to be too loose. "Estimated Prophet" *has* to be played in 7/4 time, otherwise it would certainly be a different song. But there are also many things that *don't* have to be the case. "Franklin's Tower" doesn't have to come after "Help on the Way/Slipknot", but it usually does.

To illustrate, we can return to the metaphor of the river that I used above. Imagine that the guidelines for a particular song are like the banks of the river. We know that the banks of a river change slowly and imperceptibly. They do this slowly enough that we can return to the same river and find it not so significantly altered as to be unable to identify it. But the banks of the river channel the course of the moving water. The water that flows through is always different—but the course of the water is determined by the banks. Further, there's always a subtle inter- action between the water and the bank: the bank provides a channel for the water to move, and the water's force subtly modifies the bank.

We might be tempted to say that there are *no* constraints associated with the band when they play, but this can't be right. The band must play in the same key with one another. More importantly, the band has to listen to what one another is doing, in order that they remain in the same groove. It wouldn't do if Phil were playing a bass line that was rhythmically at odds with what everyone else was doing. You can hear them listen to one another, and follow each other: one band member will play a certain line, and then another mimics or develops or accompa- nies another. This is a process that (ideally) keeps moving, developing, and growing, pushing the song in new directions, and creating a musical experience that is interesting and unique.

To answer the objection—to consider how we might be more like the river and yet still consider ourselves free—let's look at the way in which Benedict Spinoza defines freedom. He says that "that thing is said to be free which exists solely from the necessity of its own nature, and is determined to action by itself alone." First, note that Spinoza believes that only Nature (God, in Spinoza's idiom) itself is truly free, and what he means is that individual human beings aren't really free at all. Spinoza thus appears to concede to the determinist point of view—that all human actions and desires are necessarily determined, and hence not free. But there is another way of understanding Spinoza's claim.

There is a wonderful parable in the writings of the Chinese Taoist philosopher Chuang Tzu that I think exemplifies the kind of point that Spinoza is making. Here's the gist of the parable: there is a cook who is remarkably skilled in cutting meat. When asked about his skill he describes it thus: "What I care about is the Way [*Tao*], which goes beyond skill. When I first began cut- ting up oxen, all I could see was the ox itself. After those years I no longer saw the whole ox. And now—now I go at it by spirit and don't look with my eyes. Perception and understanding have come to a stop and spirit moves where it wants" (Chuang Tzu, *Basic Writings* [New York: Columbia University Press, 1964], pp. 46–47).

The first thing to note is that there is a distinction implicit in both comments, between ourselves as putative agents, and that which is really free. The implication of these comments is that our usual conception of ourselves as agents who are fully in charge of what we do is only apparent. For Spinoza, since as individual agents we are constrained by those things which we are not capable of doing, we are not completely free. For Chuang, there is a difference between acting with respect to skill and acting by Spirit. In this case, Chuang understands skill as a pattern of behavior that we can learn to perform a particular task. But Chuang insists that in order to perform a skill well, one must surpass that skill itself. What this means is that once the skill becomes second nature, and we no longer must consciously perform it, we find that we can perform the skill better. We sometimes refer to phenomena like this when we speak of someone being "inspired" or "in the zone," but the real meaning for Chuang is that when properly understood, all action is merely nature or the Way itself performing through us.

Now think about the lyrics to the song, "Playin' in the Band" to see how the Dead might be said to embody the Stoic attitude. The lyrics to the song begin: "Some folks trust to reason / others trust to might / I don't trust to nothing / But I know it come out right . . . when it's done and over / a man is just a man." These words capture two important elements mentioned above. First, there's the notion that "it will come out right." How could we know this? Unfortunately, human beings are often bad at predicting the future. Sure, science allows us to make relatively accurate predictions about the natural world, but once we factor in the complexities of human interactions, and all of the kinds of things that can happen, we *don't* really know how it's going to turn out. But, on the Stoic interpretation, we can know that it will turn out right, because it can't turn out wrong! It can't turn out any other way than it will, so that when we are upset because things didn't go the way that we want, it's not because we are not satisfied, but rather because we've failed to see the situation for what it is. This thought is confirmed by the end of the stanza: a man is just a man (for what else could anyone be?).[1]

---

[1] No need for a charge of sexism here—yes, the word is "man" but the Stoic view would apply to anyone: who or what is anyone but themselves?

Based on how the jams sound, as well as many of the Dead's lyrics (especially the quote from "The Music Never Stopped" above), it seems that the band lets the music "play" them. But we know (at least I do—I've tried) that you can't just pick up a guitar and play like Jerry Garcia. Jerry (and the other members of the band) can play what they do because of their musical skill. Much like the butcher in Chuang's story, they could be said to play music in accord with the Way, that is, beyond skill, but it must be the case that the skill is there to begin with. So the band is constrained by their skills as well—what they're capable of doing. If Jerry had lost a finger on his left hand or were tone deaf, things would have been much different.

Sometimes We Live No Particular Way but Our Own

The upshot to this discussion is that the objection to the Stoic philosophy advanced above is at best empty, at worst that it doesn't have the kind of traction that it needs to. If we can recognize that constraints that shape and affect our own lives, then we can allow ourselves to respond to them in a way that helps to mutually create a world that is more interesting, worthwhile, and freer.

Here the idea is that action that is worthwhile possesses at least two related traits. The first is that actions must respond appropriately to the environment. Among other things, in order to act well, we must pay attention to what is happening around us and respond to it, not to what we want it to be or believe it to be. The second is that actions should derive from an awareness of the particularity of a situation, and not from a tight, unbendable set of rules. Adhering too strongly to rules to guide our action often blinds us to the uniqueness of a situation. We see how the Dead, as they perform live, sometimes perform in a way that meets the two criteria noted above. And so this is ultimately what the Stoic's freedom consists in: not thinking about actions in terms of making choices but rather in thinking how we can most accurately respond to the environment we happen to be in.

This is all, of course, if we identify the jams of the Grateful Dead to possess this substantive freedom. But I think that we can see that there is this substantive freedom in the music, because what the Dead play isn't empty. They are able to create something new and interesting on the spot – a kind of spontaneous generation, if you like. If they simply played the same tunes in the same way all of the time, we'd feel as if they were slaves to those tunes. The fact that the Dead's live shows offered a growing, organic musical experience shows that by allowing the music to develop according to its own logic, something can be created that is worthwhile.

We may still wonder how the Dead's approach to improvisation can extend beyond the confines of improvisational music. To understand how this extension is possible, contrast the carnival atmosphere of a Dead show with the rigors of our day-to-day lives. Ordinary life can be routine and humdrum; if Thoreau is right, "the mass of men lead lives of quiet desperation." One might argue that this is the nature of life, and that all the Dead can provide is merely a momentary escape from that normal routine. One might raise the specter of the quietist objection again, claiming that it's all well and good to let yourself go in a concert setting, but there are rules and norms that one must follow in the context of our day-to-day affairs. Thus, whatever freedom we might claim to get from a Dead show is entirely limited to that context alone.

But why are those norms that we must follow in our day to day activities any different than the constraints placed on the band to create something in a musical setting? I have argued that constraints on our actions are something unavoidable. If I'm right, then acting well is simply a matter of responding and acting appropriately in the context of the given constraints.

We could press this objection further. Consider the short quote from Thoreau again. It's not just that we have constraints on our action, but rather that those constraints on our actions are ones that *prevent* us from being free in a meaningful way. A good example would be a person who, deep in debt, must work the only job available to them that they detest, simply to avoid the consequences of defaulting on their debt. The Dead show us a way to respond to this objection by expanding the analogy between their approach to music and how we as individuals might prosecute our own lives.

If one wanted to become a musician back in 1965, there were plenty of options of what kind of musician one could become. One could play country, blues, rock'n'roll, classical, jazz, and so on. Each of these genres has a particular set of constraints that helps to both identify the genre itself, as well as provides criteria for establishing when a particular instance is a successful instance of that genre. Consider, for example, how the groundbreaking work of The Beatles in the early 1960s led to the creation of The Monkees. The Monkees' music, as well as their personae on the television show, were designed to mimic the teen-pop aura that the pre-1966 Beatles created. On many points, the creators of the Monkees were successful. They took a highly successful paradigm, and implemented it, regardless of the actual value of the music itself.

When we ask what genre of music the Dead's music falls into, we're at a significant loss, for we find elements of many identifiable genres of music synthesized into something totally different: rock and roll, folk, rockabilly, jazz, psychedelic rock, avant-garde music, bluegrass, world music, country, and blues. What the Grateful Dead managed to do in synthesizing these styles was to transcend them, ultimately generating their own particular and unique genre of music. This example shows that some of the constraints that appear to press on creating music are not ultimately fixed, and provides an analogue to how we can transcend other constraints that threaten to prevent us from achieving a meaningful freedom. What ultimately separates those who live well and freely are those who are not constrained *arbitrarily*, but only by what is in fact necessary.

19

Death Don't Have No Mercy: On the Metaphysics of Loss and Why We Should Be Grateful for Death

IAN DUCKLES and ERIC M. RUBENSTEIN

Despite the joyful abandon people associate with the Grateful Dead, the community has suffered the loss of numerous members, most famously of course Pig Pen and Jerry Garcia. Losing a loved one, even someone you don't know personally, can be the occasion for great sadness, the celebration of their life, and also an opportunity for reflecting on life, death, and the meaning of everything in between. Thinking about death is hard. But it is important.

Most of us think that death is to be avoided at all costs and the worst thing that can happen to someone. If death is so bad, we should be able to explain what makes it so bad. Ask yourself the question: "What is so bad about death?" When some philosophers try to answer the question, they find there is no good answer. Strange as it seems, some philosophers think there are convincing reasons to see death not as bad, but actually as good. These people aren't crazy. And they don't have a death wish. This is a book about the *Grateful* Dead, after all. Is that name just a morbid joke? Forget the band's intentions, and why they chose that name. Instead, consider whether it's possible, in any sense, to understand death as good, something that we might, in some way, be grateful for. Is there any way at all one could view the death of Pig Pen or Jerry as a good thing? Admittedly it is hard to find a way to say yes. Does that mean that, as the song says, "It's better to burn out than to fade away?" Or that we should hope to die before we get old?

To ponder these questions, and more generally, to wonder about death itself, isn't to be morbid (though an obsession with it might be); it is to wonder about one of the most mysterious and difficult parts of life itself. And that certainly makes it an appropriate subject matter for Philosophy. As a guide to how to think about death (and maybe to what it is to do Philosophy at all), we might consider one philosopher's description of his day job. "The aim of Philosophy, abstractly formulated, is to understand how things in the broadest possible sense of the term hang together in the broadest possible sense of the term. Under 'things in the broadest possible sense' I include such radically different items as not only 'cabbages and kings', but numbers and duties, possibilities and finger snaps, aesthetic experience and death. To achieve success in Philosophy would be, to use a contemporary turn of phrase, to 'know one's way around' with respect to all these things, not in that unreflective way in which the centipede of the story knew its way around before it faced the question, 'How do I walk?', but in that reflective way which means that no intellectual holds are barred (Wilfred Sellars, "Philosophy and the Scientific Image of Man," *Science, Perception, and Reality* [Atascadero: Ridgeview, 1991], p. 1).

When we wonder about death, we wonder about how to reconcile the pain we feel about the loss of a loved one with the joy we feel as we remember good times we had with them. We wonder about what it means to be alive and what is valuable and important in our lives. We ask about what a good life involves and about how we should treat others. To ask about death is to ask essential questions about what it is to be human. No other being is capable of pondering its own death besides us. To not ask about death is to refuse to live a reflective life, to refuse to be the special type of beings we are capable of.

It's often remarked that only two things in life are certain, death and taxes. We know how to find help when it comes to taxes, but where do we turn to find help when it comes to death? What's the right way to think about it? As a way of beginning an answer we will explore what some famous philosophers have had to say. Of course, this can only be a start. Philosophy is a dialogue that has been going on for twenty five hundred years. The most we can hope for here is a snippet of that conversation.

If the Thunder Don't Get Ya, the Lightning Will

Most people think dying is the worst thing that can happen to them. In fact, if you were to list the terrible things that could happen, things you are afraid of, dying a terrible death would probably be on that list. True, you might believe that if you were in terrible, incurable pain, then perhaps death wouldn't be so terrible. We do say of someone who has died after a terrible illness that, "at least they aren't suffering anymore." But let us put those cases aside. Is death, in ordinary circumstances, bad, terrible, or evil? If so, why? What exactly about death makes it so bad? Why are we so scared of it? To help answer these questions we need to make two important distinctions. First, we need to distinguish the badness that might come to the person who dies, on the one hand, from the badness that results for that person's friends and family. Obviously losing someone is a painful experience, and in that way is bad. Let us focus, however, on the person who is dying. Is death bad for that person, and if so, how and why?

That leads us to our second distinction. We know that the *process* of dying can be very painful. But that is different from actually being dead. One leads to the other, but our focus is on the result, not the process or cause. While the process of dying can be terrible, it isn't clear that actually *being dead* is so bad. Let us ask: Is the state of being dead (again, not the process of dying) a bad thing? That's the more difficult question, but also the more interesting one. If we are afraid of death, it could be that we are afraid of a painful process of dying. Leave that part out. Suppose instead you were assured that the process of dying wouldn't be bad, perhaps because of heavy painkillers. Would you still view your actual death as a bad thing? The death of a loved one? Of someone you respect and admire? Why? That's our focus.

Though most people probably view death as a bad thing, not everyone does. A famous philosopher, Epicurus, thought this a terribly mistaken, limiting view of life and death. His argument is quite simple, but powerful. It goes like this. First, imagine making a list of all the things that are bad, from the mundane to the most terrible, and ask what they all have in common. Chances are, what they all have in common is that they in are in some way connected with pain or unhappiness. Just as a list of good things—from ice cream to music—would be list of things that seem to be good because of their connection with pleasure, what seems to make bad things actually bad is that they are painful. The items on the "bad list" might be actual painful items, such as ten minutes of guitar feedback at close range, or items that have pain or unhappiness as a consequence, say a month of rainy weekends. That's the first step of the argument: bad things are bad because of their connection with pain.

For the second step, consider the state of actually *being dead*. Admittedly this is an odd thing to do (not to mention perhaps impossible). But it is the crucial part of the argument. Now when we say we fear death, we can't really mean that we fear being dead because of the pain we'd experience. For if death is the end of me, when I'm dead, there isn't a me left to be in pain! Death, that is, isn't an experience you will have. It is the cessation *of your experiences*. You don't experience being dead, for being dead is nothing more than the ceasing to exist, the ceasing to have experiences in the first place. And if death isn't the having of a certain experience, it can't be the experiencing of anything bad or painful. To repeat: we might fear the *process* of dying, but being dead isn't an experience we have, so it can't be a bad, painful one, one that we should fear.

If we now put these two steps together we get a very powerful conclusion. If bad things are bad because they are painful (or connected with pain), and death isn't an experience, and so not a painful experience, then it seems that death isn't bad at all. Being dead isn't painful, nor does it make you unhappy. There's nothing left to make it bad. So, it isn't bad. Death isn't a bad thing. That should make you pause. Epicurus puts it this way. "So death, the most terrifying of ills, is nothing to us, since so long as we exist death is not with us; but when death comes, then we do not exist . . . the wise man neither seeks to escape life nor fears the cessation of life (Epicurus, "Letter to Menoeceus," *The Stoic and Epicurean Philosophers* [New York: Modern Library, 1940], p. 31).

Epicurus's argument denies one of our most natural beliefs, namely that death is terrible and to be feared. But imagine how life would look were he right. There's something absolutely liberating in Epicurus's perspective. To be sure, the argument doesn't ask us to welcome death, or to look forward to it, but it has the potential to remove much of the fear and mystery that surrounds our own eventual death. Epicurus's argument carries an additional positive force when we ponder not our own death, but those of people we love. At least part of the grief we experience when a loved one dies comes from our conviction that something terrible has happened to them. But if Epicurus is right, when a loved one dies it isn't true that something bad has happened to them. Remember, the argument tried to prove that death isn't a bad thing. When we lose someone, we will still miss them. But we don't have to worry that something bad happened to them. That might make our own grief easier to bear.

If we then use this account to look at the question of whether it is better to burn out than fade away, we find that Epicurus doesn't provide us with much insight. Essentially, it would appear that from his position there isn't really much of a difference between these two positions. They both are forms of death, and both should be treated in the same way, regardless of how much life was lived prior to that death.

To be fair, many philosophers don't accept Epicurus's argument, and think it fallacious. We will leave it to you, the reader, to decide for yourself whether you are convinced.[1] Instead of pursuing this further, however, we turn to an entirely different consideration of the alleged evil of death.

I Need a Miracle: Eternal Life

So far we've been exploring whether death really is a bad thing. And we've wondered what, if anything, makes death bad. We've tried to answer that mystery by, in essence, trying to imagine being dead. Let's now try something different. Instead of pondering our eventual demise, let's instead ponder a future where we live forever. For good measure, imagine that everyone we know and love also lives forever. Imagine the banishment of the Grim Reaper. After all, if death is bad, we would expect that not dying would have to be good. If we don't want to die, it must be that we desire immortality. So, pretend it has been granted, to you and everyone you love.

---

[1] An excellent discussion of Epicurus's argument can be found in F. Feldman, *Confrontations with the Reaper* (Oxford: Oxford University Press, 1992). Another accessible book on the subject is J. Rosenberg, *Thinking Clearly about Death* (Englewood Cliffs: Prentice Hall, 1983).

As before, we'll make explicit the elements in our reasonings about death and immortality. In what follows, we'll rely on a step, or premise, that says that among the various desires we have, some of them are fundamental and some are not. Some desires obviously are ones you'd have only if you happen to be alive—say, a desire to eat a veggieburger on a given day. But other desire are so fundamental or basic to who we are as people that they actually give us reasons to be alive in the first place. These fundamental desires are so important to us that they can help us decide whether our lives are worth living. A desire for a veggieburger, for most people, isn't that kind of fundamental desire. A desire for world peace, or maybe to collect all of the greatest Dead performances on top quality audio-visual media, on the other hand, could be fundamental desires for some people, and so give them reason to live. They want it so much that it gives them a reason to live even if there are other things in their life that make them unhappy or even suicidal. So, the first step in our argument is just the claim that for each of us there are certain desires that are so fundamental to the particular people we are, that they give us reasons to live. Each of us has, in other words, our own fundamental desires (which of course we can share and have in common with others).

With that in mind, consider more seriously the possibility of living forever. Forever is a long time. A very long time. How would you fill your days of immortality? You might decide to take up painting. And maybe you become an excellent painter—after all, you've got the time to practice. Suppose you paint for a thousand years. Chances are you'll *eventually* tire of it. So you drop the brush and pick up the piano, playing it for five thousand years before becoming absolutely sick of it. Then you might decide to be a philosopher and read all the philosophy ever written. Before, that is, you get tired of doing that, after ten (thousand?) years. A pattern now begins to emerge. This leads to our second step: Any desire you have, pursued long enough, is one you will tire of satisfying, eventually. Any desire. And that seems to include even those fundamental ones. Even a desire for world peace, pursued for twenty thousand years (on a rather pessimistic view of our future), is eventually going to cease to hold its appeal. The simple monotony of the activity itself (not to mention frustration in that example) will eventually oppress you. Even being the ultimate Dead collector, says this argument, will eventually, eventually, become terribly boring.

Consider the consequences of this pattern. If anything you do long enough is something you'll eventually get sick of (think of the expression, "bored to death"), then eventually you will run out of reason to stay alive at all. The fundamental desires will lose their appeal. But these were the very ones that gave us reason to live in the first place.

It seems that eventually we'll cease to find activities that give us enough meaning and pleasure to outweigh the growing, overwhelming boredom of eternity. Really appreciate how much time you'll have on our hands. And add to that the not unlikely chance that even people you love dearly will start to annoy you after, say, ten thousand years, a million years, more! We are bound to tire even of ourselves for that matter. Immortality, closely considered, begins to lose its charm. We'll be sick of everything, and everyone, given enough time.

Where does that leave us? Well, if immortality isn't desirable, the cure for that could only be death, right? Death perhaps looks to be almost a good thing in this case. It would be the release from the boredom of eternity. If you agree, then notice how far we've moved from our starting point- that death is the worst thing in the world.

Perhaps it isn't death itself that is so bad. In the case of immortality, death is welcome as a release. Maybe what is bad about death is the timing of it. Maybe it is only premature death that is bad. If so, we now have to ask ourselves, "How long do I really want to live? What would be a premature death, and on the other hand, how much life is too much?" Those are important but difficult questions, it seems.

Turning again to the question of which death (Pig Pen or Jerry Garcia) is preferable, we find the same non-answer we saw above with respect to Epicurus. That is, if we accept the conclusions of the above argument, we see that eternal life is bad, but we are given no insight concerning how much life is too much of a good thing. Therefore, we are still unable to determine whether it is better to burn out or fade away.

As for the argument we've just examined, death seems to be a necessary evil—the antidote to the tedium of immortality. Is that as far as we can move towards being grateful about death? Or might it be that death is not just a necessary evil, but actually a good thing, something we might be grateful for? *That* would be a most surprising conclusion, considering our starting point. And yet that is exactly the conclusion some philosophers have reached about death. To that we now turn.

I'm Begging You Don't Murder Me

One of the most famous arguments that we should view death as a blessing is found in Plato's dialogue, the *Phaedo*. This dialogue is an account of the last day of the famous Athenian philosopher Socrates, who was sentenced to death by the city-state of Athens for corrupting the youth. Much of the dialogue is focused on Socrates's belief that his imminent death isn't a bad thing at all. Quite to the contrary, in this discussion, Socrates not only doesn't fear dying, he even sees it as a blessing.

A crucial component of Socrates's view, however, is a disagreement with one of the premises we've discussed above. In the earlier discussion, death was seen as the cessation of experience, and so not a bad experience. Socrates thinks this gets the metaphysics of death wrong. He believes, in contrast, that death is really the separation of the soul from the body and its relocation to another place. We are released and freed from our bodies when we die.

Once our bodies are no longer around to distract with their pains, constant needs to be fed and protected, our souls can do what they are good for: thinking. In fact, Socrates thinks that philosophy itself is just practice for dying—the occasion to let our thoughts pursue whatever questions and puzzles they find, in a pursuit of the truth. Philosophy is literally the "love of wisdom", and those who search for wisdom while alive will of course welcome the chance to really achieve it. And that is possible only once the body is left behind. Dying is the route to wisdom, because of our soul's ability to survive and reason once the body is gone.

Though it appears different on its face, Socrates's view here is similar to Sellars's, discussed above. Both see philosophy as an intellectual rather than physical pursuit, as an activity involving reflection, where reflection involves having a certain distance or separation from the object of reflection. In Socrates's case, this separation or distance involves a rejection or suspension of one's bodily needs and desires.

Not unexpectedly, many people disagree with Socrates's views too. For while it might be that for some people, they are most happy when doing philosophy, and so might truly welcome death, not everyone shares equally in the pleasures of thinking. Nor is it clear what is wrong with deriving pleasure from sources other than thinking. Why should someone who loves the Grateful Dead and loves listing to their music deny himself these pleasures? Even worse, it seems, Socrates's views make death *too much* of a blessing. If you buy Socrates's account it's not clear why you should even bother living in the first place, and why you shouldn't just kill yourself. This would seem to save a bunch of time, and allow you to avoid all the lousy and unpleasant aspects of life. That strikes many as just unreasonable- not to mention even immoral.

Turning to the Pig Pen-Jerry Garcia question again, we finally get a substantive answer. Given that, according to Socrates, death is a blessing, and such a blessing that one might think it should be rushed, it would seem that Pig Pen's death would be preferable to Garcia's because Pig Pen was able to achieve that ultimate philosophic position found only in death much more quickly that Garcia. In this way, Socrates (despite the fact that he lived to be over seventy years old) would seem to endorse the view that it is better to burn out than fade away. However, this sort of response is troubling because of all the uncomfortable implications articulated in the previous paragraph.

Given this, it would be nice to find some sort of middle ground between a view that held that death is terrible, on the one hand, and a view that saw death as so marvelous that we should all commit suicide immediately, on the other hand. Fortunately, the work of the twentieth-century German philosopher Martin Heidegger provides the sort of position we are looking for. It is to this that we now turn.

Not Fade Away

Heidegger's most famous book is the massive, intimidating, but exciting *Being and Time*. A key theme in that book is the way in which our views of death are structured and influenced by the various goals and values of contemporary society. According to Heidegger, our deep-seated fear of death is largely a function of our culture, a culture that encourages us to avoid confrontation with the fact that we are mortal and will die. For example, let's take the sort of life that is encouraged in contemporary American society. We live in a capitalist culture in which all aspects (TV, media, the president,[2] our friends) constantly tell us that we are defined by what we own, and that to find happiness in life we just need to buy a bigger stereo and a device that will play whatever new music format the record companies come up with. This is seen quite clearly in the phenomenon of "keeping up with the Joneses" in which individuals feel compelled to acquire whatever new goods or products are acquired by their neighbors. This constant drive to acquire more wealth and accumulate more stuff is best understood as an attempt by individuals to avoid confronting the reality of death. We're distracted from confronting our own immortality, and are glad we are.

By focusing on the acquisition of wealth and consumer goods, we are able to distract ourselves from the unsettling fact that are lives are transitory and impermanent; that we are fragile beings that can perish at any time, without warning. We even come to believe that reflecting on our own mortality is morbid and "unhealthy." And we view our fear of death as just natural.

Heidegger's powerful insight into all of this, however, is that this strategy of distraction and consumption ultimately fails to protect us in the way in which it promises. Even worse, it allows us to hide from the truth of our own existence and the reality of death. Until we confront this reality, we will never be able to lead fulfilling, meaningful lives. True liberation, in other words, can come only once we strip away these society-imposed values, and once we confront head-on the fact that death is inescapable, and that it can happen to us and the ones we love at any time.

---

[2] In the aftermath of the terrorist attacks on the World Trade Center and the Pentagon, President George W. Bush encouraged all Americans to counter the terrorist ideology by continuing to shop and act as good consumers. In this way, by not abandoning our American way of life, we would not allow the terrorist to win. "I ask [for] your continued participation and confidence in the American economy. Terrorists attacked a symbol of American prosperity; they did not touch its source." This quotation comes from the President's address to a joint session of Congress on September 20th, 2001. A full text can be found at http://www.whitehouse.gov/news/releases/2001/09/20010920-8.html.

On the face of it this might appear absurd. How could it be
that a confrontation with death could enable us to lead more fulfilling, meaningful lives? Wouldn't it just make us depressed? The
answer to these questions requires us to introduce an important
philosophical concept in Heidegger's thinking: authenticity.
More than what we mean when we say of someone that they
are "authentic, not fake" (but still related to that idea), this concept of authenticity is explained by Heidegger by appeal to the
idea of "potential."

Consider it this way. Each of the individual members of the
Grateful Dead are talented musicians, but when they get
together and play, they are able to produce music that is better
than the sum of its parts. The interplay among the band members allows these individuals to excel and to play beyond their
individual abilities. We could say that each of the members has
a certain *potential*, but something has to happen in order for
these individuals to realize (or *actualize*) that potential. And we
also think that it is important that people do realize their poten-
tial- to "be all they can be". We think it even tragic when someone fails to achieve his potential or is prevented from doing so
(say by dying).

Put these ideas together and we can understand how important it is that people be able to pursue the activities that allow
them to achieve their potential. In fact, this is one way of
explaining why the death of Jerry Garcia hit people so hard. It
wasn't just that we were sad that he died, but that there was all
of this great talent and potential that would never have a chance
to be realized. So many performances and special moments that
just weren't going to happen now—for him and for us.

One of Heidegger's important contributions to the conversation of philosophy lies in his claim that it isn't just bands or talented musicians that have potential, but rather that human
beings have a certain potential solely because they're humans.
We humans are special and valuable, and we have lots of poten-
tials, whoever we are, whatever it is that we do. For anyone, it's
important that their potential be realized.

Remember the earlier concept introduced: authenticity. We
can now say that to live an authentic life is just to live in a way
that realizes or actualizes our potential as humans. An authentic
life would be one in which a person realizes his potential to the
best of his abilities, while an inauthentic life would be one in

which he fails to do so. Just as it would be a tragedy if the Grateful Dead had never come together, so too does Heidegger see an individual who fails to realize his potential as a human being as also a kind of failing, or at the very least, he sees something wrong with an individual who leads this sort of life.

What does Heidegger think is necessary for an individual to lead an authentic existence? The answer brings us right to the heart of this article. In short, we can live authentic lives only if we grapple with our own mortality. Death, after all, is the end of all possibilities for you, all opportunities for action and all projects that seemed important or compelling to you. In confronting your own death as the possibility of the end of all possibilities, you come to realize that the goals and projects that you took to define your life ultimately have no value in themselves-viewed from the outside, we might say. Since these projects and goals will end with your end, your confrontation with death reveals that these projects are ultimately limited and even perhaps meaningless. With this confrontation, you realize that your life cannot be defined by the achievement of various projects and goals, because once you are dead your money and possessions will be of no value to you. You can't take it with you, of course, and realizing this forces you to question whether any of these goals and achievements had value at all.

Here comes the crucial part. For all of this might lead you to feel hopeless, to think that nothing at all is valuable and important. If nothing is valuable, and all your aspirations and projects are ultimately valueless, you might ask about the point of it all. Philosophers call this type of despair "nihilism," and some think that this is the correct way to view your life. But Heidegger disagrees. And that's the key to his philosophy. He responds to the possibility of despair by pointing out that instead of despair, this confrontation with the possibility of your own death, this awareness that your projects are ultimately worthless, frees you to develop a new relation to your life and to the world. In recognizing the necessity of your own death, you can now cultivate a life that acknowledges this fact, and frees you from much of the anxiety and discomfort that plagued your life before. In confronting your own death, you can come to the realization that the projects and values imposed upon you by your culture and your society do not define you, and thus need not control your life. In this way, a realization of the possibility of your own death can free you from the constraints imposed upon you by society and allows you to then develop and pursue your own projects and goals that are meaningful to you as this specific individual with these specific needs and desires. You are genuinely, truly, free to create your life as you want it to be, as you think it ought to be.

From this perspective then, we can argue that between Pig Pen and Jerry Garcia, the death of Jerry Garcia is to be preferred. This is because, due to his longer life span, Garcia was able to realize his potential in a way denied to Pig Pen by his untimely demise. Thus, it would seem that Heidegger would agree with the sentiment expressed in the saying, "I hope I get old before I die."

In this way, finally, we can see why you might be grateful for death. Your awareness of your death, and the awareness of the emptiness of socially defined projects or goals mean that many of the traditional sources of unhappiness no longer need bother you.[3] As Epicurus noted, the cause of all suffering for humans is frustrated desire, but, as Heidegger argues, in confronting your own mortality in an authentic fashion, you come to see the meaninglessness of traditionally, socially defined sources of desire. Thus, you are freed to create your own values, and you are able to pursue the projects that you personally find interesting or meaningful. In this way, your death frees you from the demands of society, and allows you to pursue your life as you see fit. We expect you will be able to see for yourself now the interesting dovetailing of the way of looking at life and the spirit of the Grateful Dead and the counter-culture that sprang up around them.

I'll Get Up and Fly Away

Having briefly touched on some highlights of the twenty five hundred year old conversation of philosophy, we finally found a framework for viewing death as something for which we should be grateful. This framework also allows us to endorse the

---

[3] Heidegger is not advocating a free-for-all orgiastic hedonism. He does think that there are limits to the sort of authentic life an individual can lead. For a nice introduction to this issue, see Hubert L. Dreyfus, *Being-in-the-World: A Commentary on Heidegger's Being and Time, Division I* (Cambridge, Massachusetts: MIT Press, 1991).

claim that it is better to fade away than to burn out (in contrast to the way it is normally put). And, as we hinted at above, this Heideggerian account of death meshes quite nicely with some of the cornerstones of the movement that sprung up around the Grateful Dead in the 1960s and 1970s. This movement was characterized first and foremost by a rejection of the traditional values associated with the white, nuclear, suburban family of the 1950s. These traditional values claimed that a person's sole function in life was to get a job (if you were a man), get married, and produce and raise as many children as possible (if you were a woman). In associating themselves with the Grateful Dead and the lifestyle and culture surrounding them, Deadheads registered their displeasure and denial of these traditional values. Through this rejection, they were able to create new kinds of values and develop a new sense of community that was both different from, and in many ways in opposition to, the dominant social values of the time. Things like "free love" and the use of mind altering substances like marijuana and LSD were motivated by a desire to develop new values and ways of life that were more closely aligned with individuals' particular wants, needs and desires in opposition to the values that many felt were imposed upon them by "the Man."

Now we would certainly be going too far if we tried to argue that a close reading of Heidegger influenced the Grateful Dead or the Deadhead community. Nevertheless, the ideas and concepts developed by Heidegger out of his engagement with the history of philosophy do share a strong affinity with many aspects of the Grateful Dead. This should not be surprising, as it is often the case that ideas and systems of belief that have their origins in highly technical academic disciplines often eventually spread out into the culture at large. Though it may be mere coincidence, we can nevertheless see an important respect in which the name "Grateful Dead" makes sense. If we weren't mortal, if we didn't someday die, we wouldn't have the freedom and control over our lives and our values that an authentic confrontation with death provides. Thus, we should be grateful for death, or, at the very least, grateful for our mortality. Without it, we wouldn't be what we are, and we wouldn't be capable of doing the things we can.

Goin' Down the Road: The Grateful Dead Discography

The Grateful Dead	1967	Dick's Picks, Volume 3	1995
Anthem of the Sun	1968	Hundred Year Hall	1995
Aoxomoxoa	1969	Dick's Picks, Volume 4	1996
Live/Dead	1969	Dick's Picks, Volume 6	1996
Workingman's Dead	1970	Dozin' at the Knick	1996
American Beauty	1970	Dick's Picks, Volume 7	1997
Grateful Dead (Skull		Dick's Picks, Volume 8	1997
& Roses)	1971	Dick's Picks, Volume 9	1997
Europe '72	1972	Fillmore East 2.11.69	1997
History of the Grateful		Fallout from the Phil	
Dead, Volume 1		Zone	1997
(Bear's Choice)	1973	Dick's Picks, Volume 10	1998
Wake of the Flood	1973	Dick's Picks, Volume 11	1998
Grateful Dead from the		Dick's Picks, Volume 12	1998
Mars Hotel	1974	Dick's Picks, Volume 13	1999
Blues for Allah	1975	Dick's Picks, Volume 14	1999
Steal Your Face	1976	Dick's Picks, Volume 15	1999
Terrapin Station	1977	So Many Roads	
Shakedown Street	1978	(1965–1995)	1999
Go to Heaven	1980	Dick's Picks, Volume 16	2000
Reckoning	1981	Dick's Picks, Volume 17	2000
Dead Set	1981	Dick's Picks, Volume 18	2000
In the Dark	1987	View from the Vault	2000
Dylan and the Dead	1988	Best of the Grateful Dead	
Built to Last	1989	Hour	2000
Without a Net	1990	Ladies and Gentlemen	
Infrared Roses	1991	. . . The Grateful Dead	2000
One from the Vault	1991	Dick's Picks, Volume 19	2000
Two from the Vault	1992	The Golden Road	
Dick's Picks, Volume 1	1993	(1965–1973)	2001
Dick's Picks, Volume 2	1995	Dick's Picks, Volume 20	2001

Dick's Picks, Volume 21	2001	Beyond Description	2004
Dick's Picks, Volume 22	2001	Dick's Picks, Volume 31	2004
View from the Vault II	2001	Rockin' the Rhein	2004
Nightfall of Diamonds	2001	Dick's Picks, Volume 32	2004
Dick's Picks, Volume 23	2001	Dick's Picks, Volume 33	2004
Dick's Picks, Volume 24	2002	Grateful Dead Movie	
Steppin' Out with the		Soundtrack	2004
Grateful Dead: England		Rare Cuts and Oddities	
'72	2002	1966	2005
Dick's Picks, Volume 25	2002	Dick's Picks, Volume 34	2005
View from the Vault III	2002	Dick's Picks, Volume 35	2005
Dick's Picks, Volume 26	2002	Truckin' Up to Buffalo	2005
Go to Nassau	2002	Garcia Plays Dylan	2005
Postcards of the Hanging	2002	Fillmore West 1969: The	
Birth of the Dead	2003	Complete Recordings	2005
Dick's Picks, Volume 27	2003	Fillmore West 1969:	
View from the Vault IV	2003	Compilation	2005
Dick's Picks, Volume 28	2003	Dick's Picks, Volume 36	2005
Dick's Picks, Volume 29	2003	Live at the Cow Palace:	
Dick's Picks, Volume 30	2003	New Year's Eve 1976	2006
The Closing of Winterland	2003		

Playin' in the Band

RANDALL AUXIER is gratefully alive, although he can't be sure it's better than the alternative. He teaches philosophy at Southern Illinois University in Carbondale—at least that's what he does when he isn't playing Grateful Dead covers, and covers of Grateful Dead covers, in local bars, for small audiences who won't remember whether the show was any good, which is just as well. His father has wanted him to cut his hair since 1969, but it isn't going to happen, although both have recently noticed a worrisome touch of grey.

PETER BRADLEY is Assistant Professor of Philosophy at McDaniel College. A graduate of Antioch College, he spent the late 1990s running a series of failed dot-coms in Portland, Oregon, where he became well acquainted with the copyleft tradition. While he is keenly interested in the conflict between intellectual property and the Internet's anarchic ethos, his primary research is in trying to understand the philosophical implications of the possibility of other creatures' perception: from the fact that birds see colors that we cannot to the possibility of other sensory modalities such as pit viper's infrared sense and shark's electrical sense.

JOHANNES BULHOF is Professor of Philosophy at McNeese State University in Lake Charles, Louisiana. His interests include the history of philosophy, the philosophy of language, and logic. He blames his interest in the Grateful Dead on the corrupting influence of his older brother, Dr. Justin Bulhof, who took him to his first show at Manor Downs, Texas, the fourth day of July, 1981. He has never been the same since.

GARY CIOCCO teaches Philosophy as a Roman adjunct at Gettysburg College, York College of Pennsylvania, and Mount St. Mary's University. He has also taught English and has had poems published in several journals. He used to think of himself as a non-prolific, less-alcoholic Jack Kerouac, but now prefers to think of himself as a non-musical, unnaturally thin Jerry Garcia. As a result, he is very thankful for philosophy.

BRENDAN CUSHING-DANIELS is Assistant Professor of Economics at Gettysburg College. His research focuses on issues related to the social safety net, crime, and sexual orientation. His first tie-dyed t-shirt was of the fifteen-dollar variety and as a ten-year old Catholic school boy, decided to shock the nuns at his school, who had assigned a project on local businesses, by interviewing the owner of a music and head shop.

STEPHEN DILLINGHAM received a B.S. in physics from Wake Forest University in 1992 and (eventually) a Ph.D. in philosophy from Johns Hopkins University in 2003. His dissertation was on Einstein's cosmological constant and the foundations of the general theory of relativity, and he continues to pursue research in the philosophy of science. At present, a friend of the Devil is not just a friend of his, but his employer . . . he works as a defense contractor.

JOHN DRABINSKI teaches philosophy and related stuff at Hampshire College in Amherst, Massachusetts. He is interested in social and political philosophy, contemporary European aesthetic theory, and the encounter of European theory with the experience of the Americas. In addition to constructing pretentious, self-important areas of research, he is also interested in philosophizing about popular culture. Some aspect of that interest is an attempt to avoid facing the embarrassing fact that he went to his first Dead show with his dad. Yes, his dad. He would also (desperately) note that he saw the Dead in Eugene, more than once, which may or may not redeem going to a show with a parent. You make the call.

IAN DUCKLES has a poor sense of humor. He is currently Assistant Professor of Philosophy at Indiana University of Pennsylvania where he works on existentialism and ethics. He attended his first show at the Oakland Coliseum on December 8th, 1994.

BUD FAIRLAMB has degrees from Princeton (A.B., English), Middlebury (M.A., English), and Johns Hopkins (Ph.D., Intellectual History). He currently teaches philosophy and interdisciplinary studies at the University of Houston-Victoria. Bud caught the Dead's New York debut at the Café Au Go Go in June of 1967 where he casually chatted with Jerry between sets. His life has never been the same.

PAUL GASS is a philosophy instructor in the department of Humanities and Media at Coppin State University. His research interests within contemporary analytic philosophy include the philosophy of mathematics and logic; he has also studied Chinese philosophy in China and experienced Buddhist monastic life while living at Fo Guang Shan monastery in Taiwan. His first Grateful Dead concert was in Ann Arbor, Michigan. The concerts that followed became an annual tradition with a special group of friends.

MICHAEL E. GETTINGS is Associate Professor of Philosophy at Hollins University, and his research interests include philosophy of fiction and ontological arguments for God's existence. The best present he received for his eighteenth birthday was a ticket to his first show: Hampton Coliseum, 3/26/88. Memphis Blues blew him away that night. He also shares Mickey's birthday—September 11th!

STEVEN GIMBEL is Associate Professor of Philosophy at Gettysburg College. He has published articles on the philosophical foundations of relativity, the Kasparov-Deep Blue chess match, and the environmental ethic of the American Nazi party, as well as writing the daily weblog "Philosophers' Playground." He was lucky enough to catch both the first time Bruce Hornsby sat in and the last performance of Ripple.

DAVID MACGREGOR JOHNSTON is Assistant Professor of Philosophy at Lyndon State College, focuses on aesthetics, phenomenology, and existentialism, and is fully aware of the irony in the fact that he has never attended a Dead show. He turned down the offer of a free back stage pass to the 1988 show at Buckeye Lake, Ohio, since the date conflicted with a birthday trip to Italy with his grandmother. It wasn't an easy decision.

MARY MACLEOD is a Certified Management Account who does break even analysis for online personal injury attorneys. Every Christmas Professor MacLeod sends Bob Weir a pair of pants, but he never acknowledges receipt and has yet to wear a single pair. She also has been known to teach philosophy at Indiana University of Pennsylvania where she can be reached at mmacleod@iup.edu.

ERIC RUBENSTEIN is a wide-eyed innocent lad, from a town of three hundred people in northern Alaska. He saw a naked woman for the first time at a Dead show as she was standing in line for nachos. The shock was so great that he had to follow the Dead for thirteen subsequent years, taking time out only to race cars and smuggle arms to the Contras. He lives in a van, down by the river, dreaming of better days . . . and teaches philosophy at Indiana University of Pennsylvania.

STEVEN SILBERMAN saw his first show at Watkins Glen in 1973, before he really knew what was going on and spent the next few decades trying to figure it out. Along the way, he co-authored *Skeleton Key: A Dictionary for Deadheads*, co-produced the Dead's boxed set *So Many Roads (1965–1995)*, And wrote the liner notes for *The Golden Road, Beyond Description, Workingman's Dead, Europe '72*, and numerous other Dead/Garcia projects, as well as David Crosby's box set *Voyage*. He studied writing with Allen Ginsberg and William Burroughs at Naropa University, and is a senior feature writer for *Wired* magazine.

STEPHEN STERN is Assistant Professor of Religion and associate of the Philosophy department at Gettysburg College. His research focuses on Jewish thought and phenomenology. He is proud of the fact that out of all the shows he attended, only once, at a show in Eugene, Oregon, did he get locked inside a port-o-pot.

ALLEN THOMPSON is Assistant Professor of Philosophy at Clemson University where he works on issues in environmental philosophy (ethics, aesthetics, and metaphysics) and neo-Aristotelian ethical theory. He first saw the Grateful Dead on the summer solstice, June 21st, 1985 and subsequently attended over fifty shows while a student at the Evergreen State College and the University of Washington but, oh, those were halcyon days. Any old hippies who think they might know him are encouraged to email at athomp6@clemson.edu.

MATTHEW TURNER is Assistant Professor of Philosophy at Francis Marion University in Florence, South Carolina. Matt's current research focuses on the moral and ethical dimensions of works of art, particularly fictional literature. Matt spends most of his free time wishing he could play the guitar like Jerry.

JOHN UGLIETTA is Assistant Professor of Philosophy at Grand Valley State University in Allendale, Michigan. He earned a J.D. from the University of Michigan Law School and a Ph.D. in philosophy from Johns Hopkins University. Before arriving at Grand Valley State, he taught at Ohio State University and (very briefly) at the University of Maryland. He first heard the Grateful Dead, as he did many bands, through his older brother's stereo, but didn't make it to a Grateful Dead show until the late 1980s in Detroit.

JESSICA WAHMAN is Assistant Professor of Philosophy at Dickinson College in Carlisle, Pennsylvania. She specializes in the American philosophical tradition, most notably the work of George Santayana. She's seen a lot of shows, but one of the most memorable was Halloween 1991, Oakland Coliseum, when Ken Kesey showed up and read e.e. cummings's "Buffalo Bill's/defunct" in eulogy at the passing of Bill Graham. The richness of the American tradition was never better represented than in that moment.

CHUCK WARD has been teaching philosophy (with a touch of improvisational flare) at Millersville University of Pennsylvania since 1997. His scholarly work is primarily in the philosophy of biology and philosophy of science, with some forays into philosophy of mind, environmental philosophy, and home brewing. While he did go to his share of Dead shows in the years gone by, it just might have been the experience of *missing* a show while sleeping in a park in downtown Oakland, California, that caused the turn towards philosophy (Oh, how to make sense of it all?).

The ABCs We All Must Face

BOB DYLAN
AND PHILOSOPHY

IT'S ALRIGHT, MA (I'M ONLY THINKING)

EDITED BY PETER VERNEZZE AND CARL J. PORTER